Praise for *Terrorists in Love*

"The 9/11 Commission grappled with the question of what drove the nineteen hijackers to their terrorist acts in 2001, but we did not have time to investigate and fully understand their motives. Ken Ballen's exhaustive research, scores of interviews, and gripping writing make *Terrorists in Love* a uniquely valuable—and sometimes chilling—behind-the-scenes account of the extreme beliefs that often fuel the actions of jihadist militants."

> —Lee H. Hamilton, former congressman and cochair of the
> 9/11 Commission

"Ken Ballen not only gets beneath the skin of terrorists, but all the way into their hearts, revealing unimaginable emotional and personal secrets. Ten years after 9/11, he's shed surprising light on the never-ending question about militant jihadis—what are they thinking? Anyone who wants to know ought to read this unusual book."

> —Jane Mayer, staff writer, *The New Yorker*, and bestselling
> author of *The Dark Side: The Inside Story of How the War on
> Terror Turned into a War on American Ideals*

"Ken Ballen has managed the impossible for an American. He has worked his way into the intimate thoughts and frustrations and family conflicts that drove six young Muslims toward the jihadist movement, and he presents his findings in a series of compelling narratives."

> —David K. Shipler, Pulitzer Prize–winning author of *Arab and
> Jew* and *The Rights of the People: How Our Search for Safety
> Invades Our Liberties*

"*Terrorists in Love* shatters the dominant dispassionate treatment of modern-day Islamic purveyors of death and destruction and instead offers a profoundly intimate portal into the fragile, emotional, even sexual factors that drive their behavior. Ballen blasts past the clichés about what animates terrorists and takes readers to places that no one has gone before. The profiles and revelations in this book are at times as uncomfortable as they are vital to appreciate what lies in the mind of some terrorists. I couldn't put the book down."

> —Steve Clemons, Washington Editor-at-Large, *The Atlantic,*
> and senior fellow and founder, American Strategy Program,
> New America Foundation

"It's simply astonishing how much Ken Ballen, an outsider, penetrated the closed world of Islamic radicals. In a fast-moving, absorbing, and at times shocking narrative, Ballen destroys stereotypes and defies conventional wisdom by allowing the 'enemies' to speak for themselves. America, meet the terrorists, really for the first time. And if you find yourself in the strange position of empathizing with them, don't recoil in horror, for you might just have stumbled upon that unexpected insight that could help design a more effective response."

—Ammar Abdulhamid, former Islamic radical and leading prodemocracy activist in the Arab world

"Deploying techniques developed during his two decades as a prosecutor and investigator, Ken Ballen interviewed more than a hundred Islamist terrorists in depth, drawing from them their inner stories. Here he profiles six of these men, and the results are eye-opening and full of startling implications."

—Daniel Pipes, founder and president of the Middle East Forum and author of *Militant Islam Reaches America*

"Many authors write about terrorism. Ken Ballen took the rare step of talking directly to terrorists. If you want to understand them, read their stories, in their own words. By giving them voice, this book offers a rarely seen glimpse into another world, the world of terrorists, not just terrorism."

—Philip Mudd, former deputy director of the Counterterrorism Center at the CIA, former senior intelligence advisor for the FBI, and senior global advisor, Oxford Analytica

"A valuable, evenhanded, and insightful window into the mind-sets and emotions of jihadi terrorists. Ballen draws a telling portrait of the human side of terrorists, from childhood traumas to moments of transformation to radicalism and, in some cases, to renunciation of the terrorists' cause. A compelling if at times frightening study, one that should be read by anyone interested in the roots of—and possible deterrents to—terrorism."

—Karen Greenberg, author of *The Least Worst Place: Guantánamo's First 100 Days*

"Revealing, often touching interviews with six young Islamic men.... [Their] stories cast a revealing light on an exotic, unfamiliar culture.... [Few] readers will deny that the [stories] illuminate the frustrations of young Islamic men living in repressive societies, alternatively fascinated and horrified by America."

—*Kirkus Reviews*

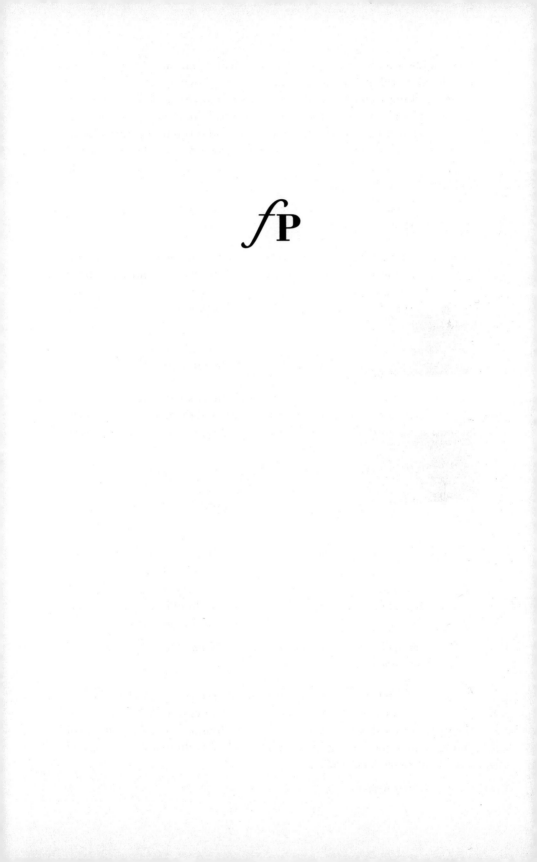

TERRORISTS IN LOVE

The Real Lives of Islamic Radicals

KEN BALLEN

FREE PRESS

New York   London   Toronto   Sydney   New Delhi

Free Press
A Division of Simon & Schuster, Inc.
1230 Avenue of the Americas
New York, NY 10020

Copyright © 2011 by Terror Free Tomorrow

First Free Press hardcover edition October 2011

FREE PRESS and colophon are trademarks of Simon & Schuster, Inc.

For information about special discounts for bulk purchases,
please contact Simon & Schuster Special Sales at 1-866-506-1949 or
business@simonandschuster.com

The Simon & Schuster Speakers Bureau can bring authors to
your live event. For more information or to book an event contact the
Simon & Schuster Speakers Bureau at 1-866-248-3049 or
visit our website at www.simonspeakers.com.

Manufactured in the United States of America

1   3   5   7   9   10   8   6   4   2

Library of Congress Cataloging-in-Publication Data

Ballen, Ken.
Terrorists in love : the real lives of Islamic radicals / Ken Ballen. — 1st ed.
p. cm.
1. Terrorists—Biography. 2. Radicalism—Religious aspects—Islam. I. Title.
HV6431.B3358 2011
363.325092'2—dc22   2011011341

ISBN 978-1-4516-0921-9
ISBN 978-1-4516-0922-6 (ebook)

To William I. Koch,
whose loyal and generous support
made this book possible

CONTENTS

FOREWORD

BY PETER BERGEN

K EN BALLEN, an American Jew, has gone behind enemy lines
to learn what makes terrorists tick. The book he's written is
his synthesis of more than a hundred interviews and five years of on-
the-ground research. It may be easier to begin by describing what this
book is not. It's not a travelogue recounting the author's experiences
throughout the Muslim world. Nor is it a scholarly analysis of the
causes or consequences of extremism and terrorism.

Rather, *Terrorists in Love* accomplishes the extraordinary feat of
delving deep into the inner lives of jihadis (Muslim holy warriors), in a
way that has never been attempted before. Telling the interwoven life
stories of six jihadis from Pakistan, Afghanistan, and Saudi Arabia,
the book shows us what's important to them; what formed their char-
acters; which beliefs drove them toward extremism and, as important,
turned them away from a life of violence.

It would be wrong, of course, to think that the individual lives of
six jihadis can reveal what motivates all Islamist radicals. But Ballen—a former federal prosecutor and congressional investigator
who brings formidable interviewing and writing skills to the task—
has gone deeper inside this closed world than any other researcher.

Uniquely, he reveals a universe of militancy that is so strange that at times it seems suffused with the magical realism of Gabriel García Márquez. The world of these extremists is illuminated by dreams and visions of great meaning, is dominated by the talismanic figure of the United States, and is shot through with intense sexual repression and decaying family and tribal structures. Ballen, a great listener who spent months with his subjects, has elicited a wealth of such insights that surprise and inform. The book reveals the impact of U.S. policy on these extremists and the stark limits of the United States' ability to shape their world. It also breaks some stunning news, from the secret war councils of Mullah Omar and the Taliban to the Pakistani army's direct support for terrorists and an unprecedented look inside Saudi Arabia's ruling royal family.

Sometimes stories—and these are true stories—can allow us to understand what motivates people beneath the surface explanations and reveal the more intangible emotional, cultural, psychological, and religious factors we often miss. *Terrorists in Love* offers in-depth understanding as never before. And, through understanding, an unexpected hope.

AUTHOR'S NOTE: Peter L. Bergen is CNN's national security analyst and the bestselling author of *The Longest War: The Enduring Conflict between America and Al-Qaeda; Holy War, Inc.;* and *The Osama bin Laden I Know.*

INTRODUCTION

A S A FEDERAL prosecutor, I convicted Muslim terrorists. I also served as congressional counsel exposing the Iran-Contra scandal and the chief investigator for Senator John McCain on a Senate investigative committee. I spent nearly two decades going after all kinds of bad guys—many much like the jihadis I now write about.

Yet I had learned as a prosecutor and investigator that, whatever crime a man had committed, empathy was the key to opening up trust and getting the hidden story. I had to place myself in his shoes, no matter how evil the deed and uncomfortably close the fit.

Over the years, I prosecuted Middle East terrorist financiers and heroin dealers, who took me inside their personal lives. I convicted Mafia hit men and capos, some of whom I gave new identities in the U.S. government's Witness Protection Program. I investigated corrupt government officials, whom I wired to capture their greed—even a son who wore a wire against his father. I also interrogated child molesters, whose confessions had to be the most vile I'd heard—and of course, terrorists and radicals themselves. It was all accomplished through long days of patient, detailed, in-depth interrogations. Sometimes, to encourage cooperation, they received benefits (for example, when I was a prosecutor, the promise of a lighter prison sentence). Mostly, there simply developed a human bond between us.

The idea that the truth could be divined from torture was something that in my experience worked only on the hit TV show *24*. In the real world of criminals and terrorists, ironically, a fleeting human connection—with sympathy and without judgment—does more to obtain truthful confessions than torture. Though rough interrogation techniques may make us feel good, they accomplish little. The far more scary reality is that sometimes empathy can bring us too close. And the interrogator sees as much of himself as he does his subject— that is the beauty and curse of a successful interrogation: it leaves everyone feeling vulnerable.

In 2004, I founded a nonprofit research institute, Terror Free Tomorrow. I gave up my legal career of nearly two decades and took no salary for three more years to find out why people support extremism. Our mission required that I spend time on the ground in key Muslim countries. I directed some thirty nationwide public opinion surveys in many Muslim-majority nations throughout South Asia, East Asia, Africa, and the Middle East.

As part of my nonprofit's research, I have also interviewed more than a hundred radicals and terrorists for five years to find out what motivates extremists in particular. There's no single path to radicalization, any more than one individual's story should be seen as representing all radical Islamists or, or course, Muslims as a whole.

I never planned to write a book and certainly not this one. But six Islamist radicals I met in the course of my work changed that. Their lives were so different from Western concepts—and what they decided to share with me was so compelling—that I felt I had little choice but to tell their stories.

I'm often asked why these Islamist radicals—or jihadis, as they call themselves—opened up in such intimate ways to me, an American Jew. I'd like to think that part of the answer lies in my nearly two decades of experience conducting interrogations of criminals and terrorists. Perhaps, though, as much of the reason comes from these six current and former radicals' own need to convey their stories—and to an outsider, where they would not lose face before their closest peers. I met two of them at the Saudi government prison established in 2007 to rehabilitate jihadis and the third Saudi through a friend of his at the prison. The Afghan Taliban fighter and Pakistani militants I met through three Pakistani reporters and a radical Islamist cleric. In the process of these intense interviews, and within an entirely different cultural context, I even befriended three of the jihadis, as you will read.

Those who have never talked to criminals and terrorists (and certainly not made a career talking to them as I have) are often astonished at their desire to talk. But most feel an overwhelming imperative to justify their lives, whether from guilt or a psychological need to purge their inner demons—or, in the case of most of the young men featured in this book, from deeply held religious beliefs. Convinced of the righteousness of the cause, they believe it is a duty of their faith to share it with others. The fact that these jihadis talked to me is not unusual. The fact that they revealed so much is.

Conventional wisdom in America and the West about the lives of jihadis is far removed from the real world of the Islamist terrorists themselves. I ask you to put aside what you've come to expect. I am going to tell the stories that follow in the same way the jihadis shared them with me—from their point of view and in their voice.

A warning: that voice can be completely disorienting. I'll offer a few examples from the stories that follow to illustrate. When Abby in chapter 2 decides to join Al Qaeda and die as a suicide bomber in Iraq, he does so because he believes he will then become married to his girlfriend in Heaven. This is not a metaphor for him, or an ill-formed romantic notion, or even his desperate escape from the strict traditions of tribal society, though to some unstated degree those unconscious factors may have played a role. Fundamentally, he believed instead that by dying for God he would live again to be married in Heaven— literally. Mullah Omar, the Taliban leader, follows Malik's dream in chapter 3 because Mullah Omar believes that this dream represents God's literal directions on why he must fight the Americans. When the Pakistani Taliban militant featured in the book changes course, he does so because he thinks that my dream meant that the Prophet Muhammad had directly spoken. The belief in dreams and jinn (unseen spirits described in the Qur'an and sometimes called "genies" in the West), interpreting God's voice through a person's physical attributes and so on, are not metaphors or my desire to write in a literary manner. They are the literal facts that motivate the jihadis to fight and of which we in the United States and the West are largely clueless.

I have made every effort to corroborate the accounts of the jihadis, which I detail at the end of the book in "A Note on Sources and Methods." These remain, however, highly personal and intensely subjective stories, where "truth" is in the possibly clouded eye of the beholder.

Seeing the lives of these six holy warriors as they chose to relate them allows us to enter the unimaginable mind-set the United States now faces fighting against the Taliban and Al Qaeda. Surprisingly, even when we are immersed deeply in the strange world of these jihadis, their stories allow us to see a way out.

Part I

SOLDIERS OF JIHAD

1

AHMAD'S TRIP TO HEAVEN
AND BACK

C NN LED the news on Christmas Day 2004:

> On the heels of a visit to Iraq by U.S. Defense Secretary
> Donald Rumsfeld, a fuel truck driven by a suicide bomber
> exploded Friday in western Baghdad....
>
> At least eight people were killed and 20 others wounded by
> the explosion.... Fifteen people, including women and chil-
> dren, were in critical condition, and many had suffered severe
> burns, hospital officials said....
>
> Baghdad police said they were looking for another fuel truck in
> the area and a BMW that they believe is associated with the attack.

My inside story of the suicide bomber responsible for this attack
actually began in Washington, D.C. Through contacts in the media
and a senior American intelligence official, in the spring of 2008 I met
one of the top officials of the Saudi Arabian government responsible for counterterrorism. The high-ranking Saudi Ministry of Interior official became my friend. It helped that he was looking to buy
a condo in D.C. and his son wanted to attend an American graduate
school—both areas where I guided him through foreign shoals. The
favor was returned inside the Kingdom of Saudi Arabia.

But my unprecedented access inside Saudi Arabia was not only the result of a personal trust between me and the Saudi official; I also benefited from timing—and luck. From 2008 through 2010, the Saudi Ministry of Interior decided to open its jihadi prison rehabilitation program to a few select outsiders. The Ministry of Interior is the most powerful government agency in Saudi Arabia, responsible for counterterrorism and internal security.

Saudi Arabia, in many ways, is the country most important to the future of Islam. Home of the faith's holiest places, it is the world's richest kingdom, with a quarter of the earth's oil reserves and wealth highly concentrated in the royal family and few others. Saudi Arabia is also the home of a strict, fundamentalist interpretation of Islam founded by Muhammad al-Wahhab, which is the source of Al Qaeda's ideology. Saudi citizens continue to be the principal financial supporters of Al Qaeda, the Taliban, and other radical Islamist groups. However, since 2003, when Al Qaeda began attacks inside the country, the government has led an official campaign against the radicals, or jihadis, as they call themselves. Still, Saudi Arabia is one of the most closed societies in the world, largely inscrutable to outsiders.

As president of the nonprofit research institute Terror Free Tomorrow, I interviewed more than a hundred terrorists and Muslim radicals throughout the world to understand what motivates them. In Saudi Arabia, over many months, I had the unique opportunity to interview at length forty-three Saudi jihadi militants who had fought inside Iraq and Afghanistan. I conducted the kind of in-depth, one-on-one interrogations that were a part of my professional background as a federal prosecutor and congressional investigator. Some people's accounts were not credible. Other radicals' activities offered little in the way of implications for future policy, while many were not insightful or self-aware. Yet, by persevering, I came to uncover a world "behind the veil."

My interviews in Saudi Arabia began during the summer of 2008. In a convoy of Ministry of Interior (MOI) black GMC Yukons, with as much security as afforded the vice president of the United States in Washington, D.C., we sped to the euphemistically named "Care

Center"—the special Saudi prison for rehabilitating jihadi militants. When I say sped, I mean it literally. We reached speeds of 100 mph or more on Riyadh's American-designed superhighways, which reminded me of "the 10" approaching Santa Monica, only without the Pacific on the horizon.

As we left modern Riyadh, the Saudi capital of nearly five million (which also reminded me of Century City with its isolated gleaming skyscrapers surrounded by neighborhoods of strip malls), I looked out at the bright brown terrain in search of Arabian life in the patches of desert that were now cropping up. Instead, I saw all manner of ATVs and 4×4s spewing exhaust and dust, with people camping next to their Land Rovers, open flames, and barbecue grills, and the ubiquitous ice cream vans that continually trolled the sands.

We sped through the "resort" northeast of Riyadh, Al Thumama, with its dusty amusement parks, finally passing Al Fantazi Land on the right. It's Riyadh's great amusement park, a Disneyland, my MOI driver said, where Islam reigned.

While I was staring at Fantasy Land, the latest-model Yukon, which still had the factory plastic shrink wrap over its leather seats, took a sudden, jarring right off the highway. Past the run-down Lebanese Fruits Restaurant, over dirt roads and sand-colored, walled-off homes, we pulled up to an unmarked security gate.

The guard waved us in before we drove through another gate, stopping at a grassy dead end and finally a sign: MINISTRY OF INTERIOR, DEPARTMENT OF PUBLIC RELATIONS, THE CARE CENTER. For two years, this would be my "home from home," as the prison warden, MOI Major General Yousef Mansour, told me. The Care Center prison for reforming jihadi terrorists offered psychological counseling, antidepressant medication, religious re-education, art therapy, vocational training, water sports—some dubbed it the "Betty Ford Jihadi Clinic." (I had mentioned to my high-ranking MOI friend the fact that the prison was part of the ministry's "Department of Public Relations" might give Americans the wrong message, and I noticed on subsequent visits that the center was renamed and the original sign had been changed to remove "Public Relations.")

Of the forty-three jihadi inmates ("beneficiaries") I interviewed, Ahmad al-Shayea, nicknamed "Bernie," had to be the most striking, his entire body bearing the scars of the first suicide bomber in Iraq who had survived his attack. His face was covered with red pustules. His nose curved to a strange hooked point, like a ski jump. The fingers on his right hand ended in a stump that resembled melted candle wax, while his left-hand fingers were twisted like the roots of a *miswak* stick jihadis regularly chew in imitation of the Prophet Muhammad (and that tastes exactly like the bitter herbs from a Passover Seder). His fingernails were little more than yellowed brown stumps, the color of toes infected with athlete's foot.

Sitting in the prison faux-tented reception area, or *majlis,* with the air-conditioning going full throttle, I was accompanied by MOI Lieutenant Majid, my favorite interpreter, who spoke in 1980s American slang (he'd grown up in Orlando, Florida), and "Dr. Ali," Ahmad's prison psychologist, a phenomenal host, with whom I shared many long dinners and who had received his doctorate in psychology from the University of Edinburgh. We were also accompanied by the usual retinue of Pakistani and Bangladeshi servants, with the endless small cups of *gahwa* (Arabian green coffee), highly sweetened black tea, and sticky dates. The occasional MOI security guards never had the patience to sit through more than thirty minutes at a time of our six-to-eight-hour-long interview sessions.

Ahmad was shy and modest. It took much prompting from me, Lieutenant Majid, and most of all Dr. Ali, who would prod Ahmad with what they had discussed in their therapy sessions. As is fitting for a student of both Sigmund Freud and the Holy Qur'an, Dr. Ali helped Ahmad begin his singular life story as a failed suicide bomber with a dream—even if a dream from Abu Ghraib.

BURNED BEYOND RECOGNITION, his skin charred and dark, Ahmad al-Shayea could dream of only one thing: dates. Not the light tan Sukkary dates his family had once so proudly grown in the center of Saudi

Arabia—"the best dates in all Buraydah," his grandfather always bragged. Ahmad couldn't stop dreaming of the rival dates from the distant eastern province of Saudi Arabia: the bitter, black Khlas dates that Grandfather scorned.

The Holy Qur'an told Ahmad that as a martyred fighter in the way of jihad, he would be eternally nourished in Paradise by "date palms." Yet instead of the sweetest Sukkary that Grandfather said would be the food of Heaven, his veins were hooked to salty water. Instead of wearing "robes of silk" and reclining on "jeweled couches," as the Holy Book pledged, Ahmad lay on a stiff white bed. Missing too were "the dark-eyed, full-breasted virgins, chaste as pearls" offered by Allah the Most High to any martyr. He hadn't reunited with his family as promised either—his younger brother, cherished grandfather, beloved mother. He was alone.

Ahmad had been "thrown into the fire of Hell," as the Holy Qur'an warned all sinners. He'd come to Iraq to fight the Americans on Noble Jihad. But his suicide mission had ended instead at Abu Ghraib.

And all Ahmad could dream of was the darkest Khlas dates.

FOOD HAD ALWAYS foretold the fate of Ahmad al-Shayea's family, as far back as anyone could remember. More than two centuries before, with literally no food to eat because of unending drought, the family had left Ha'il in the north to go to Buraydah, an oasis capital of Al Qassim in the heart of Arabia.

Then it was all about the dates.

The family became date farmers and traders, growing mostly Sukkary, unique to Al Qassim. From Buraydah, the "Date Capital of Saudi Arabia," they cultivated some of the best Sukkary, the most sought-after dates in Arabia, particularly prized during Ramadan. And for Ahmad's grandfather Abdurrahman al-Shayea, his Sukkary had no equal in sweetness of taste, smoothness of yellow meat and amber skin.

The "International City of Dates" gave them enough wealth that Grandfather could even open a small grocery store. The Abdurrahman al-Shayea Store featured the endless variety of sweetness Grand-father proudly grew and traded.

Riding the back of Saudi Arabia's first oil boom instead, Ahmad's father, Abdullah, left the world of dates far behind. With oil revenues exploding into royal government coffers, the Saudi civil service grew in tandem, becoming the largest employer in the country. Abdullah profited and, like so many others, obtained a comfortable position in the government. Starting in police administration, he rose to the middle level of health care administration for Buraydah, which has a reputation as one of the most conservative cities in the entire King-dom of Saudi Arabia.

While shunning Grandfather's dates, Abdullah kept faith with tra-dition in other respects and submitted to an arranged marriage with a second cousin. Tribal custom provided that sons marry a relative, chosen by his family. The couple had two girls and three boys, with Mother staying at home, following tradition, of course.

For tradition meant everything in Buraydah. And as Buraydah is at the center of Saudi Arabia, Saudi Arabia is at the heart of the Mus-lim world. The birthplace of Islam and custodian of its two most holy places, it is also the home country of Osama bin Laden and fifteen of the nineteen 9/11 hijackers. Buraydah and its surrounding area kept faith, giving the world most of the Saudi fighters inside Iraq—includ-ing Ahmad al-Shayea.

BORN IN 1984, Ahmad was the oldest son. He attended the nearby government Ibn Daqeeq al-Eid Elementary School, where half the classes were in religious subjects. The Holy Qur'an was his favorite class—even though his father never recited from the Book. By the time Ahmad was old enough to attend Prince Sultan Middle School, he was still small and frail at only five foot two. He didn't like to talk in class or enjoy the rough ways of Saudi soccer. He had no friends and spent his free time in front of the screen—TV or computer. That's when his father would start to yell: "Why don't you do your homework, play some soccer, something, instead of wasting away at home like a girl?"

Ahmad hated his father's shouting. Like the hot dust wind from the desert, you never knew when it would strike.

"Leave the boy alone, Abu Ahmad," his mother always said to her husband, addressing him with the honorific title "Father of Ahmad."

Umm Ahmad was his beloved mother, who always called herself by her *kunya,* the honored "Mother of Ahmad." Allah Almighty had given her the greatest blessing of a first son. She loved him "more than life itself." While the religious imams of Buraydah cried when reciting the Glorious Qur'an, Umm Ahmad cried while holding her favorite child.

"There's only one God, and there's only one Ahmad," she'd say.

Mother Ahmad always took Ahmad's side no matter what, which only further provoked his father. Indeed, Abu Ahmad almost seemed to be competing for his wife's affection with his first son. And Abu Ahmad had nothing if not a fierce temper—the only limit to which was his fear of lapsing into "a diabetic fit."

If it got too bad, Ahmad would flee to Grandfather's old-world store. The oil boom had transformed even Buraydah into a rebuilt modern city with American-style roads and strip malls of gas stations, furniture and convenience stores. But Grandfather's traditional grocery and date store on 80th Street in the Prince Mishal district felt like a relic from a former age.

Grandfather always made Ahmad feel at home, kissing him warmly on both cheeks, embracing him with his old smell of sandalwood oil and incense smoke. Ahmad supposed that if his grandfather had a computer or even a TV, he would move right into Grandfather's "land of dates": Sefri, Khudairi, Suqaey, Safawy, Shalaby, Anbarah, Ajwah, Helwah, Madjool, Rothanah, Maktoomi, Naboot Seif, Rabiah, Barhi, Rashodiah, Sullaj, Hulayyah, Khlas, and most of all, of course, Sukkary.

Ahmad could name them all. Some boys could recite the Holy Qur'an, yet he could recite all the distinct variety of dates and explain how each had its own unique color, taste, texture. And while he couldn't recite Qur'anic chapters, he could point out each of the twenty-nine times dates were named in the Holy Book. Reciting their Qur'anic attributes, Ahmad and his grandfather savored every date. And Grandfather's shot was the stuff of legend: spitting each pit through his missing middle front teeth into a large brass bowl, which had been passed down in the Al Shayea family for generations.

But sweet dates weren't Grandfather Al Shayea's only love. Grandfather's other secret passion was Arabic love songs, most of all, those of "the Noble Lady," Umm Kalsoum, the legendary "Star of the East." The great Egyptian contralto continually sang in the background on the old record player. Grandfather loved all her songs but perhaps most of all "Lissah Fakir": "Do you still remember all that was in the past?" Ahmad's favorite was the classic "El Atlaal," especially one version that lasted more than an hour: "Give me my freedom, untie my hands!"

With the grand lady of Arabic song wailing of unrequited love, the old man and the boy mouthed a date at exactly the same time, eating its yellow flesh at the same speed, in rhythm with the Star of the East's syncopated beats and whirling trills. They'd finish together and, as Umm Kalsoum moaned or cried at the end of a verse, would spit out the date pits like soccer balls into their goal. This was a sport Ahmad excelled in, even though Grandfather enjoyed the advantage of missing his front teeth.

The singing of their recorded "mother" egged them on and became a vital part of the "date game." As Umm Kalsoum tackled a particularly high note, the date pits would launch together. Sometimes Ahmad felt that the clapping on the old records was not for Mother Kalsoum but for Grandfather and Ahmad, as the pits hit their spot. Score! The people clapped! Umm Kalsoum trilled her deep voice again as only she could! The pits would launch once more. Some people claim that the Noble Lady sparked *tarab*—ecstasy—in her listeners. Ahmad didn't know about that. But Mother Kalsoum had certainly provoked the firing of many a Sukkary pit from the lips of Grandfather and Grandson al-Shayea.

Grandfather only played his cherished Umm Kalsoum records in private with Ahmad. When Saudi television and radio stopped broadcasting Umm Kalsoum after the 1979 attack on the Grand Mosque in Mecca, Grandfather didn't understand why. How Umm Kalsoum could be considered un-Islamic when her father was an imam, descended from the Prophet himself, and when she even sang verses from the Holy Qur'an, eluded Grandfather. But to be safe from the *mutaween* (religious police), the date game, with Umm Kalsoum providing the musical sound track, became Grandfather and Ahmad's secret from the world.

By the time Ahmad turned sixteen, he was only five foot six and still thin as a date pit. He looked more like a twelve-year-old boy than a man. But he now felt Mother Kalsoum's lyrics from "Inta Omri" growing inside him too:

"I started to worry that my life would run away from me."

His family went to mosque on Fridays, observed Ramadan and Eid, but his father never prayed five times a day. Instead, he complained about getting diabetes, and though he avoided dates like desert locusts, he still constantly drank cloyingly sweet tea, even ate baklava and all kinds of honeyed pastries. Ahmad's father, who said you should be observant but didn't make the holy pilgrimage, and who extolled the Book but would smoke his hubbly-bubbly in private when no one was looking—never even listened to the Noble Lady.

IT WAS THE first Eid celebration after 9/11. It was also the first time since Ahmad was little that the entire family went to dinner at a restaurant. The Jerusalem Restaurant, one of the oldest in Buraydah, was the only place Grandfather would eat out since it bought his very own Sukkary dates.

The Eid dinner at the Jerusalem Restaurant was a feast with Lebanese food the family was not used to. The family ate separately, with the women apart. Unlike many families in conservative Buraydah, Ahmad's family always ate as one at home, the men and women together.

Ahmad couldn't remember eating separated like this before. But he was sixteen and couldn't be his "mother's pet" for the rest of his life.

At the end of the meal, when the overly sweet pistachio baklava came, Ahmad went to stand alone on the sidewalk outside. The desert night air was cool. Perhaps he should turn toward religion, he thought. He had never truly known God. Under his breath, Ahmad was busy mouthing the words of a prayer to himself, moving his hands up and down in the air, like an imam at mosque giving a sermon.

Ahmad was so engrossed in his daydreams that he didn't notice his father leaving the restaurant. He came from behind and, startling Ahmad, began to mock him, waving his hands wildly in the air.

Father Ahmad always made sure his head was meticulously covered with the customary red-checkered *shemagh* headdress. Continually taunting his son to "crawl out from under Mama's *abaya*," he had even threatened Mother Ahmad that if she didn't leave the boy alone, he would take a second wife. But Grandfather didn't approve of having more than one wife, so Father Ahmad showed him the "tribal honor" that was due any father—why couldn't his own son show the same? All he wanted was for his eldest to "wear the white"—become a man.

Ahmad turned toward him and blushed like a boy. He felt humiliated to see his father mocking him.

"Stop," he cried. There was no sin worse than to talk back to your father. It could send you to Hell. Hell, the religious teachers told him, where fire seventy times hotter than the earth's would burn off his skin only to grow back and be roasted off again; where he'd carry his intestines in his hands, chains binding him while he hung from his boiling feet, bitten by scorpions the size of donkeys and snakes as big as camels, and his dry, cracking desert mouth would beg for the only drink ever offered: his own pus and blood that never stopped flowing.

No sooner had the word "Stop" left his cursed lips than he regretted it and his father's open hand slapped Ahmad's left cheek.

As Ahmad then raised his arm to stop another blow, it hit his father's hand, which enraged his father even more.

Ahmad saw his father's brown eyes turn black with hate. "How can a little mama's boy strike *me*?" he yelled, balling his fist in full fury.

Ahmad fell back and instinctively spat, as if a date pit were leaving his mouth at full speed, as if an evil jinn were caught inside his throat. It wasn't as if he were trying to spit at his father, God forbid, but he tasted pus and blood.

His father hit him again before Mother Ahmad came between them, as she always did.

"Abu Ahmad," she cried, deliberately addressing her husband by his *kunya*. "He was just talking to himself. Where's the sin in that?"

"Out of the way, Umm Ahmad." His father wasn't finished, his face now red as pressed date paste.

"By the Word of God, you'll have to strike me first before you hit him again," she said. She didn't flinch.

Mother Ahmad was imposing in her own right. She too loved food and was the reason the family never ate out. A wonderful cook, her *jareesh* was the sweetest in Buraydah. She was equally strong in or out of the kitchen. She was the love that held the family together.

"Damn you both," Father Ahmad muttered.

"Jafar," she now said firmly, using the secret name only she called him. "You keep this up, and you'll send yourself into a diabetic fit."

At that the father dropped his fists to his side and loosened his fingers. The wife's plea for his survival worked better than a mother's plea for her son.

Or perhaps it was that Grandfather had finally left the restaurant. Ahmad felt sure if Grandfather had been outside with them, his father never would have struck.

That night, his mother came to kiss him good night, as she always did. She brought his glass of hot milk to help him sleep and repeated her customary bedtime greeting: "How's my favorite son I love more than life itself, the very best son in the whole wide world?" He did not reply, as he always did in turn, "He kisses the hands of the very best mother in the whole wide world."

Instead, after his mother shut the door behind her, he couldn't stop crying. It was the first time he remembered crying like that in years. Maybe because he saw a tear in his mother's eye before he rudely just told her good night. Maybe because Grandfather never saw what happened or said anything to come to his rescue outside the Jerusalem Restaurant—Jerusalem, where the Prophet Muhammad ascended to Heaven. Because of his father's eyes, Ahmad was headed to Hell: he saw the black hate inside them, and nothing was the same again.

THE NEXT DAY, Ahmad dropped out of school. His father refused to get angry. "You're not worth a diabetic attack," he said.

Ahmad wanted a friend. He had none in school. He'd used to hang with his cousin all the time when they were little in primary school. Even some in Prince Sultan Middle School, until they fell out of touch in secondary school. Adel was everything Ahmad was not. Tall, with dark eyes and wavy black hair, he even had the beginnings of a manly beard sprouting on his face. Adel played soccer and drove his very own "love car": a neon-red Chevy Camaro with tiger gold stripes. He even smoked when no one was looking. There was nothing awkward or shy about him. What would he want with puny Ahmad?

Ahmad was so nervous when he first tried to call, he dialed the wrong number.

"Adel? It's Ahmad, Cousin."

Adel was more than a year older and had just turned eighteen.

"Hey, Cousin."

Ahmad's fears melted away.

"Long time no hear, Cousin." Adel peppered his speech with "cool" American slang.

"I dropped out of school today and figured you'd help me celebrate."

"Cool. I'll pick you up, Cousin. Long as your old man doesn't see me."

"Fuck him." Ahmad thought of "El Atlaal": "Give me my freedom, untie my hands."

Adel laughed. He was the one who seemed nervous now, but came to pick Ahmad up in his blazing red Camaro. Everybody saw the classic. It was a head turner, the hottest car in Buraydah or even its twin city, Unayzah. It had everything: a carbon-fiber hood scoop, signature turbocharger, custom hypersilver wheels, and of course those gold tiger racing stripes.

As Adel almost "burned rubber" speeding the Camaro away from Ahmad's house, he raised his right hand to give him a high five American style. Ahmad slapped his hand like an American too and never felt so happy in his whole life.

From that day, they hung together nonstop. More, Adel brought him into his "posse." With a core of six boys, the posse sometimes grew to eight, even nine.

They raced the classic Camaro against another gang's souped-up Mustang. Adel was one of the best at drag racing. More than drag racing: *tafheet,* or "drifting," where Adel would spin out and skid the Camaro sideways, down the parking lots and deserted side streets of Buraydah and Unayzah in the middle of the night. The gang also went to the Al Nafud desert outside Buraydah, racing 4×4s over the rocky, steep dunes and sand hills. Camping in the desert, the boys tormented the poor *dhub* lizards around them, never bothering to cook them over an open flame in true Bedouin tradition. They were not about tradition.

With so many boys, there sometimes was a free house to hang at when the parents were at mosque. But the gang usually went to *estirahas*, small houses outside town, where they could play video games, watch TV, smoke cigarettes. "Hot cars, cool friends, and free air," they said.

Soon the posse started to score hashish. Getting high on hash helped pass the time. Getting high made Ahmad better at the video games and surfing the Internet, something new and cool.

"To kick it with girls" was the posse's main drive, or so they'd say.

The boys would roam the streets and "spy girls." They'd follow the girls who shopped in groups. And if the girls had no adult man with them, it'd be open season for "spying": asking them to take a ride in the hot Chevy, come back to the *estiraha,* and hang out. They asked if the girls found them sexy. They'd even ask for a quick peek behind the veil. The boys would also "spy" from the street, driving in the Chevy or in Mohsin's Impreza. Of course, a girl riding with another Arab man would be off limits. Only if a Pakistani, Filipino, or Bengali servant were driving would the boys feel free to spy.

But nothing ever happened. The boys were all talk, and the girls, while sometimes giggling, never ended up meeting a single boy. The game of spying seemed more important than a real girlfriend or the arranged marriages that tradition would eventually grant them.

Ahmad passed the next year like this and hardly slept at home. Every time he did, his father would repeat the same litany. He'd begin by yelling, you're supposed to be the eldest son, but what kind of role model are you? Then, still red, he'd yell how Ahmad was not even worth a diabetic fit, while his mother always sided with Ahmad, telling her husband that he was the one driving Ahmad away. It ended with his mother in tears and Ahmad fleeing with Adel and the posse: scoring hash, drag racing the Camaro or drifting the Impreza, spying girls.

UNTIL THE DAY Adel came back to the guys boasting of his conquest.

"My-ree-ah, oh, My-ree-ah," Adel said. "I did her."

The boys, always ready to shout at any mention of girls or sex, didn't know what to say.

"She's Pinoy, *kafir*. Small, skinny body, but man, what big tits," Adel said in their cool boy talk.

The entire desert *estiraha* was swimming with hashish smoke. Of course, Adel waited to tell his tale when they were quite high and giggling like babies. If Adel wasn't the hero, the leader of the group before this, he'd certainly be so now: the only one who had a girl, even if she was a Filipino.

"Ya fuckin' liar. Bet'cha didn't fuck no one, smart-ass," Farid said, almost tagging Adel with a large wet clam of spit. Farid had the deserved reputation of having the juiciest spits of the whole posse.

Adel's manhood challenged, the happy hash laughing stopped.

Ahmad was afraid Adel might hit Farid, though he'd never seen him turn violent. Whatever mischief the boys got into—spying girls, drag racing, drifting cars, smoking dope, or drinking still-made liquor—they never looked for fights or stole or really got into deep trouble with the *mutaween*. What if all the boyhood bullshit suddenly escalated into something really sinful?

"A man doesn't kiss and tell," Adel said at last.

Farid just repeated, "Ya fulla shit."

The other boys were now quiet and seemed to move toward Farid. Adel's leadership of the gang was on the line. Despite the red Camaro, scoring hash and booze, always the loudest when spying girls, if he now lied to the boys about actually having a girl, his role as leader would never be the same again.

Ahmad wondered what he was doing there. The hash smoke was suffocating.

"Okay, she's my Filipino maid," Adel said.

"The maid," Farid shouted. "That doesn't fuckin' count, man." He now spat on the ground directly in front of Adel.

Ahmad imagined the Filipino maid's eyes looking at Adel. And felt certain Adel's story was just made up to impress the boys. But what was the point?

That night, his father started again: when would he get a job, or at least go back to school. Mother Ahmad warned her husband to stop or he'd get another diabetic attack.

It was the first night Ahmad had gone home in more than two weeks. He now felt sorry he had. At least he was glad to see his mother, brothers, and sisters.

In the middle of the night, he turned on the TV, then, next to it, the family computer newly set up to dial the Internet. Adel had told him about a porn site online. He couldn't find it. Farid had told him about some other site, he didn't remember the address.

Trolling the Internet, he went from the news sites of Al Jazeera and Al Arabiya to social sites where he couldn't get access, to religious sites where he could. He couldn't find the right home page. He hardly slept that night but remembered a dream he'd had sometime during the morning when he should've already been awake and praying.

A DREAM—it caused Ahmad to hesitate and Dr. Ali to spring to life. I would soon learn that dreams held a powerful place in Saudi culture and their fundamentalist Wahhabi Islamic faith and are often considered the harbinger of divine prophecy.

Dr. Ali started in, encouraging Ahmad to reveal his dream. "Leave nothing out, Ahmad," the doctor said. *"Inshallah"* (God willing).

In the Care Center prison, facing a man whose entire body was permanently disfigured from his suicide attack, I knew I needed Dr. Ali's help if I was ever to truly know what mix of religious, cultural, political, and personal factors had led Ahmad to blow himself up.

"Inshallah," I now knew to respond.

IN THE DREAM, his father was praying before asking Ahmad, in a very calm and sweet voice, to pray with him before he died. That was when Ahmad woke up. The news the night before had said that the king had a dream that foretold his death.

The following day, Ahmad left the house in the afternoon to hang with Adel and the gang as always.

He coughed with his first draw on the hash pipe. Maybe it was something he'd seen on the Internet or the TV the night before. He didn't feel like being there.

Maybe it was the dream. It had been so long since he prayed. "What's the point of all my sins?" he thought, though was quick to stop as he remembered how talking to himself had gotten him in trouble before. Instead, he asked, "Where's Farid?"

The boys were in the middle of a video game, high anyway, and said nothing as Ahmad walked out.

He didn't pray. His whole life didn't amount to anything. He felt sorry for the Filipino maid, sorry for his mother. His sins would send him to Hell.

For the next couple of weeks, he wandered in and out of the gang and his house, not knowing where to go or where home really was. Then Abdurrahman, his younger brother, who had looked up to him, dropped out of school, saying he wanted to join a gang too. Mother Ahmad now pleaded with Ahmad for the sake of his brother to be a better role model and quit the gang.

Abdurrahman always got along with both his father and mother. Ahmad hoped that one day he could get along with his father too, as he did with his grandfather and mother.

Ahmad told Abdurrahman that he had quit the posse.

"Better to be a good Muslim, a good human being. Why would you want to practice a life of sin and end up burning in Hell for eternity?" Ahmad said.

"You did it," Abdurrahman retorted.

"And now I need to repent for my sins," Ahmad said.

Just saying the words changed him. But he didn't know how.

He started going to mosque. And he soon got a job as a delivery boy. That lasted only a couple of weeks. He hated driving around, as he had endlessly with Adel and the other boys. No one from the gang ever called him, not even his cousin. His "friends" dropped Ahmad without a single call.

Ahmad found another job at a call center and several weeks later a better one at the Al Qassim Chamber of Commerce and Industry, near Prince Abdullah Sports City. He started with data entry, advancing to computer training. They began him at a low salary, only 1,500 riyals ($400) a month, promising to triple that after six months. After nine months, when he complained that he'd never gotten a raise, he was fired.

Ahmad couldn't find work again, not even his old job as a delivery boy or at the call center. For a high school dropout in Saudi Arabia in 2003 and 2004, that was hardly unusual. At least half of all men under age twenty-five were unemployed.

His brother never joined a gang. Mother Ahmad doted on Ahmad as she always did. His father's temper seemed to worsen, so he just avoided him as much as he could. Ahmad watched TV, trolled the Internet, but felt "each day was like a year," as the Star of the East sang.

But he also went to mosque every day and said his five daily prayers. He thought of growing a beard. He wanted to redeem himself from his sins.

On Fridays, he would go to Jumu'ah prayer and hear sermons in different mosques throughout Buraydah and Unayzah. Many of the

sermons were from radical clerics. Buraydah was a center of fundamentalist Wahhabi thought, and after the U.S. invasion of Iraq, jihad
against the infidel invaders of neighboring Iraq became the call from
the pulpit.

It was the spring of 2004. Ahmad had gone alone to a new mosque
with a fiery imam on the other side of town. Then, after Friday
Jumu'ah prayer and sermon, he was struck as if by a miracle from
God.

He saw Adel, and Adel was transformed. Adel looked much taller
than Ahmad remembered. Maybe all the time that had passed was just
playing tricks. After all, it had been more than a year and a half since
they last saw each other. But he could swear that Adel had grown or
was holding himself taller. And Adel had a beard, pious dress. The
beard changed the man.

"Cousin Adel." Ahmad was the first to speak.

"Cousin Ahmad, God has blessed me in seeing you again."

AHMAD HAD TURNED nineteen and Adel twenty, and they went
together to Grandfather's favorite, the oldest restaurant in Buraydah.
Sitting at one of Jerusalem's old tables, they drank *gahwa,* followed by
sugared tea. Shunning baklava and other honeyed pastries, they ate
just dates—sweet Sukkary, of course.

Adel told him all about jihad. He had learned from the imam how
jihad could be a shortcut to Heaven and allow them to repent from the
sins of their gang days.

Ahmad started to hang with Adel again. Rather than video
games, they watched videos about Americans bombing schools. In
place of surfing for porn, they surfed for jihadi websites together.
They no longer talked about girls they were going to "spy" or maids
they could boast about raping but together were moved by TV and
Internet reports on how American soldiers were raping Muslim girls
in Iraq.

Ahmad was struck by an interview on Al Jazeera of an Iraqi girl,
maybe sixteen or seventeen, which the boys watched together. She had

large black eyes and full lips; she showed her face but covered her hair. The poor girl could barely talk as she described how the Americans had raped her. Ahmad thought of the Filipino maid and could tell Adel was thinking of her too. It didn't matter whether his story had been true then, it became true now.

For the next several months, they were friends again. Instead of driving fast cars, they fasted. Instead of chasing *dhub* lizards in the desert, they prayed in the mosque. Instead of smoking hashish, they watched a sheik on DVD issue a fatwa, which held that jihad was the surest path to forgiveness from sin. A religious friendship replaced their gang bond.

Then Ahmad saw the TV pictures that changed him.

They were of Abu Ghraib. The Americans had strung up a Muslim man as if he were about to be hanged, except his face was hooded in black and his body was completely naked. The American soldiers exposed him: everything was stripped away. The news said he had been raped.

The next shot was even more devastating. It showed the man afterward. He wasn't any older than Ahmad. He hardly looked much different either. Ahmad could even see into his eyes. They were brown, like his, not the raging black of his father.

Ahmad could never remember feeling so moved in his life.

"There's no greater sin than rape," Adel said.

"We must stand up for our brothers in Iraq," Ahmad replied, choking on the tears caught in his throat. He didn't eat for days.

He would go to Iraq to defend his Muslim brothers. An invading foreign army was attacking innocent Muslim women and children. It was his religious duty to protect them. He was at last on the side of the good, on jihad in the way of God.

Ahmad fixed himself to follow the righteous path. The photos of Abu Ghraib called him to Holy War. To see this abuse and humiliation would call any good person, any good Muslim, to arms.

"You must swear on the Holy Qur'an not to tell anyone," Adel said.

Ahmad stayed mute and told no one—not his grandfather, brother, or even mother. He knew his mother would just cry. He had to do this to be a man. He didn't want to disobey his parents, but thought Grandfather would be proud. Grandfather was a good Muslim. He knew all twenty-nine times dates appeared in the Holy Qur'an; he prayed five times a day; he fasted during the month of Ramadan. And he was strong enough to know for himself what was right. Even though the Saudi government had banned Umm Kalsoum, Grandfather listened to her sing.

It was the beginning of Ramadan in October 2004. And because it was the holiest month of the year, no one would suspect he might not obey his parents.

Ahmad collected his passport, $1,600 in cash and wore his favorite leather jacket for good luck. He had gotten the jacket from his father when he was thirteen and wore it everywhere. His mother even joked that he slept in it (he sometimes did), went to the bathroom with it (well, not really), and took a shower with it still on (obviously not!).

The morning they left Buraydah, Adel and Ahmad together trimmed their beards and took on the look of their gang days. Transformed back, they seemed no different from before, but felt truly proud for the first time in their lives.

Taking a taxi from Buraydah on the highway through the desert to the capital, Riyadh, Ahmad wanted to swing by his grandfather's Prince Mishal store on the way out of town.

"We can't take detours from our mission, Cousin," Adel said.

It was the first time that Ahmad had ever left his hometown, the International Capital of Dates. Now he'd be truly international—not something just any boy from Buraydah could boast of.

They stayed in a run-down hotel, the Al Mutlaq, which Adel had found in the center of Riyadh on the Old Airport Road. It was not much better than the *estiraha* near Buraydah they had hung at: smoky old lobby with deep red curtains and paintings of date palms and camels peeling from the cracked green walls. Their room was small and smoky too.

Ahmad had trouble falling asleep that night without his mother's glass of hot milk. But he hoped that "the best mother in the whole wide world" would one day understand.

Adel gave Ahmad the contact phone number and meeting place in Syria he got from his imam and said from now on they must act as if they didn't know each other. Each taking their own taxi to King Khalid International Airport, they checked in separately. Ahmad did not need a visa for Syria.

The Saudi Airlines flight to Damascus put pressure on his ears. He could barely hear all the instructions the flight attendants gave.

He took another taxi to the Marjeh Square Hotel, off the town square near Old Damascus. It was another beat-up hotel like the Al Mutlaq. This time the paintings of date palms didn't even look like the real thing. He supposed the Syrians didn't really know.

They played Umm Kalsoum in the lobby, music now forbidden to him as a jihadi. It was even "Aoulek Eih" (What Should I Tell You?). He recognized every sway of the violins, every off beat of the drums—most of all that voice, wailing, pleading, crying for mercy, moving up and down scales, from her deepest guttural pleas to her fluttering, gasping trills, giving him goose bumps all over. The Noble Lady had once held millions of Arabs in *tarab*. On every record, you could hear all the men screaming, clapping, and singing along with the world's greatest singer—no Arab was more beloved. Ahmad imagined that it must have been a simpler time than now. Why did the Americans have to attack? He even remembered another of Grandfather's favorites, "The Time Has Passed": "Tell Time to turn back, turn back for us once more . . ."

Ahmad never left the hotel to explore Old Damascus. From the taxi, it looked so much more crowded than Buraydah. Leaving separately, he hadn't seen Adel at the airport or hotel. Ahmad was sure he was on the right path, even if sweating. It was a great feeling of adventure he had never known before. It was a duty to God. He had seen Abu Ghraib. If those photos didn't move you, nothing would.

Ahmad called the number from a phone booth in the hotel lobby at precisely 20:00 hours, just as he was supposed to. After he made the call, he saw a guy walk by and signal him with his eyes. He followed the man outside, who told him to follow another man at the next corner. It was hard to keep up with the next man through the back alleys of Damascus, but they soon arrived at another hotel, climbing the narrow stairs to the third floor. The man, whose face was covered, asked for 500 riyals ($150) and Ahmad's cell phone. He told Ahmad to keep wearing his black leather jacket (no problem!) and carry today's newspaper in his left hand ("More American Massacres in Iraq," the headline).

"Go to the Al Amir Hotel in Aleppo and the phone booth in the lobby, call this cell." He handed him the back of a folded cigarette box with a number written on it.

Every time he had to move, Ahmad felt important. What was he doing in Buraydah? Now he was helping his Muslim brothers against an infidel invader. Every time he had to go to a back alley or make a phone call, he was following in the way of God. It didn't matter that he had lost touch with Adel. He was on jihad. Ahmad al-Shayea was living Islam.

He took the bus to Aleppo at six the next morning, found the hotel near Aleppo's Old City, and made all the calls he was told to.

At last he saw a taxi pull up to the hotel and Adel come out with a Syrian. They all went off in the cab together.

It was wonderful to see Adel again, even if they didn't talk.

Mazen was the new Syrian handler from the "Tawhid and Jihad Group," under the command of the famous Abu Musab al-Zarqawi, Al Qaeda's commander in Iraq. Mazen was short, no taller than Ahmad in fact, but had an enormous chest with bulging biceps and a three-day growth across his face. His words were clipped and harsh. He told the boys to read their newspapers in the cab and not look where they were headed.

They came to another decaying building in the old souk and climbed the steep stairs to an apartment on the second floor. The Syrians led Adel in a different direction, and Ahmad was now with two Moroccans, another Saudi, and a Syrian. They were curtly told not to leave the apartment, just watch jihadi videos set up for them, and in the evening, for *iftar* to break the Ramadan fast, eat the hummus and Syrian bread. It was a pale imitation of the Lebanese dishes at the Jerusalem Restaurant. Ahmad missed his Sukkary dates.

None of them talked much. The guys were here to defend Muslims, promote Islam, and expel a foreign invader. There was no room for chitchat. Or for Ahmad to wonder where Adel was.

The next day, Mazen drove them in a van with curtains to a farm outside Aleppo. There were more Saudis and North Africans, only no Adel.

Mazen was in charge. He said that the road to the battlefield in Fallujah was not clear. The men spent the next ten days watching jihadi videos of the suffering of Iraq.

Ahmad got up all his courage to speak to Mazen. He asked the burly Syrian to contact his parents and let them know he was safe. He handed Mazen his father's number in Buraydah.

"Don't worry 'bout it, kid," Mazen said, pointing his stubby index finger. Ahmad noticed that he had no nails.

On the tenth day, Mazen took each man into a private room. He sat Ahmad down. Without saying a word, Mazen handed him a fake Iraqi ID, 500 Syrian liras, and a bus ticket. He told him to leave tomorrow, wait under the pharmacy sign at the end of Tal Abyad Street in Raqqah. The pass code was *"helilmoya"* ("sweeten the water"), a traditional Bedouin greeting.

"Did you reach my parents? Let them know I'm all right?" Ahmad asked.

"Told you not to worry 'bout it, kid. Not a problem."

Mazen needed Ahmad's Saudi passport and any money he had left. Mazen didn't say anything but motioned with his hand for more.

"That's all I have," Ahmad said.

Mazen kept calling with his hand: "The jacket, kid."

It was Ahmad's prized possession. The lucky leather jacket his father had given him and his mother had always joked about. He'd promised it to his brother Abdurrahman. He now wished he'd just left it at home in Buraydah. He was sure it wasn't worth much. Why did the Syrian need it anyway? It was just lucky to Ahmad. It made no difference to anybody else.

He didn't know what to do. Tell Mazen it was lucky? He'd sound like a kid, not a jihadi fighter. A lucky jacket was hardly pious.

"You're a soldier in jihad. I'm your superior officer. I've given you an order. You want me to call your father, don't you?" Mazen barked.

He took off his lucky jacket and handed it to the Syrian, wondering whether he'd sell it in Aleppo's famous souk the next day.

Mazen just said, "Dismissed." Ahmad felt his throat well up and was about to say "Please call my parents," when Mazen shouted "Dismissed!" almost at the top of his lungs.

Ahmad felt like crying, but wasn't a baby, he told himself. He was here as a jihadi to fight for justice. What did a silly childhood jacket mean? And if the money went for jihad, it would bring him even more luck in the battles ahead.

UNDER THE SIGN, Ahmad waited. It was only a couple of minutes. It felt like forever. He was cold. He'd gotten so used to that stupid jacket. He wondered where Adel was. No one had ever told him they'd be separated like this. His ears felt full, as on the plane. It almost made him feel dizzy.

He began to pace under the sign. The pharmacy looked like his grandfather's Prince Mishal store, if you thought hard enough.

At last, a stranger came and muttered *"Helilmoya"* under his breath so quickly Ahmad could barely make it out. They all talked so curtly. But that must be the way of real soldiers, he thought. Told to look down, they walked in circles around Raqqah town, to a ground-floor apartment and a group of four other Saudis and Adel at last.

Ahmad felt so relieved to see him. They embraced but didn't talk. It was not the jihadi thing to do. He knew he couldn't tell Adel about his jacket, even though he was dying to. Friendship now meant something different. They were comrades in arms, not boys from Buraydah.

Two days later, they left Raqqah for the town of Dayr az-Zawr, closer to the Syrian border with Iraq. Riding in another van with curtains, they were like women veiled. Still, Ahmad was happy: Mazen had put Adel in charge of the Saudis.

Ordered into the back of a truck, hiding underneath soap, laundry detergent, and other cleaning supplies, the men then went to Abu

Kamal on the Syrian border with Iraq. At near midnight, the Syrian smuggler, "Abu Muhammad," he called himself, wearing his night-vision goggles and Kalashnikov, led the men on foot into Iraq. They crossed near Al Qa'im, the Iraqi border town in Al Anbar Province.

They had made it inside. The Syrian now handed the new jihadis to an Iraqi, "Abu Asil, the Prince of Arabs," he called himself. The prince led Ahmad and the other boys to the safe house, a farm near Al Qa'im.

The prince cut a commanding figure. Unlike the Syrians, he was tall and thin, with full Arab headdress and beard.

Gathering the group together the next day, Abu Asil, prince of the Arabs and emir of Al Qaeda in Iraq in Al Anbar, addressed them as "valiant jihadis." Twenty-four men from all over the Arab world: five Saudis and nineteen from Jordan, Morocco, Yemen, Libya, Tunisia, Algeria, and Egypt.

At last they were in Iraq, ready to fight for their Muslim brothers and defend Islam against the American torture and humiliation of Abu Ghraib.

"You soldiers of jihad have arrived at the time of God's greatest glory. The battle against the infidel American invaders is joined. Your sacrifice at Fallujah can defeat the Jews and Crusaders," Abu Asil said.

Ahmad had never felt so proud.

"How many of you will die to avenge Abu Ghraib?" the prince demanded.

"*Allah-u-Akbar!*" (God is great) they all cried, to a man willing to avenge the shame visited on Muslims at the satanic Abu Ghraib.

"Those most blessed among you in God's eyes," the emir continued, "are noble *shaheed* ready to go to Heaven on a martyrdom mission for Allah Almighty. Whoever wants can leave with me at the vanguard, leading all of you."

There was silence. Maybe the boys had not clearly understood the prince's words.

Abu Asil explained with a fatwa: "Every martyr will go straight to Heaven, in ultimate glory, there is no higher calling. So each of you is called, so each of you shall go."

Again, there were no cries of *"Allah-u-Akbar,"* not even a word.

Ahmad came to Iraq to fight to defend the honor of Islam against Abu Ghraib and American torture, not die right away in a suicide bombing before he could even save a single soul. Ahmad thought Adel and the others must feel the same way, as Abu Asil continued to exhort the group to suicide missions but no one volunteered.

"Soldiers of God will do what jihad requires. Every one of you will in time be worthy of Al Qaeda in Iraq."

The next day, Abu Asil led the new soldiers in more vans to another safe house in Rawah, near Anah. And farther down the Euphrates River in Al Anbar Province awaited the scenes of battle and glory: Hadithah, Ramadi, and Fallujah.

But the men just waited. Day after day. The dirt stuck to the food— not like the real Arab food Ahmad was used to eating. Iraqi flat bread, *khubz* mostly or *samoon,* hummus, sweet watery tea, crusty date jam. The Khadrawy dates were dried and hard, not Sukkary sweet and moist. Ahmad had diarrhea and was embarrassed how much time he spent at the shithole.

There were some forty-five jihadis now, many just returning from battle in Fallujah. They didn't say much except pray five times a day. None of them was Iraqi, except for Abu Asil the emir, who took his orders directly from Zarqawi, the highest commander of Al Qaeda in Iraq. The days were spent waiting. They did allow the men to hold a Kalashnikov, but not shoot it. The *shamal* winds were fiercer than in Buraydah.

At least Adel was there. Ahmad always prayed shoulder to shoulder with him in true jihadi fashion. Adel was the only one he talked to. But all Adel kept saying was "Remember Abu Ghraib. Never forget what you saw with your own eyes, Cousin."

Who knew TV photos could call you to fight, give up your whole life?

After almost three weeks, the emir told Ahmad that he and another Saudi would go to Ramadi, closer to the front.

But the other Saudi wasn't Cousin Adel.

Separated from Adel, Hamzah made a poor substitute. Fat with a long stringy beard and crooked teeth, his skin was dark as a dried Khlas. Hamzah didn't seem to know much about anything. He was from Asir, the southernmost province in Saudi Arabia. A real tribal, he kept saying that the emir had promised him "sweet Heaven" and seventy-two *houri* (virgins) in a martyrdom mission. Hamzah was just after some reward. What about helping his fellow man on Earth right now? Ahmad thought. Weren't they fighting to stop Abu Ghraib and the infidel Crusaders? He wondered how Hamzah could stay so fat on such lousy food. Ahmad could hardly sleep, waiting and waiting, while Hamzah just got fatter and fatter.

The next long month and a half brought no fighting. Ahmad and Hamzah would shuttle from Iraqi safe house to safe house to avoid the Americans, though Ahmad never saw any. And there was no training at all. Not even how to shoot the Kalashnikov that they had once been allowed to hold.

His diarrhea wouldn't stop. There were no real dates to fortify him, no Cousin Adel to urge him on. Hamzah, the hick Asiri, would talk of the "eternal beauty" of the virgins and how he'd drink the "sweet juice of Paradise while a virgin beauty wiped his mouth." Ahmad hoped to God that nasty Syrian had at least called his parents. He tried to remember Umm Kalsoum, "Hadeeth El Roh" or "El Atlaal," but there was no music. He worried Grandfather might be sick, or maybe his mother. Ahmad could cry with her as he'd never cried while reciting the Book.

Ahmad kept telling himself it was time he became a man, stand and fight for his Muslim brothers. Remember Abu Ghraib. Finally, when Abu Asil stopped by to check on them, he got up all his nerve to complain.

"I want to fight like a soldier for jihad," Ahmad said. His stomach hurt, he even felt tears.

The Iraqi told him security was hard now and be patient. They always said be patient. "We will give you a sacred mission," he promised.

Shortly after, another emir, higher up than Abu Asil, came. He called himself Abu Osama and said he was the highest leader of Al Qaeda in all of Al Anbar Province. He would take Ahmad on a mission to Baghdad.

"Al-Hamdulillah," Ahmad said, nodding. Praise God.

Ahmad felt his whole life leading to this point. After nearly three months in purgatory, he would finally have the chance to help others and serve God.

Taken to the safe house of Abu Omar al-Kurdi in Baghdad, he spent the night with two other Saudi soldiers of God and a Yemeni. He wondered where Adel was now and what his brother Abdurrahman, his whole family was doing. He wished he could just call them.

Three days later, Ahmad was taken to yet another safe house, still in Baghdad, this time with nine Iraqi fighters.

Adel wasn't there. In fact, there were no foreign Arabs. Ahmad was now the only Saudi among all the Iraqis.

His new emir, Abu Abdul-Rahman, hardly looked the part of a pious jihadi. He had an oily stubby beard and always a cigarette in his mouth—or was busy lighting one to stick inside. The cigarettes even had an American name: Miami. Ahmad found it strange that this great Iraqi jihadi with yellow fingers and hands always smoked a Miami. Even his toes were stained yellow. He felt like asking if the emir smoked with his toes too, but Ahmad had a sacred mission for jihad.

And his first mission, Abu Abdul-Rahman now told him, was to deliver a fuel tanker to Al Mansour, a Baghdad neighborhood, where it would be picked up by other jihadis.

"I don't know Baghdad at all," Ahmad said.

"We'll help you, my son." The emir managed to smile without ever removing the Miami from between his lips. But Ahmad could see that his teeth were yellow and tobacco-stained like his fingers and toes.

Ahmad felt cold. The headache between his eyes grew stronger. He had never trained for this. He didn't even know how to drive a tanker. Then again, he had never trained for anything. And after almost three months of waiting, waiting to fight, to help, to do anything at all, he didn't want to refuse.

That evening, Ahmad performed final Isha prayer with the Iraqis and had dinner—a dish of chicken and eggplant, the best since he had arrived in Iraq. It tasted almost as good as the food at the Jerusalem Restaurant, but not as good as the Sukkary-sweet *jareesh* of "the best mother in the whole world."

His stomach was on edge again. He tried to think of something that would help him sleep. Umm Kalsoum. He wasn't allowed to sing any-more, even to himself. Sukkary dates. He had a hard time remember-ing their sweet taste. The eggplant stuck in his mouth. He was scared it would give him diarrhea in the middle of his mission tomorrow.

Ahmad had to find the strength. He called the pictures of Abu Ghraib to mind. One of the Iraqis had said the hellish prison was not that far from them. He thought of all the young men like himself being held there, raped and beaten by the American Crusaders. He felt their pain in the pit of his stomach, his head pounding as if he too was hanging by his neck at Abu Ghraib. The jihadis told him the American Crusaders and Jews would not rest until they killed every last Muslim. Ahmad knew that only God could give him the strength. He just hoped his father would know all he'd sacrificed.

It was a rather cool day for Baghdad, even at the end of December 2004. Ahmad wished he still had his leather jacket. The emir handed him a simple hand-drawn map from his yellow fingers. With a Miami firmly stuck between his crooked teeth, the emir assured him that two Iraqi jihadis would be with him every step of the way.

"Abu Abdul-Rahman, my emir, I have but one request." Ahmad tried to talk in the most formal florid Arabic, with its traditional words of deference and obeisance. Maybe the emir didn't even understand.

"Stop worrying, Abu Omar and Muhammad Odeh are going with you. You'll not be alone." The emir's foul tobacco breath made him want to recoil.

"Not that—" Ahmad said. He lost his words. His hands were shak-ing. His cheeks were red, even though his beard was now fuller and longer than it had ever been in his life. His whole body was cold. He was afraid he'd shit in his pants.

"I have but one request," he repeated in formal Arabic.

"Spit it out, my little son," Abu Abdul-Rahman said, inhaling his Miami with such force he could've swallowed the lit cigarette whole.

Ahmad thought of his grandfather—and Farid, "the Spit Champion of Buraydah."

"After the mission, can you arrange for me to call home?" He didn't want to sound like a kid.

The emir smiled through his tobacco teeth. "Of course, it would be my greatest pleasure, my smallest son," he said in the most formal manner that apparently he could muster.

AHMAD WALKED BEHIND Abu Omar and Muhammad Odeh. The two Iraqi jihadis were not much older than Ahmad. Not much taller or bigger either.

Each step Ahmad took his stomach turned, until he let loose a large fart. He hoped to God the other men didn't hear it. But he farted again even more loudly. The whole neighborhood could hear it now. Ahmad burst out laughing. He couldn't stop.

"You're a real Saudi," Abu Omar said.

"It's the eggplant," Ahmad said, still laughing like a desert camel.

"No, you're Saudi. You guys are the loudest." Abu Omar chuckled now too.

The tanker truck parked around the corner was much larger than Ahmad had imagined. The other jihadis told him to get in the driver's seat. He had no clue how to drive it.

But the Iraqi jihadis were nice. Before they drove anywhere, they let him practice. The clutch worked smoothly. And he didn't have to worry, they told him: they'd start driving the tanker first toward the center of town themselves.

Abu Omar took the steering wheel. He was the nicest of the Iraqis. Ahmad sat in the middle. The other jihadi, Muhammad Odeh, was close beside him in the passenger seat. Ahmad felt warmed by their bodies. They were joking around.

"Don't fart again, Brother Ahmad. You might send us sky-high," Abu Omar said.

"Yeah," Muhammad Odeh said, "I want to breathe, fart-face."

"How come you Saudis are the best at farting?" Abu Omar said. "Maybe we can use your farts as our secret weapon against the Americans."

"Don't encourage him, Omar," Muhammad Odeh said.

Ahmad saw Baghdad from the tanker's front window. While Abu Omar avoided the American roadblocks, the blackened buildings and ash reminded Ahmad of the end of the emir's burning Miami.

Abu Omar successfully drove the eight-wheeler to Al Mansour, one of Baghdad's "best neighborhoods," he said. In the last hour of driving, the two jihadis talked to him more than anyone else in the three months since he'd left Buraydah. While he wondered why he'd never been trained and didn't have a weapon, Ahmad felt proud he was finally doing something. Abu Omar and Muhammad Odeh were both "really nice guys," and Abu Abdul-Rahman, smiling at him, had promised he'd call home after. The emir must be a man of his word.

A thousand yards from where they were supposed to park the truck and go to a waiting car, the Iraqis suddenly jumped out, shouting at him to pull the tanker up to the concrete blocks.

Ahmad could see the concrete barrier just ahead. He didn't know what to do but had to grab the wheel quickly as the truck was sliding forward. It was only a thousand yards to the end. There he'd meet Abu Omar and Muhammad Odeh, park the truck for the other jihadis to drive away, and go back to the smiling emir. Mission accomplished.

In what seemed like a matter of seconds, perhaps twenty at most, he made it. His first mission of jihad completed, he could return to the safe house and call home. That was the last thought in his mind as he stopped before the concrete.

A powerful explosion, remotely triggered, then turned the back of the tanker, filled with twenty-six tons of liquid explosives, into a powerful fireball that could be seen miles away.

The bonfire below shot upward, lighting the desert sky above Baghdad like a comet, a sign from God Himself.

———

AFTER THE EXPLOSION, someone from Al Qaeda called Ahmad's parents in Buraydah. It was the first time they had heard about him in the three months since he'd disappeared.

"You can be proud. Your son has chosen the path of martyrdom. For him and all of his family, Allah the Most Beneficent, the Most Merciful, reserves an honored place in Heaven." Then the phone went dead.

The pain Father Ahmad felt, holding the dead receiver in his hand, was greater than any diabetic fit he could imagine. He wanted to scream but couldn't. He wanted to cry, but his eyes were cold and dry. His first son. His beloved Ahmad. He could barely bring himself to mouth the words to his wife, whose wailing and screaming wouldn't end, and then to his own father, who, though now quite old himself, had never been seen to take anything so hard. The whole family was turned on its head. They had never felt such sudden and complete grief. No one thought of Heaven and its rewards, only their pain and loss right here on Earth.

Within days, a prayer and mourning. With no body to bury, the Al Shayea family felt greater grief and shame.

While Ahmad's father and grandfather held her on each side, Mother Ahmad could not stop softly wailing. It was as if the old record player froze on Umm Kalsoum, the needle stuck in the cry, playing her deep wail over and over again.

"I SEE THE world melt," Ahmad said to me, the air-conditioning in the Care Center *majlis* cranking loudly. "Everything turns black. My hands disappear in more black. My throat leaves me in screams. Hellfire is licking up everywhere. My mind is dead numb. The flames are shooting at me from every direction.

"Suddenly I fall; jump out, without even knowing where I am or what I'm doing. My body on fire, running, falling down, rolling on the ground. I couldn't move. Didn't know what happened or who I am anymore. I am frozen in shock as my body is burning, as the world burns to the ground," Ahmad remembered.

He turned toward me. Dr. Ali the psychologist and Lieutenant Majid the translator were silent before Ahmad finally said, "I hope one day we can meet again in America."

AHMAD AL SHAYEA was the martyr who never made it to Heaven, even though the blast from his bomb was strong enough to kill eight bystanders.

While frail, Ahmad had always been a handsome boy. Now all that was left was his round brown eyes. His face had become a bomb crater, his hands twisted red stumps, what remained of his fingernails on his left hand were a yellow brown, like the rotten teeth of Abu Abdul-Rahman's smile when he promised he'd call his parents. Every time he looked at his deformed nails from that moment on, he saw the teeth of Dajjal the Deceiver.

Lying on the Baghdad ground, literally smoking from the fire, the truck still on fire, a man—no, a hero—ran up to his body.

Thinking he was an innocent Iraqi Shiite victim by his fake ID, the man and other passers-by carried him from the blackened earth to a Shiite-run hospital.

The pain he felt lying in a cot with the other bodies all around him was unlike anything he'd ever felt. His burnt skin and flesh left him naked. His heart burned too, his stomach in ashes.

He just lay there like a corpse, no doctors or nurses, the other bodies crying in pain, their souls mixed with the unseen spirits of jinn.

Ahmad felt that the fire never stopped. The only thing that cooled his barbecued skin was the pee and shit that uncontrollably came out and covered his oozing, pus-filled flesh, as if he were in Hell. For three days it seemed, he lay silent in a hallway like a *dhub* lizard he'd once tortured over an open flame in the desert, squirming reflexively in its last throes of life.

When an Iraqi doctor finally came, cleaned and dressed his wounds, Ahmad couldn't keep silent. He told the doctor everything: who he was and what exactly had happened.

Ahmad was sorry he had. Hours later, Iraqi security men surrounded his hospital cot. He could barely see them, his eyelids were so swollen with burns. He told them everything, but they wanted more. They took the back of a cold knife and ran it against his burns, poked it into his charred eyes and melted nose. His face looked like bubbled tar. He let out the screams of a fiery *dhub*. His tortured pain drew out every breath of life he still had in him. He could never imagine pain before.

"You fucking dog!" they yelled at him. "Taste what it feels like!" The knife pulled at the remnants of his skin. He didn't know whether the liquid he felt was his blood or more pee or pus or diarrhea. Ahmad now knew what it must feel like to burn in Hell. The pain took over everything.

The only thing that made the Iraqis stop was TV.

The world's first encounter with Ahmad al-Shayea was on footage sent to the Al Arabiya news channel and then broadcast throughout the globe.

It was the first known case of a suicide bomber in Iraq who had survived his immolation and ended up "back on Earth instead of Heaven," the announcer said.

Back in Buraydah, Ahmad's parents saw their son, face charred, head heavily bandaged, but alive. They immediately recognized his eyes, though most of the rest of him was wrapped like a mummy. For the first time, his parents felt like their own kids, stuck to the TV.

They had already held a funeral prayer. His mother thought she must be having a vision. His father just broke down in tears.

The deputy minister of Iraqi security led the interrogation, followed by other Iraqi security men. Ahmad told the truth. He told his interrogators where to find a senior Zarqawi lieutenant in Baghdad and revealed all he knew about Al Qaeda. They kept him from sleeping, kept threatening and rubbing his burns until he screamed, before the Americans showed up.

He was scared to death: Ahmad was told he was going to Abu Ghraib, the prison of torture and humiliation, the place of death that had caused him to come to Iraq in the first place, the American infidel hell on Earth he had come to fight against—though he didn't see how it could be any worse than his hell now. And when the Iraqis told him that innocent people had died when his truck exploded, Ahmad felt a different kind of hell—one inside his own heart.

Yet inexplicably, at that moment, he also felt something unexpected: God had saved him from the hellfire. God wanted him to live for a reason.

Ahmad no longer thought of his own pain. He mourned for those who had died and prayed for the injured to recover. He didn't think of his own fate but that of his mother, grandfather, brothers, sisters, and father too.

Three days after Iraqi security started its interrogation, the Americans arrived.

Ahmad, covered in burns and barely able to walk, was stunned. The careful way the Americans helped carry him down the stairs to the waiting U.S. Army jeep was nothing less than another miracle.

One of the American officers even spoke in Arabic. Ahmad didn't speak a word of English. The American told him, "Don't worry, it's all good."

When he arrived at Abu Ghraib, instead of prison, the Americans immediately sent him to the hospital. Spending three months in ICU, he received over thirty operations, including skin grafts, cellulite transplants, and other plastic surgery from the American doctors. The American medicines helped his raw, wounded flesh too. And the physical pain was salved by the balm of caring.

Sergeant Crystal Evans was the army medic who helped him the most. She had a soft voice. That's all he heard. His eyes were still bandaged from the surgery. And he didn't understand a word of her English.

Ahmad had never talked with a woman before, apart from his own mother, aunts, and sisters, of course. But he thought maybe this American army nurse didn't count since he couldn't understand her anyway.

Each time Sergeant Crystal touched his face with alcohol, the burns felt cool. Each time she swabbed his charred arms, it didn't matter how much the pain ate away, her fingers were cool. As she washed his swollen feet, he felt his whole body shiver with goose bumps. It was the first time he'd been touched by a woman. He never could have imagined before what it would really feel like.

As she fed him small bites of food, Ahmad felt his appetite come back. Oh, he'd read of the angels in Heaven, the virgins who'd serve the men—how was she different? Could he fall in love with an American nurse he couldn't even see? Couldn't understand a single word she said?

She continually healed him with soft unknown words; she continually healed with soft light hands. If he were in Saudi Arabia, they'd get married.

Ahmad thought that if Umm Kalsoum had talked and was an American wherever Crystal Evans was from, that was how she'd sound!

Her name alone healed him. "Crystal." He asked an interpreter what it meant. *Light.* Yes, Crystal was his light. Ahmad had never dreamed an American could be so nice.

He asked the Iraqi interpreter to be there once with Crystal so he could find out about her: the light of Crystal that he couldn't see but with every cell that was still alive on his dead skin, he could feel warming his heart, cooling his hot flesh, bringing him back to life.

Ahmad was so happy finally to talk back. He told her about the dates and *dhub* lizards, Buraydah and Camaros.

Crystal told him about Texas, Ahmad wasn't sure where, Temple, he thought she said. He knew she had to be a person of faith. Crystal said she was "in her family's shoes" in the U.S. Army, following her father and grandfather.

Ahmad then told her about his grandfather, with Umm Kalsoum singing at full volume while they shot out their date pits.

Crystal started laughing. Ahmad now felt sure she had the same deep voice as the Star of the East. She was the music of life; she was Grandfather's secret born again, for this laughing American, like his grandfather, defied what others thought. This laughing American helped save his life.

"God has saved me," Ahmad now said.

Crystal stopped laughing. "Amen," she said.

"The worst thing about being here is that I haven't been able to pray five times a day, in the way I should," he said.

"I believe you," she said.

"But the Holy Qur'an says that if you're sick or ill, God forgives you," Ahmad said.

"Amen," Crystal said.

"I still pray five times a day in my heart," Ahmad said.

"I pray for you too," Crystal said.

Ahmad could feel her smiling at him, even if he couldn't see it.

Then he told her the story of how Mary ate dates before giving birth to Jesus. He didn't know whether that was just his grandfather's story or really from the Qur'an.

"It's from our Holy Book," Ahmad said.

"We're related by dates then, Bernie," Crystal said, laughing.

That was the one word in English he now understood. She called him "Bernie." So did all the other Americans.

He wanted to correct her. But he liked the sound of "Bernie." The truth was, he liked any word that came from her lips. And he figured the Americans just couldn't pronounce Ahmad, that's all. He knew he could ask Crystal.

"Where did Bernie come from?" he said.

"That's not your name? I thought it was just short for Bernardo or some Arab thing," she said, laughing again. Crystal had a wonderful laugh.

"I don't mind," Ahmad said.

He felt like saying he didn't mind it as long as Crystal spoke the word, sang it to him. Ahmad had never thought that English could sound so sweet.

One day Crystal came in with an American officer and Iraqi interpreter, who told him that the Americans had called his parents in Buraydah to say he was all right.

Crystal said something in her soft English words, and the Iraqi interpreter translated: "Your mother and father give their love."

Ahmad now knew that the cool liquid he felt on his scarred cheeks was tears.

He'd never forget Crystal. He'd always keep a secret place in his heart for the American nurse who never scolded him, who laughed him back to health, and who prayed to God too.

But after three months in ICU, Ahmad was transferred to physical therapy. The room now had more light and more things to do. And the bandages were taken away. He could now see.

While he missed Crystal, at last he could see all the Americans who healed him. All the nurses and doctors, who helped him move his charred arms, taught him how to use his stumps of hands, helped him to walk on broken feet, breathe through smoky lungs, and eat again from burned lips. In the next three months, he regained life.

Ahmad now knew that the Americans he had come to Iraq to kill had saved his life. And the Iraqis he had come to fight for had tried to kill him like a dog.

The Abu Ghraib that tortured others saved him.

He told the Americans the truth, just as he had his Iraqi interrogators. But unlike the Iraqi security men, no American ever hurt him. He was treated with respect. He was treated with kindness. It was Al Qaeda that "used me like a tool. I was a piece of rotten bait to lure a *dhub* out of his dry hole."

Ahmad thanked God every day for the chance to see life again. And a lesson for others, he now told me: "I came to help the Iraqis. But when I needed help, Mr. Ken, the Americans were the ones who helped me, not my fellow Arabs, my brother Muslims I came to help."

After almost six months of medical care and interrogations, three Saudi Ministry of Interior officers arrived at his hospital room.

One of them was Captain Fahad.

"We're from the ministry," he said. Everyone in the entire kingdom knew that could only mean the all-powerful Ministry of Interior.

"Americans treating you well, *Burn-nee*?" Captain Fahad said, laughing.

"How did you know that's what the Americans call me?"

"We're the ministry. Tell us what we don't know," the captain said.

Ahmad took the captain's response literally, for there was one thing that he had wanted to know for the last six months. In the past, he never had the courage to ask, especially someone in authority like the MOI. But after all he'd been through, he was no longer the shy little boy from Buraydah. Still, he couldn't quite bring himself to ask, not yet.

"How's my family?" he asked instead.

"They're fine. They're dying to see you, no pun intended," the captain said, joking again.

"There is one question I'm dying to ask." Ahmad tried to joke as well.

"Fire away, *Burn-nee*," the captain, who was known for his joking ways, said.

"Do you know about Adel, the guy who came with me to Iraq?" Ahmad showed his newfound courage, the new strength he had inside.

"Sure enough, told you, at MOI, we're in the know," the captain said.

But Captain Fahad didn't say. Was he waiting for Ahmad to ask again?

"Do you know why the Americans call me *Burn-nee*?" That popped out of his mouth instead.

The captain started laughing like Crystal. The other men joined in. Ahmad smiled but didn't know what was so funny. Finally, the captain got ahold of himself, cleared his throat and said: "Ahmad, you're the lucky one. Adel died in a suicide attack about two months ago, here in Baghdad. Allah Almighty has saved you to come back to the kingdom, *Inshallah*." The captain was now dead serious.

"*Inshallah*," Ahmad said. Adel's fate made him feel sad and blessed at the same time. He couldn't help it and even felt his eyes begin to gather tears for his favorite cousin.

But above all, he knew the captain was right.

"God has saved me for a purpose, *Inshallah*," Ahmad repeated.

He told the MOI officers that he wanted to go on Saudi TV to speak directly to the young people of the kingdom. Al Qaeda was not for Islam; it was not for humanity.

"I don't want what happened to me to happen to others, like Adel," Ahmad said. "I want everyone to look at me. To see my burned body. My scarred face. All that is the same is my eyes. I am a living example of Al Qaeda's hellfire. I want them to see Al Qaeda in the flesh. I want them to see how Al Qaeda tricked me into killing innocent people. I want them to see the lie that is Al Qaeda."

The captain said that was what the MOI wanted too, but first he had to go home, be checked out medically, and go before a judge to receive a sentence for leaving the kingdom without authorization.

"Probably no more than a year," the captain said.

Ahmad would also be sent to the MOI's Care Center, a special half-way house to rehabilitate jihadis, where he'd receive religious reeducation, psychological counseling, physical therapy—all with the goal of having him return to Buraydah as a loyal Saudi citizen. Ahmad was just one of many young Saudi men who had gone to fight in Iraq— Saudis made up most of Al Qaeda's foreign fighters.

"As soon as you come home, you can see your family too," the captain said. In fact, he said, he'd take a letter to his parents and grandfather and personally tell them their son was on his way home at last.

"*Hamdillah,*" Ahmad said. "*Allah-u-Akbar.*"

After the MOI officers left, an American general, with his Iraqi interpreter, came to see him.

"You don't have to go back to Saudi Arabia unless you want to," the general said.

Ahmad was quiet. He didn't know what to say. He wanted to ask the general about Crystal. He thought maybe he could go to America and start a new life.

But he knew God wanted him back home in the Kingdom. God had saved him for a reason. Ahmad wanted to see his family. He wanted to taste the dates.

"Thank you, General," Ahmad said. "Thank God."

The general had a release form to sign. It said he agreed to go back to Saudi Arabia of his own free will.

Ahmad signed it. But he really agreed to go back to Saudi Arabia not of his own will but because it was the right thing to do. It was God's will.

Two weeks later, in mid-2005, Ahmad was flown home.

His parents were at King Khalid International Airport.

Ahmad first saw his mother and hugged her. As she cried, tears welled up in his eyes. Then his father was standing next to them. Ahmad didn't know what to do.

"I took my dad in my arms, crying out loud, and kept asking for forgiveness," Ahmad told me. "I can never forget that moment."

His father had also brought with him Grandfather's Ramadan box of Sukkary dates.

OVER THE NEXT several years, after his release from the Care Center, Ahmad lived with his family in Buraydah. He spent most of his time taking courses to learn English. Though he still didn't have a career in mind, his dream of going to America never died. With his Al Qaeda past, I didn't see how it would be possible, but I didn't want to give up either. This failed Al Qaeda suicide bomber had become more pro-American than some of the soldiers he went to fight against.

In an e-mail, he wrote:

Dear Mr. Ken☺

Ahmad will never forget You.☺ Thank God. Thank you for your interest in me and my family. We are fine, praise be to God.

My English is not very bad, I walk slowly but in the right direction.☺

Mr. Ken, you have recording machine with you? In the Capital of the United States, I want You and Me to hear Umm Kalsoum singing again.☺

Al Atlaal.

"It was a palace of dreams but it has crumbled;
Now give me back my freedom, untie my hands."

2

ABBY AND MARYAM:
A JIHADI ROMEO AND JULIET

I MET ABDULLAH AL GILANI, or "Abby," as he preferred to be called, not in the Care Center prison's comparatively grand *majlis* for honored guests but in a plain concrete conference room Abby had specially prepared for me, his very own honored guest.

The room was decorated with all manner of homemade banners and photographs of Abby at the Care Center (though the critical one of his "true love" was missing). The largest banner, hung from the fluorescent lights of the acoustic tiled ceiling, was made of a kind of shiny fabric, with awkwardly hand-painted black-and-green lettering: "Welcome Mr. Ken." Another one propped against the back of an empty metal folding chair, written in the same slanting hand but in red magic marker on a square piece of white letter board, promised "Enlightened Welcoming." Next to it was a series of color photographs of Abby. Each photo showed him, with his thin Ottoman-style black mustache and customary white full-length Saudi *thobe* and red-checkered *shemagh* headdress, standing at attention in different places around the Care Center: the entrance to the prison swimming pool, the art therapy center, the Care Center public relations welcome sign, and more. Finally, Abby made a sign I cannot forget (and never had the nerve to ask what it really meant). Much less grandiose, it was in small letters, more a note than a sign or banner, though written in his same crooked handwriting. In a peculiar bit of Christian iconography for an American Jew in this most Islamic of all Muslim countries, it read, "Hello Mister Saver."

When I first came into the room decorated by Abby with Lieutenant Majid the translator and Dr. Ali, Abby was not alone. He was surrounded by almost twenty other inmates, all boys between the ages of fifteen and twenty-four.

Abby wanted nothing to do with them. He was a fervent jihadi who had gone to Iraq to fight for Al Qaeda against the Americans for one reason. And that was a secret he'd tell only me: he was in love.

If Ahmad's (Bernie's) quest as a jihadi had him looking for love in all the strangest places, Abby was a jihadi literally dying for love. Not just Abby. You couldn't talk about Abby or even think of him without his girlfriend, Maryam, who sought to become one of the first female suicide bombers for Al Qaeda. It was all about Abby *and* Maryam. You couldn't say one without the other.

Abby and Maryam had found a love so passionate that they were willing to die for it. Lieutenant Majid—"the Orlando Majid" (his nickname, after his favorite basketball team)—scoffed, "the Arab Romeo and Juliet." But I wondered if I had ever felt a romantic love so consuming. Abby and Maryam seemed to breathe the air of other planets. A jihadi Romeo and Juliet for our times, however, spells a far more lethal end not just for the lovers but for all of us.

Abby asked Dr. Ali to clear the room before we began. And though Abby desperately wanted to tell me his story, Dr. Ali's prompting of what Abby previously had told him once again proved essential to uncovering the kind of secrets Saudis—or anyone, for that matter—usually guard closely.

WITH HONEY, the Book of God says, there is a cure for men.

In the cool mountains of the Kingdom of Saudi Arabia, Abby's grandfather was one of the best beekeepers in Al Shafa, indeed in all of greater Taif. But his honey seemed to lead his family into a rather different cure for men.

There's no doubt. His bees made a golden sweet brew, which Saudis had a soft spot for. Intoxicating! You could almost say they fell in love with the Al Gilani honey. And just as Saudis loved their honey, the Al Gilani men loved their women. Yet unlike most Saudi men, they had an equally strong sweet spot for only one wife.

Grandfather Al Gilani and all of his sons had married only once, a strict family tradition of monogamy. And the Al Gilani men showed their special one-woman-love by each new child. Grandfather had some twenty children. That may not be a lot by Saudi standards with the customary multiple wives. But, *wa'Allah,* it was a lot for one woman to bear!

Mahal was the eleventh and last son and Abby's father.

Al Taif al-Ma'nous, or "Taif the Friendly," as its people prefer to call it, is a cool and green city lying over the Al Sarawat Mountains, an hour's drive from Mecca in western Saudi Arabia. Famous for the scent of its roses and other flowers, it is a popular resort for tourists and doubles as the summer retreat for many of the Saudi royals as well.

Riding the tourist wave, Abby's father pioneered the art of hawking the sweetest Taif souvenirs: locally grown pomegranates, grapes, dates, and of course, his family's own Al Shafa honey.

Following in the Al Gilani family tradition, Abby's father also faithfully dedicated himself to his only wife, Rana. The young couple had six girls and seven boys in as many years. With so many children for one woman to bear, complications such as stillbirths, miscarriages, birth defects, or even death could be expected to occur. They did not. Instead, when the last son, Abby, was born, the father died at childbirth.

A father doesn't die in childbirth, especially this father, who welcomed the joy of every child as God's expression of love for his one and only wife. But a heart attack felled him when he first saw his final baby boy.

Rana's mourning was intense yet short-lived. She would never question God's will. Besides, God had blessed her with so much. And the advantage of such a large family clan was that one of her husband's many brothers quickly stepped in to take over the fatherly duties. But Rana finally ended up as a second wife.

THE LAST OF the line, Abby, was a skinny boy, sickly and overprotected by his mother. Abby had one peculiar stomach ailment after another. The boy was constantly nauseous. It was a strange symptom for a boy to have. It was as if he suffered from morning sickness.

First they tried honey. It had many medicinal proprieties, according to the Holy Qur'an and the imam. But not in this case. Strange: an Al Gilani boy immune to the power of honey!

Next, they took him to Jeddah Clinic Hospital. The doctors x-rayed, MRI'ed, probed with a barium enema, and found nothing.

Then they held a round-the-clock prayer vigil by his bedside. When that did not work either, Muslim healing ointments were rubbed on his belly before bed. Next came swallowing the *habbatul barakah,* the black oil of the blessed seed, which the boy just threw up.

Finally, they took little Abby to Mecca to drink the water from the famous Zamzam well at Al Masjid al-Haram (the Holy Grand Mosque), near the Ka'abah itself. It was the well of Ishmael, the son of Ibrahim, from which Allah quenched the thirst of Ishmael when he was an infant.

Abby didn't like it. The water tasted salty, not sweet like honey. And since Abby was supposed to drink until it filled his ribs, according to the Hadith of the Prophet Muhammad, the holy water made him even more nauseous.

When Mother Abby washed his bare stomach with the Zamzam, as the Prophet's chest had been washed, it felt much better. But by the time they got back to Taif, the Zamzam did not last. Abby still suffered from his mysterious morning sickness.

Missing much school from his stomach ills, the boy fell behind, though his mother did her best to tutor him. Half of the classes in Saudi government schools are on Islamic teachings. And those were the ones Abby liked best. By only eleven years old, Abby had memorized much of the Holy Qur'an.

Whenever Abby became sick, he would recite Qur'anic verses and pray he would not die like his father. Surah 36, Verse 56, in particular, was his favorite, where one day a true believer could reside in Paradise with his wife "in blissful shade, reclining on thrones."

Abby knew the Holy Qur'an worked best, not any old herbs or chants or even the Zamzam water. If only his father had found the love of the Qur'an too, maybe he wouldn't have dropped dead when Abby was born.

ALL THE STOMACH sickness and nausea suddenly stopped the year Abby turned seventeen.

Abby was over at his sister's house near the center of Taif watching TV, the American show *Perfect Strangers* dubbed in Arabic. A little boy from the neighbor next door, who couldn't have been more than seven or eight, knocked loudly on the door.

The boy was barefoot, his toes black with dirt. He kept his dark coal eyes fixed to the ground the entire time. While rubbing the dust with his toes, the boy pushed the paper he clung between his dirty nails in Abby's direction.

"For you," he mumbled, still staring at the ground.

Abby could see it was a handwritten note, sealed inside a light brown envelope. At first he noticed its distinct smell of cloves and jasmine.

After the boy ran next door, Abby left the TV on and went into his sister's bathroom. Her husband wasn't home. For that matter, he had no idea where his sister was either, probably making more lamb *kabsa*.

The bathroom overwhelmed the scent of the letter. Maybe this was the wrong place to open it. He went back to his spot in front of the TV. *Perfect Strangers* was still playing.

Sliding his first finger under the carefully sealed edges, he slowly opened the ends of the envelope. He never remembered feeling so nervous, as if he were getting one of his endless stomach maladies. He couldn't open the letter in a straight line and had to make a jagged tear, which ripped the entire envelope. Extracting the small note that hid inside, he let it delicately unfold before him. The handwriting was small but careful and neat, with finely etched, indeed stunning, calligraphy: "Ana Fintizarak: 'I'm waiting for you at my window, the fire inside my veins,' Maryam." The boy's eldest sister quoted from the famous love ballad.

Abby felt his stomach sink into his toes, and ran to the toilet. He was used to the wide hole in the ground at the honey farm or the family house on the other side of town. His sister had a white chair that was elevated in the air, so half his vomit landed on the floor. He could've given birth at that moment, his morning sickness was so strong. He wished he had the Zamzam. He began to recite the Holy Qur'an, Surah 36, Verse 56, over and over again.

He soon felt better but did not go to the girl's window that day. Instead, he asked his sister about her.

"*Ya'Allah!* She's here all the time. She even asked about you from our family portrait," his sister said.

That stupid photo where Abby looked pale and sickly, almost a jinn! Why did he have to be so sickly? Why did he have that stupid, cursed stomach? How could she look at that ugly photo?

The next day, Abby skipped school and headed to visit his sister. Reciting the Qur'an to give him strength, he went to the window instead.

It was a large window on the side of the house that directly faced the alleyway. He stood there, kicking the dirt at the ground with his sandal so that his toes became as black as those of her little messenger brother. Five minutes felt like five hours: he felt like a fool until she came to the window, uncovered.

Abby now knew why the Holy Book required women to veil.

He'd never seen a woman before, outside his family. She made him wonder what his father had seen right before dying: when his father looked at Rana giving birth, did he see an angel taking him to Paradise too?

Everything melted when Abby now saw her. He was filled with the Zamzam water without drinking a single drop. It sweated from his pores; it ran through every one of his veins. And for the first time in his short life, his stomach just left him.

Abby said nothing. Maryam said nothing. Maryam was named after the mother of Isa (Jesus), the last prophet before Muhammad— Maryam who'd delivered Isa in a miracle of virgin birth.

Abby felt the miracle now.

From that moment, Abby went to see Maryam every day. Only after the first miraculous day, they actually started to talk.

For two weeks when school was out from noon to four in the afternoon, Abby showed up at the window. He hid behind her father's rusting VW in the alley until the pale green window opened and Maryam appeared in uncovered splendor.

For two weeks, they just talked, and Abby couldn't remember a single word that was said. It felt almost as if he were reciting the Holy Qur'an. Every word was sacred, of unending beauty, taking the breath from each syllable and sending it in flight above.

Thursdays and Fridays—the weekend—were hellish. Though her parents went to Friday mosque, they took afternoon naps at home, so Abby had to stay away.

AFTER TWO MORE weeks, Abby felt the miracle again: he decided to accept Maryam's invitation and go inside.

Maryam's elderly father was a security guard at an elementary school for girls while her mother stayed nearby with family. They were faithfully and safely away during school hours. So now Abby would cut school himself and come to her very room. Behind the world, there was another world.

He'd lie next to Maryam, hoping for another miraculous birth like Baby Isa. And Maryam would hold him tenderly. At first he thought, why not just play with sex, as the other boys bragged about, but he suspected most never did. Maryam said she wasn't that kind of girl.

She wanted to marry him sacred, as a virgin. Being a virgin only made Abby love her even more. She wasn't like any other girl. She was the only one; she was his angel Mary. He gave her his heart.

They made a family. First, they would have a girl and name her Shahed (nectar). Then came the boy, little Abdullah of course, followed by three more boys and three more girls: Jamal, Zaki, Karim, Wafa, Zahra, and Sakina. They picked out wooden cribs, a cherry-wood poster bed and a white Chevy Caprice and painted the bedroom a bright green. Maryam now lovingly called him "Hubby" or sometimes even "Abu Shahed," the honorific name common to proud Arab parents, meaning "Father of their first daughter, Shahed."

They had children in their dreams because Maryam remained pure. But the children could have been real. For the young couple figured out every kind of sex possible—short of the ultimate union—to make their dreams seem real, while keeping Maryam a virgin like her namesake.

Abby was Maryam, and Maryam was Abby. They were married in spirit before they legally could be in the presence of their own families and tribes.

Abby saw his school grades drop until he just barely passed. He now spent every weeknight at his sister's and five days a week with Maryam. He wrote her poetry and brought her Al Shafa honey. He sang "Ana Fintizarak." He carved wooden rattles and toy cars for Shahed, little Abdullah, Jamal, Zaki, Karim, Wafa, Zahra, and Sakina.

Sometimes they watched American TV dubbed in Arabic. *The Honeymooners, Perfect Strangers* again. Sometimes they ate Ajwah dates from each other's mouths. They kissed and dreamed their family into life.

And Abu Shahed wrote his virgin Maryam bride-to-be sacred poems to their blessed love:

Your eyes are my stars,
Your lips my door,
I open to go inside.
You've opened my window;

You've seen my heart;
I have given you mine.
Together, we serve God in all His Glory.
Together, we conquer the world.
Together, we love.

They made more dreams together. Abby would study in Mecca, maybe poetry, maybe math at the university. It was only an hour away. And like many other girls her age, Maryam soon dropped out of school entirely; her head and heart would wait for her Abby, her Abu Shahed.

Maryam was a precious emerald, the most striking girl in Taif, and she would fetch a *mahr* (dowry) greater than what her father earned in an entire year as a guard at an elementary school. But Maryam's resolve made her father back off, his greed no match for her faith. She thought her name really should have been Aisha, the Prophet's favorite wife, or better yet, Khadijah, the Prophet's first wife, whose practical ways first helped Prophet Muhammad.

Maryam told Abby he had to get a university degree and work on the side to earn enough for the *mahr*. Of course, every man had to pay a handsome dowry to marry a worthy woman.

Men are so impractical, Maryam told him. Praise be to Allah that He knew what He was doing when He placed a shrewd head on the shoulders of the female race! Maryam took sewing, cooking, and even personal computing classes, so whenever her dull-hearted father raised the prospect of marriage, she could fend him off, saying she was preparing to be the perfect bride.

But practical Maryam wrote Abby poetry too:

You are my soul.
Through the darkness, I carry you,
A winged servant on God's shoulders;
I am your Maryam,
I am your light and life.
You are my Man, the Abby of dreams,

My Abu Shahed—
The Father of my Nectar,
The temple of faith,
The witness to God's great and everlasting beauty.
I am your Khadijah.

Abby agreed to be practical because Maryam had asked him. And he had to get a job, a degree, a dowry, or there could never be a marriage before the imam and God. He lingered at school and tried to work but saved little. His heart was with Maryam. He could think of nothing else. Their love would carry them through.

Maryam, you are the greatest Virgin:
You are greater than all the virgins of Heaven,
Who greet the greatest martyrs.
You are my Virgin, and
I am your Martyr.

THIS LASTED FOR some five years, until Maryam's older brother Ayman returned from his post in Dammam, dismissed from Crown Prince Abdullah's National Guard. Ayman had the smell of an infidel.

"Why shouldn't the girl get married? She's already twenty. If we don't hurry, no respectable man will want her. We'll lose the *mahr,*" he ranted. Ayman conspired with his father for the dowry, even though the word of God in the Holy Qur'an said that the *mahr* should be paid only to the bride herself.

Abby had managed to save $8,000 toward a dowry, but that fell way short of the $20,000 Maryam's father and brother would insist on as their right as her *wali al-amr,* or "marriage guardians." Even the poorest Saudi man had to come up with $15,000 for a suitable dowry. Maryam told Abby he must at least have his uncle come to her father to make a verbal agreement for marriage. If there were an agreement, she thought, Abby could pay the $8,000 as a down payment, and Maryam could be preserved for the full bride price later.

But Abby dithered. His brothers had managed their own dowries. How could he ask his uncle for any special favors? The man wasn't even his real father.

"You need to hurry up," Maryam pleaded, trying to force some practical sense into his dreamy head. "My brother's yelling I'm not a virgin. What does he know of love? My excuses have run out. Even my father's starting to believe him."

Men! What was wrong with them? She had kept herself for Abby, and now he'd risk letting his foolish manly "tribal honor" get in the way of their happiness.

Abby said his uncle was from "the Army of the White." He followed tribal customs and would never deign to ask Maryam's father for marriage without a proper dowry. Still he promised to go to his uncle. He loved Maryam too much not to try.

He dragged his way to his uncle's auto body shop that catered to vintage American-made models. For Maryam, he gathered his courage from the pit of his beating stomach. His poor stomach indeed turned upside down for the first time in five years. But miraculously, his uncle agreed to help, though he could hardly afford the full bride price either.

Abby immediately called her mobile. His fingers were sweating and slipped off the cell phone as he dialed. He had to dial three times and switch wireless networks from his normal carrier, Mobily, to STC to get through. He couldn't believe his dream was about to come true. Maryam would soon be his bride!

Only he reached voice mail. A good Muslim knows what it's going to be like to be sent to Hell, and Heaven too is described in exact detail in the Holy Qur'an. But it seemed to Abby that day if there were a place between Heaven and Hell, it would be in voice mail.

Message after message, call after call, fell silent. He didn't know what to do. He went by her window and waited.

THE ORLANDO MAJID now laughed. He couldn't control himself.

"Again with the window, the Arab Romeo," the translator turned to me and said.

Abby asked what the joke was, and Dr. Ali had to reassure him that it was something that Lieutenant Majid knew from growing up in America.

I now had to reassure Abby that he could trust me too.

"Mr. Ken, this is hard," he said in broken English.

Abby had saved all of his and Maryam's poems. He had also saved Maryam's final letter to him. He showed the poems to me because Dr. Ali said he should. He showed them because I was the one who'd tell the world. He'd honor Maryam one last time.

Dr. Ali temporarily picked up the translation as Majid downed more *gahwa* before starting to translate again.

FOR THE NEXT five days, waiting to hear back from Maryam, Abby's nausea returned. He drank all the honey at his sister's house and went on a crazed shopping spree for more. He even found a place that sold bootleg Zamzam, drank that with the honey before washing it over his pulsating belly, anything to stop his stomach, which now resided in his head.

And at the end of the five days, he finally got a voice mail. It was her voice. He'd never heard her sound so quiet, so low, so sad: "I was expecting you to go to your uncle sooner."

He played the message over and over again, each time the words, one by one, like knives cutting into his fingernails.

He found out later that Maryam had been presented with an ultimatum: get married or be disowned, thrown to the street as a dishonorable orphan.

"Where you can be raped," her brother Ayman chortled.

"Maryam, dear, he is really a good man." Her father tried to soften the blow. "From a fine family, noble man," he added, as if throwing camel fat to a dog.

They showed Maryam a hideous photo. Her chosen keeper, Hisham, had to be at least sixty, with a big bushy black-and-gray mustache and a potbelly large enough to give birth. He was a brigadier general in the National Guard and had commanded her brother. From a noble tribe, he'd bring honor to the family, even if Maryam would become his fourth wife. To the point: He brought a handsome *mahr* that he'd pay "in trust" to Ayman and her father. As *wali al-amr,* they had the legal right to determine her spouse. The dowry was $30,000.

Maryam said nothing. Fleeing to the toilet, she vomited violently, as she imagined Abby would do when his stomach attacked. She took one of her brother's razors and made a small incision on her wrist.

She wanted to show her "family" that they had killed her, even if only symbolically. She left the toilet, vomit over hair and dress, blood dripping from her wrist. "I . . . will . . . not!" she bellowed from her gut, as loud as she could.

The next day, Abby saw cars pulling up in front of her house, like a burial procession. He called her mobile relentlessly. But Maryam never answered. Her little brother, now a snotty teenager, gleefully delivered the news: Maryam had been "officially married," even though she was at Al Ameen Hospital getting her stomach pumped.

Abby couldn't think. He felt like the baboons dying of thirst who ransacked much of Taif during droughts. In a frenzy of violence, they attacked everything, seeking the bright red juice-laden pomegranate they needed to live. Abby tore to Al Ameen. It seemed fitting that Maryam was at the hospital near Masjid Abbas Cemetery.

"We only allow family to visit," the nurse said.

ABBY SNUCK BACK to the hospital in the middle of the night. Going to the side of her metal hospital bed, he kissed pure Maryam on the forehead. Her eyes were bloodshot and puffy. He'd never seen her miraculous lips so pumped up, so large and swollen.

"I . . . am . . . sorry, Abu Shahed," she whispered to her only love. He could barely hear her fading words. It was as if she lay on her deathbed.

In Islam, a girl cannot be forced to marry. When the imam asks her before God if she accepts, she must answer of her own free will.

So the devil of the earth Ayman made a satanic bargain, bribing an imposter, a pretender, to pose as the bride. It seems that her second cousin Aisha was chosen to play "Maryam" and agree to marry Hisham.

Maryam had always dreamed of following in the righteous path of the Prophet's faithful first wife, Khadijah, or even the Chosen One's later wife, Aisha. She was strong like Khadijah; she helped Abby become strong; she would do something important in her life like Aisha.

But standing before the extended family and imam that black Thursday, it was this fake Aisha who became "Maryam" instead. The imposter was completely covered in a black *abaya*. You could barely see the narrow slits of her treacherous eyes, hidden under the bridal deception.

When the imam asked the imposter whether she consented to the union, she let out a squeaky high-pitched "yes" as "Maryam." Anyone who knew Maryam could have detected the fraud. Anyone who truly worshipped God could tell He was not present among the "witnesses."

At her hospital bedside, Ayman had delivered the verdict: Maryam was now legally married whether she liked it or not. She belonged to Hisham, and unless she wanted to be stoned to death as an adulterer, the National Guard commander would soon come and claim his wife. And if she tried to kill herself again, she would go to Hell, for suicide is the greatest sin of all for a Muslim.

Maryam was already in Hell.

Abby wanted to go straight to the commander and tell him the truth. How he and Maryam had been in love for five years and married in all but name. He'd tell him they even had children, though she was still a virgin—he would never tarnish her honor—how could the commander then even want a "used woman" like Maryam?

"Abby, you're a romantic fool," Maryam murmured. "You're lucky if he just has you arrested, never mind slits your throat."

"Why would he even want you if he knows the truth?"

"He's already paid for me."

Abby stood empty by the hospital bed. His stomach was beyond nausea.

"We will always be married before God." Maryam now tried to smile for her Abby.

"You'll always be my only love."

"I love only you," the tears of Zamzam water fell from his eyes.

"One day, we'll be together," she said.

"On Earth or in Heaven," he said.

"You'll always be in my heart, Abby."

"You'll always live in mine, Maryam."

THE NEXT MORNING, the National Guard commander came to Maryam's sickbed to claim her. Sick or not, that very morning, the commander took his new "wife" back to the northern city of Ha'il to her new jail.

It was Eid al-Adha, the Day of Sacrifice, when Muslims commemorate Abraham's willingness to sacrifice his son as an act of obedience to God.

Abby drove up to the edge of a cliff outside town. His life was Maryam. His life was gone.

He stopped his yellow Sebring and stared out of the front window over the cliff's steep edge. All he had to do was drive straight. But confronting the sin of suicide, he didn't want to go to Hell. He knew that the punishment in Hell for killing yourself with a knife was never to stop stabbing yourself, or for drinking poison to endlessly drink nothing but poison. And by throwing himself from a cliff, Abby would constantly fall in the flames of Hell for eternity.

Instead, like Abraham, he'd now make the real sacrifice before God. The Holy Qur'an told him that if he died as a martyr for God, he would meet Maryam in Heaven, where they could be married at last. He now wrote the ultimate love poem to his everlasting bride, so she would know:

God performed a miracle
I was His humble servant.
Once I was a lost boy; then
God gave me Maryam.
She gave birth to me again,
Without sin.
In the purity of virginal love.
How can I let God's Miracle die?

If God has now chosen to let my only love marry another,
He alone knows why.
I must deliver my life to God,
And marry my love in eternal Paradise.

Abby went to a famous tribal poet of Taif and asked him to publish the poem in the *Arab News* so Maryam could read of his sacrifice. He then gathered the funds he'd saved for the dowry and headed for Dubai without telling his family.

Flying to Lebanon, he stayed in the Hamra district in Beirut, before going to Al Masna to cross the border into Syria. He'd die worthy of his love. Together, as the Holy Qur'an promised in his favorite verse, Abby and Maryam would lie "in blissful shade, reclining on thrones" as husband and wife in never-ending Paradise.

He walked the streets of Damascus looking for jihadis—long beards, pious clothes. God would lead him.

He continued that way for five months, one month to match each year he'd loved her. Renting a small room in Zabadani, not far from Damascus, Abby walked the streets in search of long beards.

The room he rented was from a gentle, God-fearing elderly couple in a farm area, near a narrow river. They gave him a small room and good food with much kindness.

When not wandering the streets and alleys of Damascus, Abby would spend most of his days sitting by the river, thinking of marrying his love in Paradise as a martyr to God. All he could do was write:

Jihad turns loss into gain,
And love into God.
Jihad is the only oath of loyalty,
Every true Muslim swears by its love.
Jihad is a revealed gift; only the lucky ones will gain its love in ever-
  lasting Paradise.
Jihad teaches how to love; only those who love will live to die and
  love again in Heaven.
Jihad is the deepest of feelings.

Jihad is the stand for truth;
Never to go back once you have taken the first step.

God finally answered him and sent his neighbor in Zabadani, an Algerian man, Arubi al-Makhlouf, "Maloof" for short. Maloof was a security guard at a ski resort in Bloudan. Though clean-shaven, the man was pious and talked about Iraq.

His money running out, Abby had to take a chance. Maryam deserved more than a suicide; she deserved a hero's martyrdom. Abby told Maloof his whole story.

"The first problem is, you don't look pious. Rather than a jihadi, you're likely to be made for intelligence," Maloof said.

Abby gave him 3,000 riyals ($800) and his poem to jihad. The Algerian was impressed. He took the money, posted the poem with Abby's byline to a jihadi website, and agreed to help. But first, he said, Abby needed just to show people the poem on the jihadi website and not mention Maryam to anyone. He needed to make himself a real jihadi—nothing to do with a girl.

Abby gave Maloof another 2,500 riyals ($675). The Algerian took him to the Old City of Damascus, where Maloof vouched for him to three other Algerians. They led him to a safe house in Aleppo. He had to hand over his passport, mobile phone, and remaining money to the Syrian emir. It was his first step to Iraq and martyrdom.

WE STOPPED FOR Asr prayer. Abby now asked me to pray with him, Dr. Ali, and Lieutenant Majid. I didn't know what to say.

"No worries, Ken, I already gave Romeo the skinny. That's not your *thobe*," Majid said, winking.

They went to the opposite side of the conference room, unfurled prayer rugs, and, bowing toward Mecca, prayed in unison (though Majid was slightly behind each step of the way).

After prayer, Dr. Ali and Abby started to argue feverishly in Arabic, while Majid started joking with me. "No woman's worth that bullshit," he said. "You married? Kids?"

"I have a son and daughter."

"That's the real marriage, not Mr. Romeo here."

I asked Majid what Dr. Ali and Abby were arguing about, but all he said again was "No worries."

Ten minutes later, Abby and Dr. Ali sat down with me and Majid. Dr. Ali explained that Abby now agreed to share Maryam's last letter with me. She had written it to Abby several months after he had left for Iraq.

FULLY VEILED FROM head to toe for the first time in her life, Maryam sat alone in the back seat of the Mercury Mountaineer, along the hot highway to Ha'il, she wrote in her letter to Abby.

She said nothing to this Hisham, her so-called husband. At the hospital, the commander simply issued an order for her to follow. She obeyed. He told her to cover. She obeyed. As he raised his hairy hand to lead her away, Maryam's instinct was to jump.

"I'm not going to hit you," he barked.

Commander Hisham said almost nothing during the ride either, or she didn't pay attention to what he was saying: about his other wives and kids, the new house he'd just built himself, more empty and useless words.

She was just a new doll for him, to be played with and thrown away. Why should she bother to pay attention to what he said? It made no difference anyway. He certainly didn't care about anything she might say.

But Maryam couldn't possibly know the real terror that waited.

The house and yard were still under construction. Pakistani and Bengali workmen sat in a narrow wooden shack outside; green plastic soda bottles covered the dusty marble floor.

"Don't worry, your room's away from this mess," her keeper said.

The entrance was grand, almost regal: a circular rotunda with a beautifully painted cupola and fine mahogany trimmings. This must be the way King Fahd lives, Maryam wrote in her letter.

The National Guard commander led her to a separate building, next to the outdoor kitchen, far less grand than the main house. Her room was small and square, but considerably bigger and more modern than her room at home, with a large bed, a TV, even a computer to occupy her. A boy's room, his son, where was he? Maybe this Hisham had told her, but she didn't listen. It was nothing more than "a luxury cell," she wrote.

Maryam lay on the bed and could feel nothing. She wanted to cry, to scream, to laugh, anything at all, but nothing came out—not even the little squeak of her imposter, Aisha, who'd dared to steal the holy name from the Prophet's wife.

Maryam had nothing, not even her own name. A dog comes when you call its name. What would this swine call her now, Aisha? She wished she really had tried to commit suicide. "Tell me, who is it that committed the real sin here?" she wrote in the letter.

The idea of the night froze her. She refused dinner but did say Maghrib prayers. She believed God would save her. She was a good Muslim. He must have a plan for her.

After final Isha prayer, Hisham turned the doorknob and entered without knocking. Maryam was as much his as the bed or TV. Do you ask the TV's permission to turn it on?

She was already lying on the bed, staring at the cement ceiling with its swirling paint like clouds. Maybe she'd will herself to throw up all over him. Abby's revenge! Surely then Hisham would beat her silly. She didn't care. It would be worth it to see him covered in vomit, smelling like the garbage he was.

But Maryam could will herself to do nothing. She was limp. He came down next to her, unbuttoned the *abaya* she'd never bothered to take off. Put his thick iron hands on skin that only her true love had ever graced. His stubby fingers with sharp nails fastened to her like steel. He ordered her with just two words: "Don't move."

"Don't move" was all he said. "Don't move," again and again.

She wanted to let out a glass-shattering cry, a high-pitched lie as if she were the imposter "Maryam." She recited Abby's poems to herself and even the ballad she'd sing to him, "I keep waiting for you, the fire in my veins"—anything to keep on living "for you, my love," she wrote.

Maryam didn't have to vomit. Her blood now covered all.

She couldn't imagine a greater death. The sin of suicide is nothing, nothing compared to the sin of rape. Her whole body was nothing more than a worthless rag one of Hisham's many maids would use to wipe the toilet.

But Hisham made one fatal mistake. Or God in His infinite wisdom showed Maryam the way.

WAITING TO GO to Iraq, Abby spent what seemed like unending weeks in the Aleppo safe house. Told to be very quiet, the men couldn't leave and didn't even train. With two Yemenis and four Algerians, he watched nonstop videos about jihad and the American atrocities in Iraq.

After almost a month like this, the Syrian emir finally told them the night had arrived to enter Iraq and the first step to Jannah (Paradise). Seven jihadis in all, they left in a Nissan van with dark blue curtains, driving down the long road following the Euphrates River to the Syrian border town of Abu Kamal. Taken to a Syrian smuggler, the seven men had to leave behind any money they still had in Syrian hands.

The Syrian smuggler led them across the border at night to the Iraqi town of Al Qa'im. At a safe house, Rauf, from Al Qaeda in Iraq he said, gave the seven men fake Iraqi IDs and split them into groups of two and three. Rauf took Abby with a Yemeni to a farmhouse and its Iraqi farmer, Abu Reda.

Abby felt numb to everything. He was on a sacred mission that he kept locked close to his breast. While his secret burned his heart, his stomach didn't throw up. It still had the same peace as if he were in Maryam's arms, in her embrace, in soft, warm, blessed love. Abby was on the path of love in jihad to God.

The Iraqi farmer trained Abby and the Yemeni on a Kalashnikov. The Yemeni developed a friendship with the Iraqi, but Abby remembered what Maloof the Algerian had told him and kept to himself.

One month later, Abu Obadiah (Ghassan al-Rawi), an emir of Al

Qaeda in Iraq, came to the farm. A former Baath officer in Saddam's army, he said he reported directly only to Zarqawi, the leader of Al Qaeda in Iraq. Ghassan took Abby and the Yemeni with eleven other men to the town of Rawah, near Anah in Al Anbar Province.

Abby and the others stayed in Rawah for two months in complete boredom, punctuated only by fleeing from safe house to safe house whenever the Americans raided. The jihadis never trained again.

Inside the brown cement walls, there was little to stop the emptiness. Only five prayers, three meals, jihadi videos, and broken sleep.

Abby tried to keep to himself and think of Maryam. He wanted to fly to her like a jinn, unseen by men, and for one final minute, in a smokeless flame, envelop her, if only to hear her give him a single word. Just to hear "Abby."

It didn't matter how the dust of the safe house buried him and the hard bread sank in his stomach. It didn't matter how the rabid dogs never stopped barking and the black flies never stopped flying. Abby would do anything for Maryam.

The worst was the constant *shamal*. The dry wind was unlike anything he had ever felt in the cool mountain air of Taif. This wasn't air. It was the breath of death. Not just from the desert, it mixed with the foul cigarettes Iraqis always had planted between their brown teeth or yellowed fingers. Didn't they know that a good Muslim never smoked? It didn't matter: Abby willed himself to think of nothing but flying on the wings of noble jinn to meet his beloved.

The jihadis ate whatever the Iraqi family brought. After months like this, Abby's stomach finally rebelled. The endless nausea started all over again. He tried to calm himself by bringing Maryam into his bed, dreaming of how he was there just for her, but time, like acid, began to eat a hole in his useless stomach.

The other men told him not to vomit but pray instead. He prayed; he vomited. There was no honey balm or Zamzam, only some yellow dates. The vomiting only made him more of an outcast. He lost weight and stuck to the flat *khubz* bread.

When another Saudi in the group asked when they would ever see any action, "perhaps I should join the fighters of Ansar al-Islam instead," Ghassan the Al Qaeda leader said. "Here's the door. First we will kill all the Shia, and then, when we're done, we'll kill you."

The next morning, the Saudi's body was in the back courtyard, hacked into pieces.

AFTER HISHAM LEFT HER, Maryam continued to bleed. She felt nauseous, as if she had morning sickness already, as if she were Abby. She couldn't stop coughing but had to be strong, like the real Aisha. God would show the way.

She turned on the TV. It was not covered, as in a proper Muslim home. But of course this was anything but a true Muslim home. She thought she heard him say the boy was no longer there. Had he died? Had Hisham raped him too? The room itself stank of rape and broken blood, Maryam wrote in her letter to Abby.

Maryam turned to KSA2, the Saudi government English-language channel. She didn't want to understand anything on TV before she switched to Al Jazeera and all the victims in Iraq. She'd heard before that the American soldiers raped little girls. How was that different from her rape now?

A wave of loss ran over her. Perhaps if she had planned everything sooner, Abby would still be with her. If only she had started earlier, if only. She couldn't stop blaming herself.

She'd lost the only person she had ever loved. From the first time she'd seen his picture until now . . . she finally felt the tears well up, then drop from her puffy eyes, landing in this stranger's bed, this dead boy's white linen burial shroud.

The tears that left her could never be dried. Nothing could ever replace the emptiness she felt.

What happened to her was shameful before God. This was *haram*. She'd never been married in the sight of God. And to think that she had saved herself for Abby to please God and be a good Muslim. This must be *haram*, to be had by a man who deceived God. There could be no greater sin: it was the act of an infidel, a *kafir*. The rage she felt inside could never be satisfied with anything from this earth.

She could never make peace with her loss. All that was left was to make peace with God.

KSA1 had a preacher; then back to Al Jazeera. But wherever she turned, the TV had no answers. She felt a rash, her skin peeling back like a desert lizard.

Maryam turned on the computer, also uncovered. He had forced her to cover, yet left the TV and computer uncovered. He was a liar before God.

She had no trouble logging on. She went to Al Jazeera online. Same news, same innocent deaths, same rapes.

She couldn't sleep. Where was her love? Her Abu Shahed?

She now realized that the name of their first child, their daughter Shahed (Nectar), was close to the name of a martyr who dies in jihad and goes to Heaven (*shaheed*).

Maryam Googled "Abdullah al-Gilani."

And from that warm computer screen staring back from her dark, shameful night, God answered, as He always does, for He is All-knowing, All-merciful, and All-compassionate:

"Jihad turns loss into gain,

And love into God . . ."

ABBY'S DAYS WERE EMPTY. Hearing gunfire in the distance during one American raid, the men, their faces covered like ninjas, were moved to a farm outside Rawah. As they ran, Abby twisted his ankle. After the raid, the men moved back to town, but Abby couldn't walk. He stayed at the farmhouse for six weeks.

The owner of the farm was Abu Sa'if. His son was called "Safe." Safe took care of Abby. First he wrapped the swollen ankle in a bandage made of car rags. Then, every day, he'd bring him food, help him walk to the bathroom, and, most of all, talk. For the first time in months, Abby's stomach settled.

Safe had strong black hair and eyes, with a small nose, and quick smile. No more than twenty years old, he also showed miraculous strength, though he'd lost his left leg and part of his left arm. Safe helped Abby to stand and walk, even if in truth he was far more infirm than his ward.

Like a "boy graced with eternal youth" pledged by God to every martyr in Heaven, Safe was indeed a noble servant, as the Holy Book promised. God alone must've sent him.

They passed the time watching Al Jazeera. The TV was supposed to remain covered, with only the news ticker at the bottom of the screen left visible.

But Abby and Safe, in secret communion, watched it in full view. And they talked about the Americans, Saddam, the Sunnis, and how Al Qaeda was now killing the tribal chiefs.

"Al Qaeda's killing Iraqis more than Americans," the boy said. "What kind of jihad is that?"

At the end of six weeks, Safe brought a Holy Qur'an.

"You must swear by our Holy Qur'an never to tell a living soul what I'm about to tell you," Safe said.

Abby swore, staring into the boy's unblinking black eyes.

"The group doubts your righteousness."

Abby didn't understand.

"They noticed that you only do five prayers a day, never the voluntary."

"I do my five required prayers. Always."

"You watch TV uncovered."

Abby could say nothing. He wondered if Safe had betrayed him.

"Please be honest with me," Safe said. "Tell me the truth, and I swear on the Holy Qur'an, I will help you. I will protect you. I'll make sure on my life that you're okay."

The pain inside Abby was so much more powerful than the pain of his twisted ankle, his loneliness so much more vast than the dusty boredom of the Iraqi desert that everything came pouring out from his heart, his whole story of Maryam, how he now wanted to end his life to marry her in Heaven.

"You can't trust them," Safe told him. "They'll kill you on the spot sooner than let you die for your love."

———

MARYAM WENT TO the jihadi website's chat page to find Abby live online.

She stayed on the site most of the night. Since Abby's jihadi poem was blazoned across the home page, she felt sure she'd find him online. She read all the chat. Even signed in as Shahed1 (Nectar the First), the name of their first "daughter," before changing to Shaheeda2, the name of a female martyr. But no one knew the author of the poem.

She slept little. The Indonesian maid, Yuli, brought her some food. The only time she left the room was to go to the toilet next door.

God answered her prayers and the Devil himself, Hisham, did not return after that first night.

Almost three weeks passed while she spent her days on the Internet looking for Abby, chatting on the jihadi site, taking her meals from Yuli.

Maryam had just finished her evening meal, and Yuli was sitting on the bed with her. The TV was on in the background when the door flew open like a *shamal* sandstorm.

Before Maryam could even see what happened, the back of his hand struck Yuli across the face.

"*Pergi,* go back to work," Hisham commanded in a mix of Indonesian and English.

"You're next," he yelled at Maryam in Arabic.

Her body felt cold but stiff. She'd rather be hit than raped again. But Hisham just left, slamming the door behind him. *Hisham* . . . the very sound of the name made her spit it out like poison.

Maryam turned to the Internet that night with a vengeance. Desperate to find Abby, anyone, she found a jihadi women's chat room and "Nadia" instead.

Nadia wrote that she was from Jeddah and her husband had left for Iraq too.

"Jihad is the stand for truth; Never to go back once you have taken the first step," Maryam replied on the screen, quoting from Abby's poem.

"We should go and be martyrs with them," she then wrote to Nadia.

Maryam faithfully followed Abby's words.

ABBY WANTED ONLY to die a hero's death worthy of Maryam, not be killed as a traitor by one of Saddam's officers or an Iraqi boy who betrayed him.

He felt the sweat collect on his stomach. He thought of running, but where could he flee? He thought of trying to kill the crippled boy with his bare hands. He didn't know what to think, where to run or even die—

"I can explain to Ghassan how we couldn't fix your ankle," Safe said.

Abby just nodded in disbelief.

"I give you my word. I can take you out of Iraq, but don't tell a living soul," the boy said.

Abby didn't know what to say. He'd come to Iraq to die for God and meet his love in Paradise.

"There's no jihad," Safe said. "You'll go straight to Hell instead," the boy continued. "Who do you think Al Qaeda is killing? What jihad? They're either killing Iraqis or making a lot of money like Ghassan. He doesn't care about one lousy lovesick Saudi with a broken ankle," Safe told him.

His dark date eyes narrowed, his face became pomegranate red. "Fuck them." Safe spat out the words.

Abby swallowed the dry air and felt it sink all the way down into his empty stomach.

"I lost my limbs because of them," Safe now said. "That's what you want to die for? Their earthly greed? It's not jihad. They made my father take you or they'd kill him, just like they did my uncle. So tell me, to put those corrupt assholes back in power you want to sacrifice your life?"

Abby could only nod. He had come to Iraq for jihad, for Maryam, and found neither. He had come to fight the infidels and seen that the fighters were after money and power. But Abby had no money to give Safe. He had nothing.

It didn't matter. Safe would take him the next morning. They'd hobble to the border together.

"I know the way," the boy said, smiling. His teeth were crooked and yellow. He had just a stump for one arm and a little more than that for a leg. But Abby thought he was—after Maryam of course—the noblest person he'd ever met. This boy cared for him with nothing in return. He didn't want money, glory, or power. God could ask for no more.

They left the next morning, and Abby's ankle felt just fine. But more than anything else, he had to know why. Why was Safe helping him? Why risk his life for someone he barely knew, someone who had come to kill his countrymen, all in the dream of just saving himself?

"I believed it once like you. How do you think I lost my arm and leg?" Safe said.

They took his father's old van and drove toward the border. Safe was quite adept at driving with one hand and leg. Abby felt he could never repay his debt to the boy. If he lived his whole life, he'd never forget this simple but profound act. This is the true jihad, he thought.

MARYAM STARTED TO chat online with Nadia. Every day without Hisham was a blessing from God.

Yuli returned, still bringing food, though always looking over her shoulder. It didn't matter, since at least for now, Hisham had gone off on some kind of trip.

Over the magic screen, Maryam and Nadia chatted jihad. They chatted martyrdom and would follow their true husbands to become *shaheeda*s. Nadia even had some money. She said her cousin could help get them to Syria. Maryam didn't have a passport. Nadia's cousin could arrange for a fake one. They just had to have the courage to try.

Maryam felt the crush of time, the sudden jolt of Hisham returning. She was a rape victim in jail. She had no other way out. Besides, she always stood tall. She wrote that first letter to Abby. She gave "birth" to all their children and thought of each name. The truth was that if only Abby had listened to her and acted sooner, she'd be married and living happily in the cool mountain air of Taif and not this desert hell with a rapist infidel.

A month later, when the second wife was visiting relatives in Medina, Maryam slipped inside the real wife's bedroom. Invisible as jinn, Maryam knew that God was with her at last as she blessedly found several gold rings, necklaces, and bracelets.

After Fajr prayer the following Friday, when Hisham was safely away at mosque, she waited by the back entrance of the house. Nadia had written that her cousin would come in a white Ford Ranger. Maryam hid the gold in her black leather purse, the only thing left from her former life.

When the Ranger pulled up, she ran so quickly the hot desert wind tossed her *abaya* to its ends. She could barely open the burning white door; her head barely felt moored to her body. She spun into the backseat. Nadia's cousin was at the wheel. He completely covered his face with his red-checked *shemagh* headdress. Though Nadia's hair was covered, her face was exposed.

Nadia looked entirely different from what Maryam had imagined online. Her face was swollen and fat, her nose strangely pushed in as if someone had punched her dead on. And she had no chin; it just merged into her thick neck as one. Maryam thought, if anyone, this girl should fully veil but smiled instead. "*Salaam,* my online buddy jihadi," she said. "I have some jewelry, some gold."

The cousin said there'd be no need for that yet.

They were headed for Riyadh, where they'd stay overnight and the cousin would obtain her new identity. Maryam asked if she could be called Khadijah.

SAFE SAID GOOD-BYE. Abby felt tears. He didn't want to say good-bye to the one friend he'd found. The one person who was honest with him and wanted nothing in return. The one person who'd fought a real jihad—and won.

Abby now knew: Safe was no less than the "immortal boy," as the Holy Book said, whose thin hair glowed with the smokeless flame of a noble jinn.

"You've done God's work," Abby told him.

"Inshallah," Safe said.

Safe had brought him in sight of a border crossing with only several Syrian guards and no Iraqi or American checkpoints. Abby would turn himself in to the Syrians and ask to go home.

"KHADIJAH," THE PASSPORT clearly said. She was ready at last. Boarding the Emirates flight at King Khalid International Airport with the cousin and Nadia now fully covered, the 777 rose like an eagle toward Dubai, and Maryam—no, Khadijah—took flight as if she were on the Prophet's white winged steed, Buraq, on the way to Heaven.

They stayed overnight in Dubai. The plan was for the cousin to accompany the girls to Damascus and leave them in the hands of a trusted jihadi, who would spirit them to the border and on to martyrdom in Iraq.

Staying in a small hotel room, she realized this might be her last chance to ever contact Abby, at least on Earth. While they'd surely meet in Heaven, there was no telling who'd get there first. Yes, truly like the Prophet's wife Khadijah, she remained practical, her feet still planted firmly on the ground.

Failing to find Abby online, she decided to write a letter instead. She'd send it inside a sealed envelope to his sister as she had once so long ago—indeed it felt like her whole life. From the letter, even if Abby might never read it, at least the family—his and hers—would know her whole story. She left nothing out and postmarked it the next morning from Dubai.

THE SYRIAN GUARDS arrested Abby at the border.

One called him a "filthy rich Saudi dog." The others laughed while shoving Abby into the back of a van with two other arrested jihadis.

"Welcome to the Syrian Arab Republic," said another tall Syrian with a thick, oily mustache.

The long ride to the prison was bumpy and dusty. They called it "Palestine Prison." The guards said that this was what happened to "apes, pigs, and Jews."

As soon as the arrested jihadis arrived, the Syrian officers ordered them to strip naked and stand in the sun. The Syrians took any money or valuables they had. Abby had none. That earned him a quick slap on his bare butt. He had never been hit before.

After several hours standing naked, the men were ordered to dress. Shouting like animals, the Syrians herded the once proud jihadis into a cement room that looked as if it had once been a kitchen, but all the appliances were now stripped bare too. Abby threw up in the corner, which earned him the quick disdain of the others.

Forty-seven men were crowded into that narrow space. There was no bathroom or toilet. The guards allowed them to go to the toilet only three times a day, for just ten minutes at a time. The old kitchen reeked of piss and sometimes shit when a man could no longer hold it. And vomit. Not just Abby's, thank God. The moldy, stale food was thrown into the same room as they slept and shat and crowded together with the fleas, ticks, cockroaches, lizards, and rats.

The cell was hosed down several times, but the men only got to take a real shower once a week, naked in front of each other and the guards.

Abby had never been so alone and felt selfish for thinking only of his love. The suffering he saw had changed him. Safe had changed him.

But the maggots wouldn't stop. One jihadi had injured his leg in Iraq. He tried anything he could to cover the wound, but slowly, surely, the puffy yellow maggots began to crawl in and out of his open sore. The other men finally put him in a corner because the maggots kept multiplying, growing, crawling, until the guards one day just dragged him out, never to be heard from again.

The men thought he'd been shot. That would be a mercy from God, because the other men were simply beaten and tortured, to the ceaseless amusement of the guards. The free-and-easy torture was as much a part of the daily prison routine as the stale, moldy bread and muddy water. The other men told Abby that whatever he did he must never talk. The Americans, through the Iraqis, had given the Syrians lists of wanted jihadis.

After several weeks, Suleiman, a "maggot-face" guard, ordered Abby out of the shower line.

Abby was naked and little more than skin and bones, looking like "a Jew from the Nazis."

Suleiman yanked him by the arm so hard that Abby heard it crack. The guard pulled him like a dog to a small reinforced concrete room, with a single rusty metal chair. He ordered Abby to lie on the cement floor and put his bare feet up on the chair. The guard took some coarse rope, tied Abby's ankles to the cold steel chair, and took out a wooden stick to begin the *falaqah*. Suleiman beat his soft soles and flat arches with the thick wooden stick. The more the Syrian guard struck his feet, the more Abby felt the pain in his head. He felt like passing out until he began throwing up.

With that, the guard, who had a black, scraggly mustache and protruding belly, stopped the *falaqah*. He untied Abby's red, burning feet and threw the chair to the corner. The cement floor was cold. The guard told him to turn over. Abby could barely see. The pain attacked him from every direction.

"Not like that, you Jew." The guard grabbed him by a fistful of hair and swung his head facefirst into his own vomit.

The Syrian took his boot and used it to push Abby's head back into the ground and sticky vomit. He then endlessly hit his feet as if the *falaqah* had never stopped, until Abby let out a cry that the whole prison could hear.

God finally gave Abby the gift of leaving this earth, at least for a while.

PALESTINE PRISON WAS the worst. Abby learned afterward that he'd spent six weeks there and in two other jails. The last jail could have been Heaven compared to Palestine. They didn't beat him. He shared a cell with just three other guys, could relieve himself in private, and they actually had real food to eat. He was there for a little more than a week when two Saudi officers from the Ministry of Interior took him away.

They might as well have been messengers from God. They took him to Taif Prison. Abby was home.

Taif Prison felt like Heaven too, next to Iraq and Syria. Abby prayed five times a day, had real meals and real dates, and no guard ever hit him. Instead, they gave him a TV, newspapers, and a Holy Qur'an. They even gave him honey.

His favorite sister regularly came to visit him in prison. Every time she came, he would ask about Maryam. The thought of her had sustained him throughout his entire time in Syria—the thought of Maryam and his deeper faith in God. And what it meant to have a friend like Safe.

But his sister wouldn't say anything. Finally, after what seemed like five months of endless pleading, his sister handed him Maryam's letter, postmarked from Dubai.

After reading it, Abby felt the pain in his stomach, the blood on his beaten soft soles and flat arches, the *falaqah* hitting him like Satan himself.

Yet, only God knows why, he also felt a certain peace.

Sentenced by the judge to twenty months in prison for unauthorized exit from the Kingdom, Abby promised the judge he'd never leave Saudi Arabia again.

After serving his sentence, he was sent to the Care Center. He was now a different person. He wanted to help others. He wanted to work at the Care Center and with the ministry to warn people off the path of false jihad.

Abby wasn't in the news like Ahmad al-Shayea, the suicide bomber who survived his attack. Nor was Abby singled out by God, like the boy Safe or the new, mysterious Kamal, who stayed at the Care Center for only a short time.

Yes, Abby now also told me, he'd never be famous like Ahmad, or

God-blessed like Safe. But he still wanted to warn against Al Qaeda. He wanted to dedicate his life to serving true Islam.

He never heard from Maryam again or ever learned what really happened to her. His sister thought that she'd heard that Maryam was still alive and now married, happily living in Medina. She might have even given birth to her first son and named him Abby.

But when I later asked Lieutenant Majid and Dr. Ali if the MOI knew where Maryam was, they said the Saudi government had no record of her—leaving Saudi Arabia, becoming a female suicide bomber in Iraq, sold into "white slavery" in Dubai, or even if she was in Saudi Arabia living with her first husband or a new one. Like so many young Saudi women who try to flee their legally assigned husbands, Maryam had simply joined the ranks of the "women disappeared."

"I just ask God every day to tell me whether she's alive or dead," Abby said.

3

MALIK, MULLAH OMAR'S SEER

AHMAD ("BERNIE") learned the true character of Al Qaeda. Abby also saw how it led vulnerable young men down the path of violence and hate.

Inside a hotel room in northwest Pakistan, I was again with someone who seemed to be the enemy. I was certainly everything he hated: an American, a Jew, and once a prosecutor of terrorists like him. He was everything I hated too: a Taliban jihadi and sworn killer of Americans, Christians, and Jews. Yet, like Ahmad and Abby with Al Qaeda, Malik had witnessed the inside workings of the Taliban, seen firsthand its corruption, and now questioned its ways.

Besides Saudi Arabia, Pakistan is the most important country to the future of religious extremism in the Muslim world. The only Muslim country with nuclear weapons, it is the home base of Al Qaeda, the Pakistani Taliban, and a large indigenous radical movement. Pakistan is also the base of the Afghan Taliban, which fights against the United States in bordering Afghanistan.

In Pakistan, the work of my nonprofit organization, Terror Free Tomorrow, had become front-page headlines and lead stories on the TV news. It gave me important media contacts who knew radical clerics and the Taliban themselves. Introduced through these connections, Malik was the kind of man I had devoted my career to putting away. And now here I was, listening to his secret confessions.

Malik told his story from the heart. He spoke softly, always waited for me to speak first, never interrupted or showed any anger, and was, by his own admission, a killer. Born of Afghan Pashtun parents who fled the Soviet invasion of Afghanistan in 1979, Malik grew up in refugee camps in Pakistan and joined the Taliban at its very beginning. From his meager childhood in the camps and madrassa schooling to his time as a soldier and reign as a high-level enforcer for the religious police, Malik fought for the Taliban throughout Afghanistan. He helped liberate his home province of Laghman; he fought for the Taliban in northern Afghanistan; and as a chief of the Virtue and Vice Police, he "commanded good and banished evil" in the capital, Kabul, and then in Jalalabad and eastern Afghanistan, a base of Al Qaeda.

Most significantly, Malik became the spiritual guru to Mullah Omar, the leader of the Taliban. For many Taliban, dreams can bear the power of prophecy. And Malik's "true night dreams" guided Mullah Omar himself. After the fall of the Taliban from power, Malik acted as Mullah Omar's seer during a pivotal secret *shura* (council) meeting of the Taliban leaders. His story took me behind enemy lines in a way few outsiders had ever been, to the religious visions and dreams that shockingly determined the course of the war against the United States.

Yet Malik's deep faith led him, over time, to question the actions of the Taliban. Its corruption, heroin trafficking, and alliances with the Pakistani intelligence agencies all struck the deeply pious Malik as "the work of the Devil." As with both Ahmad and Abby, Malik's story seemed to be one that led him away from the violence of his colleagues.

I was all set to learn from him how we in the West can respond to the Taliban in ways that will lead to, if not peace, then at least not endless war. Here it was from the mouth of Mullah Omar's very Rasputin—the key to an American understanding of the elusive Taliban. The triumph of faith over terror was at hand, or so I thought.

———

MALIK'S FAMILY HAD come from the Land of the Two Holy Places: Mecca and Medina, the Land of the Holy Prophet.

They had come to Afghanistan to farm in its fertile valleys. Malik's great-grandfather, Mullah Muhammad Ayub, became one of the greatest mullahs in Afghanistan. He was not only a famous mullah—Islamic teacher and mosque leader—he was a mullah to King Amanullah, the last king before Mullah Omar to wear the Cloak of the Prophet Muhammad, some seventy-five years ago.

Mullah Ayub was revered by all and grew great quantities of almonds, apples, apricots, wheat, and maize in the overflowing valleys of Laghman in eastern Afghanistan. The soil was wonderfully rich then; now it is desert from all the wars.

Malik's great-grandfather had seven wives and forty-eight children. The old mullah was as fertile as the rich Afghan land.

Malik's grandfather continued the family tradition, farming his small plot of Laghman earth in the village of Lara Mora in eastern Afghanistan, near Jalalabad, and founding a madrassa, an Islamic school to teach the Holy Qur'an. Becoming a learned mullah himself, the people called him Mullah Lara Mora. Even the Afghan king, Zahir Shah, came to pay his respects. But Mullah Lara Mora had just three sons, and Malik's father, Abdul Khaliq, was the only one to survive.

As Abdul Khaliq grew up, he had to trade to earn his way. Yet Abdul Khaliq continued the family tradition, teaching in the madrassa and marrying his young Pashtun first cousin, as was custom. For though the family could claim to trace their ancestry back to Arabia, they had been Pashtuns for many generations now, firmly settled in Lara Mora. Lara Mora the peaceful. Lara Mora the pious. Lara Mora the beautiful.

BEFORE THE DEVIL Shaytan shakes the ground . . .

No one in Lara Mora knows what it means. They hear the rumbling from afar. Malik's father, Abdul Khaliq, and his new wife are together. They hear the noise, the gunshots. There's fire. They run behind a door. The noise comes closer. There are screams, people pleading, monsters shouting in an unknowable tongue.

Their front door flies open. These soldiers from the North, they speak a language like Tajik. They shout with heavy accents, *"Dost ya dushman!"* (Friend or foe!) That's all they know, and don't wait for a response. They fly through the house with the speed of evil jinn, turning over all its rooms, but never open the side door. They grab Abdul Khaliq's aunt and uncle-in-law from the room next door. There's nothing Abdul Khaliq can do with just a *shalwar* covering and no weapon, half naked and shaking behind a side door. They drag his uncle and aunt away.

When Abdul Khaliq looks out several minutes later—it seems like a lifetime—he sees Akhtar the milkman.

What he then sees he will never forget.

A soldier knocks the milkman to the ground with the butt of his bayonet. Taking its sharp end, he brings it down with all its force. Moving the bayonet back and forth like a pendulum, the soldier severs the milkman's leg from his body. The blood won't stop. Another soldier begins to pour Akhtar's milk into the open wound. The milkman's screams pierce through the soldiers' laughs. Abdul Khaliq holds Malik's mother tight until dusk. She can barely breathe.

The peaceful village of Lara Mora is silent. Malik's father and mother finally leave their hiding spot and nervously get dressed. They take what little food they can find and the family's Holy Qur'an and leave their small home next to the madrassa.

The poor milkman lies dead in the middle of the dust-filled road, the milk he carried in peace poured into his blood, a reddish frosty white curdled over the dusty earth. Not far is Abdul Khaliq's uncle-in-law, his throat cut, his body stiff. There are children, his students, his *talib*s, slaughtered like sacrificial goats. And a sight from Hell, worse than anything Abdul Khaliq could ever imagine. There is a young woman, her burka violently ripped and her eyes gouged out, two bloody yellow holes staring out at him, asking for help, dead on the ground.

The young couple is sweating and can hardly breathe the thick, rotting air. They run like rabbits, searching desperately for their aunt. Maybe she lives, *Inshallah*. But all are dead. The small, peaceful village of Lara Mora has become a violent open grave, its pious, peaceful people slaughtered by the invading infidels.

The fires are eating the village. Abdul Khaliq knows they have to flee. He leads his crying wife, running toward the mountains. Not far from town, in the farm fields, they meet their neighbors from Lara Mora, those who fled and managed to live.

It's the Russians, the neighbors tell them. They've been coming from the north, Communist infidels killing all the believers. God has sent them to test our steadfast faith.

The escaping fortunate few of Lara Mora climb past Mehtar Lam to Jalalabad, down the Trunk Road through the heights of the Spin Ghar and the Khyber Pass, over to the border and Pakistan.

The Lara Morans, almost a hundred surviving families and parts of families, make their way as a single group inside Pakistan. Tired and hungry, with blisters on their feet, broken bones, open sores, and undying faith in God, they find their way with other Laghmanis and Pashtuns to a UN refugee camp in Badaber, a suburb of Peshawar. They are soon moved to another UN camp at Barakai in the Swabi District.

The wind is cold. Inside the tents, Malik's father and mother just have each other, an open fire to cook the flour rations, and the occasional milk. The family Qur'an is all that is left from Lara Mora, the mullahs, and Mecca. Every night, Abdul Khaliq kisses its spine three times before going to sleep.

They shiver through the nights of the spring. The summer holds nothing new. Malik's mother sweats through her pregnancy. Everything is brown: the stick that holds up the canvas tent, the constant diarrhea and dogs, the dusty rats and rationed UN porridge, even the dirt and sand they have to use to wash for prayer when there is no water. Brown covers them all.

———

CONCEIVED DURING the fall of Lara Mora to the invading infidels, Malik was the first boy born in their part of the camp—the first refugee son. Pakistani soldiers guarding the camp fired in the air to announce his birth.

There was celebration but not much food. Allah Almighty's grace fell on the family that morning in the camp, as it had on the blessed couple in Lara Mora who survived the infidel slaughter and found their way through faith to the camp, through suffering to the birth.

The guns now shouted in celebration; guns that had once killed now shouted for life, for Allah's great glory and the Lara Morans' unbroken faith. Malik's father, Abdul Khaliq, knew his son's birth meant he must start a madrassa for the refugee boys. But he had nothing. He even had to go back to trading whatever few vegetables he could to eke out a living.

Malik was often sick, but his mother was sicker, losing two boys and a girl in childbirth. As soon as he could walk, Malik carried water in small tin cans from a well a mile away. Barefoot, he trekked through the tough dirt and developed callused feet. He collected dog poop for the fires to cook the rations.

He always felt hot with fever, his throat burned, and his feet were sore. He "played stones" with the other boys. Many boys and girls died, like his lost brothers and sister.

When Malik and his family finally moved out of the tent to a mud house, he went to refugee school in a mud building. He was seven. A sweet and loving teacher, with her blond hair from Sweden, taught the kids English at the UN school. Malik learned the ABCs. He had never been so happy. Before he had been hauling water, sticks, dog poop or playing stones. Now he could sit on the wooden bench and say, "A ... B ... C ..."

The UN gave them tents, rations, this school. But did the UN stop the godless Communists from invading, from massacring Muslims? His father wanted him to learn the Holy Book. That was the education a boy must have.

———

WHEN MALIK turned ten, his mother fell ill. Three sisters had finally survived childbirth. And she was full with another son, they hoped, when she became hot in the cold night, sweating like the brown dust earth.

The next morning, after Fajr prayer, Malik went to get the water. He knew where the camp doctor was. His father had refused to get the doctor. Each step Malik took, a tear fell from his eyes, like the drops of sweat falling from his mother's forehead.

His mother was good like the English teacher from Sweden. Of course, his beloved *mor*'s soft eyes were brown, not blue. And she didn't teach him English. But she was always kind, always told him to play with the stones, that's enough chores. His mother always told him she loved him. If his mother was like the English teacher, couldn't the doctor be kind too? His father said that infidels like the doctor could never be trusted. But Malik's eyes burned, and his mother lay moaning.

Malik took a detour from the water and went to the camp doctor instead. He just didn't want the doctor to tell his father that he had asked for help.

He ran home without the water. His mother was lying on the bare ground. His father had stolen an extra *patoo* full of holes to cover her and placed the *taweez,* a verse from the Noble Qur'an written in his own hand, next to her heart ("Neither slumber nor sleep overtakes Him"). Malik could see the brown diarrhea running down her legs. What looked like blood began to form as his mother wailed and tears fell.

It wasn't long before his brother-to-be was born dead. His father cried out in pain with the blood. Oh, where is that doctor? Malik thought. But he said nothing, as an evil jinn now entered his mother and she began to shake without end. His father cursed her for giving him another dead son. His poor mother shook harder.

"I love you, *Mor,*" Malik cried at her.

But the unseen jinn continued to eat inside, the heat coming from her body warming their small mud house. Malik's father screamed at his sisters to play outside.

There was a silence worse than the noise of her pain. His father began to sob. Malik now cried too.

When the doctor arrived an hour later, it was too late. He was kind and tried to help, but there was nothing he could do.

His father now held Malik and his sisters for the first time.

"She was the most wonderful wife," he told them, "but she's now with God."

A YEAR LATER, when Malik turned eleven, the UN school closed, and he never saw the Swedish English teacher again, the way he never saw his loving mother.

His father had remarried, and Malik now had two little stepbrothers. It was time he went to a madrassa, his father said.

The same day Malik started at the local madrassa, Darul Hifz, in a nearby village, the mujahideen freed Kabul from the Communist infidels. Cries of *"Allah-u-Akbar"* went up everywhere. Like the day Malik was born, Kalashnikovs were fired in the air.

At Darul Hifz madrassa, Malik learned the Uncreated Word of Allah. The madrassa was under the control of the famous mujahideen commander Muhammad Younis Khalis and his radical Party of Islam, with some three hundred students, all Afghan refugee children.

At first Malik didn't care. Sleeping in a large room with the other boys, he wet his thin bed, had more brown diarrhea and sweat like his mother. Everything left him, and he felt weak and empty. He couldn't lift his head up. Until he had a dream.

It was the first dream he ever had. In it, he heard his mother's voice coming from Heaven. All the evil jinn who had visited her were banished, and she told him, "You can find me now with Allah the Most High."

Malik told his dream to the mullah, the religious teacher who was the madrassa's headmaster. The mullah told his dream to the whole school. They all knew what it meant. It was the Word of God Almighty.

In a miracle, Malik soon learned by heart 22 of the Holy Qur'an's 114 surahs and was one of the three best students in the entire madrassa. A favorite of the mullah, Malik now loved every word out of the mouth of God.

But the defeat of the Russians in Afghanistan didn't lead to peace in his homeland. The mujahideen lost their way to God. With Shaytan at their side, they fought among themselves for the Devil's sins of power, glory, and money. Malik's madrassa was closed. He returned to his father's mud house, where he did nothing among the brown.

He carried water from the well a mile away, played marbles with stones, but refused to collect the dog poop for the fire. His father's new wife could do that. He kept asking his father to send him to another madrassa, and his father, being a man of God, finally sent the idle Malik to an even more radical madrassa, the great Ahya-ul-Uloom madrassa in Maneri village. The madrassa was free, reserving many spaces for Afghan refugee children—indeed, it was the only education available.

FROM THE HAND of God, Malik recited by heart the Uncreated Word of Allah. In the Ahya-ul-Uloom madrassa, with three times as many *talibs* as Darul Hifz, Malik continued to walk resolutely in the path of God. But when the senior students began to hoard all the good food and nobody did anything to stop them, he stood tall. The mullah beat him for writing a letter in protest.

Malik had his mother's sweet smile. He was thin, a lanky six foot two, soft-spoken, with tapered feet and hands—the palms of which the mullah beat red. Malik did not flinch. He was steadfast during the beating. The senior students shouldn't hoard all the good food. It was un-Islamic. All the other boys admired his courage, and he had fully memorized 42 out of 114 Qur'an surahs. He was a hero to all the boys, even the seniors.

The day after the unjust punishment, an ISI—Pakistani army

intelligence—officer came to the madrassa to urge the boys to join the Taliban (religious students) and wage jihad in Afghanistan. One of the Taliban commanders, Mullah Ehsanullah Ehsan, came too and told the students to join their "new Muslim movement of Taliban," to take back Afghanistan "for God alone."

It was the spring of 1996, and Malik was sixteen. At first he and his friends did not agree. But that night, he had another "true night dream." In the dream, all his fellow students had turned to girls. Except for one—he couldn't make out who—was dressed in the white flowing robes of Prophet Muhammad.

The next morning, Malik told his fellow students the dream. No boy wanted to be a girl.

Mullah Ehsan explained the meaning of the true dream to the chosen Malik and all four hundred boys. The Taliban commander told them about the Honored Cloak of Prophet Muhammad, kept at a shrine in Kandahar, the capital for the Pashtuns in southern Afghanistan: "Simply by standing near the Holy Cloak, the lame will walk and the sick will be healed. Though only when there is grave danger to the Afghan nation and a true leader from God stands before it will the Holy Cloak come out. In the past hundred years, the Honorable Cloak came out only once when King Amanullah wore it to save our country and once to stop a cholera epidemic more than sixty years ago.

"Now, in a miracle by Allah Almighty, I have received word that the leader of the Taliban, Mullah Muhammad Omar, just went to Kandahar's Shrine of the Blessed Cloak seeking the holiest: the Cloak worn by the Prophet himself. A camel-fur garment without seams or color, the Cloak was given by the Prophet Idris to Prophet Muhammad on the *Mi'raj* [Prophet's Night Journey] to Heaven.

"The Prophet's Cloak is kept inside a small, padlocked silver box, which in turn lies inside two larger boxes. The locks can be opened only when touched by a true *Amir-ul-Momineen,* or Leader of the Faithful.

"Mullah Omar had the right touch. So Allah Almighty opened the chests for him.

"Mullah Omar stood trembling when he first saw the Blessed Cloak and was so overcome that, for a moment, he lost sight of which direction to pray to Mecca. Yet after praying, he knew to lift up the very Cloak worn by Prophet Muhammad, which took to his own body with the breath of God, fitting to him like his very skin.

"After the Fajr prayer, on the roof of the old mosque in the center of Kandahar, Mullah Omar then wrapped and unwrapped the Holy Cloak around his body. Putting his palms through its sleeves, he held the Noble Cloak aloft, letting it be taken by God's breath Heavenward. As the Cloak touched the clouds, the people below cheered in glory. Many fainted. Many threw their hats and other clothes in the air in the hope that they would touch the Holy Cloak. The learned mullahs, who had assembled together with the crowd, embraced Mullah Omar. Shouting as one, all proclaimed Mullah Omar 'the Leader of the Faithful.'

"Malik's dream had foretold the miracle of Mullah Omar and the Blessed Cloak," Mullah Ehsan now explained to the madrassa students.

All the boys, the Pakistani ISI officer, even the school's mullah were stone silent. They all knew the power of dreams.

Mullah Ehsan concluded by saying he would take Malik, "this boy of God's dreams and prophecies" to Mullah Omar himself.

Every *talib* in the entire madrassa—all four hundred of them— then followed Malik's dream and left that very day with the Taliban leader Mullah Ehsan. Malik and the other boys took off without telling their parents because they might stop them. And like the other boys, Malik left with just the clothes on his back and 100 rupees (about a dollar) in his pocket.

"God and the Taliban will take care of everything, *Inshallah,*" Mullah Ehsan said.

They went first to the city of Peshawar, then the town of Torkham at the Pakistani border. They waited at the border. The Taliban fed them rice and sent word home that they were now fighting in jihad. They crossed the mountains. When Malik first touched Afghan soil, Mullah Ehsan told him again that, with his power of dreams, he would personally take him to Mullah Omar.

———

MALIK AND HIS madrassa friends trained under the famed mujahid commander Mullah Abdul Salam—"Mullah Rocketi," nicknamed for his skill in shooting down Russian aircraft with Stinger rockets. Mullah Rocketi was disciplined and shrewd. He expertly trained the boys at a camp near Jalalabad in basic training and firearms—the Kalashnikov, of course, and even his prized Stinger.

At the end of August 1996, the Taliban launched a surprise attack to liberate Jalalabad. In a row of lightning-strike pickup trucks led by Mullah Borjan, Malik helped free Jalalabad, which quickly fell. Within days, Malik had the honor to help free his home province of Laghman for God. After battle, Malik and his friends continued to train with Mullah Rocketi, before, several weeks later, the Taliban liberated the capital, Kabul, and Mullah Ehsan sent for the boys.

Mullah Ehsan had become the governor of the Bank of Afghanistan. He told them that he would soon lead a select corps of a thousand fighters under his personal command to liberate the North. They would train in Kandahar, the southern city and Taliban stronghold.

"I have not forgotten your power of dreams," he said to Malik.

Malik looked down at the floor. He never had been in a place like this. Shiny white marble floors and endlessly high white walls. Great chandeliers of lights, which made it bright like outside. And Afghanis. The bills, cash, lying in stacks, growing in tall columns toward the great sunlike ceilings. Mullah Ehsan was the new governor of the Bank of Afghanistan, after all.

Mullah Ehsan explained to Malik and the other boys, "Our leader, Mullah Muhammad Omar, understands the power of dreams. Each true night dream is a prophecy of God. When he had the dream where Almighty Allah appeared in the shape of a man, Mullah Omar knew to lead the believers. When he had another vision with the flash of cruise missiles blinding all in a white blaze until one man stood tall, Mullah Omar knew it was time for him to wear the Blessed Cloak."

Mullah Ehsan pointed at Malik and said, "I will tell Mullah Omar the night vision of this poor *talib* refugee boy, who dreamed of Mullah

Omar wrapped in the Blessed Cloak the same day it happened. Mullah Omar will know then that Mullah Ehsan delivers the voice of God the Most Merciful."

For Mullah Ehsan was not only the new bank governor and new Elite Corps commander but also a rising member of the Supreme Shura Council, the top leaders of the Taliban.

But Mullah Qalamuddin needed men now, and since Mullah Ehsan hadn't received orders to report to Kandahar, he let the boys go.

Unlike Mullah Ehsan's grand office filled with Afghani bills, there was nothing in Mullah Qalamuddin's bare office in the center of Kabul. He told the men—boys, sixteen, seventeen, and eighteen years old—that they would have important districts to command in Kabul.

"You will be high officials on the front lines of virtue, bringing the peace of Islam to city sinners," he said, for the learned mullah was in charge of the new *Amr Bil Maroof Wa Nahi Anil Munkar*—the General Department for the Promotion of Virtue and Prevention of Vice.

Yet it was only a matter of days before Mullah Ehsan came back to take the boys to Kandahar as part of his chosen corps of the "Holy One Thousand." On Toyota Hilux pickups, they made the long dusty ride to another camp. They trained again with Kalashnikovs, grenades, and explosives, though none of Mullah Rocketi's famous Stingers. Malik knew the drill by now: he was there to fight for Islam.

IT HAPPENED RIGHT after Asr prayer. The ground shook throughout the entire camp. The rumble of Toyota Land Cruisers and Hiluxes and the firing of Kalashnikovs in the hot midday air chased away any evil jinn. Mullah Omar, Mullah Ehsan, and the other Taliban leaders came up to the boys, close to Malik.

Malik was now almost seventeen. He knew it was time for him to stand and let Allah's holy power come to Earth, through his feet. For the Noble Book told him that his feet shall bear witness before Allah the Most High if he has earned a place in Heaven.

The Leader of the Faithful, Mullah Omar himself, looked like anyone else, except taller. He had a thick, long black beard and black turban. It was said that he had pulled the shrapnel out of his right eye after battling the Communists. Malik couldn't see his lone eye.

But he could now overhear Mullah Omar telling Mullah Ehsan and the other mullahs how he would personally lead his men in battle for the liberation of Mazar-e-Sharif and the north of Afghanistan.

"You are a brave fighter, but you must be our leader here in Kandahar," the other mullahs told Mullah Omar.

Then it struck, as God Almighty Himself delivering a fire sign in the night sky:

"A young *talib,* just like you, had a dream," Mullah Ehsan now said in a loud voice to Mullah Omar.

The guns stopped firing in air. The mullahs stopped arguing. All the men turned dead silent, as the power of a dream took over.

Mullah Ehsan addressed them with Mullah Omar by his side: "I was in Pakistan, recruiting the *talib*s to fight. At first they didn't want to go. Then that night, one of them, Malik, had a dream. Malik dreamed he saw a *talib* just like himself, with no tribe or pedigree or money, an unknown man whom Allah *Subhanahu Wa-Ta'ala* [Glorious and Most Exalted] chose from the masses to bring the peace of Islam. In his dream, Malik saw this humble *talib* wrapped in the Holy Cloak of the Prophet Muhammad. It was a miracle. And all four hundred of the madrassa students then knew they must follow me to jihad. It was that very day, of course, that you, Mullah Omar, our great leader, stood before the masses in Kandahar, wrapped in the Holy Cloak of the Prophet Muhammad, peace be upon him." Mullah Ehsan took a breath.

The dusty earth was so quiet you could hear him let out the air. "Allah *Subhanahu Wa-Ta'ala* had given the prophecy hundreds of miles away," Mullah Ehsan proclaimed. All were silent.

It was in that moment that Malik felt his feet grow larger.

"Rise, Malik," Mullah Ehsan said. "Attest to your dream before the Leader of the Faithful."

His friends from the madrassa all looked at Malik as he rose before Mullah Omar. One of their own was standing before the brave warrior, the leader of the Holy Soldiers of the Pure, sent to fight against sin and make Islam reign.

Malik stood up, trembling as Mullah Omar had trembled before he wore the Holy Cloak.

But Mullah Omar said nothing. No one knew what to do. Even Mullah Ehsan, who was never at a loss for words, couldn't say one.

The sun was hot above them, not a cloud from Heaven in the blinding sky. Not a single word from man or animals. Even the dogs were silent. The wind stopped too. The dust didn't move. Even insects were still.

Mullah Omar opened his palms, as he once had through the Blessed Cloak of the Prophet Muhammad, as if to pull Malik toward him.

Malik heard each of his sandaled steps in the dust make a sound with the same beat as his heart, which now beat so loud it left his chest. He began to feel faint. He could hardly walk, even move. His head was so dizzy, it left his body. He was so light, he left his own body too. He couldn't see straight. He was sweating like his mother before death.

Now, God alone in all His wisdom must have led him, because he no longer remembered where he was or even who he was. All he could recall was, as he thought he fell forward, he coughed. Then somehow he was pulled upright. It was as if God's Hand had reached from behind and caught him by the back of his neck, yanking the fallen boy toward Heaven.

Suddenly Malik was wrapped by Mullah Omar's arms. Held in his embrace, Malik felt every thread from the Blessed Cloak of the Prophet touching his skin, absorbed inside him by his own sweat. His nose too drew in the perfume of Prophet Muhammad that Mullah Omar wore, a scent of musk and camphor. The sacred scent went straight through his nostrils to fill his lungs and every breath Malik would ever take, before the tears that formed in his eyes touched the skin that touched the Holy Cloak, racing through his blood until they pumped inside his very heart.

"Allah-u-Akbar!" he heard Mullah Ehsan cry. Others joined in.

In that moment which lasted a lifetime, in that moment when

Malik couldn't see, was dizzy and weak, and died in his mother's sweat and tears of blood, in that moment when Mullah Omar held him up, Malik was embraced by the Holy Cloak of the Prophet Muhammad forever.

And by the Hand of Allah the Most Glorious and Exalted, Malik immediately grew another inch or two, so he now approached even Mullah Omar's great height.

TWO DAYS LATER, Mullah Ehsan led his chosen corps of the Holy One Thousand—including Malik and his madrassa unit—from Kandahar on jihad to liberate the North from infidels. Malik's true dream had confirmed Mullah Omar's standing as the Leader of the Faithful, and the boy's presence among the Holy One Thousand was a blessing from God alone, Mullah Ehsan told all the men.

Mullah Ehsan's men and thousands of other Taliban moved north as one, crossing a rough terrain most of them had never seen before. Speaking Pashto, growing up in Pakistan, they now entered unfamiliar Afghan country, where the language was Tajik or Uzbek and the people, towns, and land were almost foreign, Russian.

Racing northward on the rocky dusty roads, the wind from Almighty Allah carried them, not the Toyota Hilux pickups. Death meant Heaven, and life meant they could fight for God. The men would never forget the inspiration of the Leader of the Faithful. Mullah Omar was living proof that Allah's Hand could raise any one of them up from the brown earth. They could all indeed now bear witness to how tall Malik had become.

Malik still felt the sweat from the leader's embrace. The threads of the Blessed Cloak of the Prophet Muhammad around him grew into thin hair on his arms and chest. Though he performed *wudu* (ablution) for prayer, he hadn't washed the rest of his flesh. He felt the sweat from his fever enter his blood: the sweat from the Cloak of the Prophet and the skin of the Leader of the Faithful. Even when his madrassa friend Adeel was killed in battle, Malik saw that he was quickly taken to Heaven. He could see the light of faith illuminating his friend's face and the smile come over his lips. Malik could even smell the sweet scent of musk, Adeel's entire body fresh as a newborn boy.

Moving swiftly, with God at their back, the northern provinces fell to the soldiers of God. Mazar-e-Sharif was their prize. Led by Mullah Ehsan and his Holy One Thousand, Taliban Foreign Minister Mullah Muhammad Ghaus, and Mullah Abdul Razaq, more than three thousand Taliban fighters advanced on Mazar at the end of May 1997.

But on the eve of battle, as they were moving north, Mullah Ehsan ordered Malik and about sixty of his loyal madrassa followers to return to Kabul. Malik didn't know why, unless it had been an order from Mullah Omar himself. Still, Malik told no one his dream that night. He saw his mother cloaked in white, dripping blood. He woke up knowing that God would try His truest soldiers.

Five days later, Malik and his madrassa companions again reported to Mullah Qalamuddin, the commander of Virtue and Vice in Kabul. During that time, Mullah Ehsan and his crack forces were the first to take Mazar, followed by Mullah Abdul Razaq and his men, the first to have taken Kabul some nine months earlier. Indeed, it was Mullah Razaq who had personally captured the Communist president Najibullah, castrating him with his own knife before shooting him at point-blank range in each eye and hanging his bloody corpse from the center traffic signal in Kabul. Yet soon after conquering Mazar, infidel Shiite Hazaras rose up and slaughtered the true believers. It was the greatest defeat for the Forces of God since they had begun. Not only were the city of Mazar and three thousand Taliban fighters lost, but noble leaders such as Mullah Ehsan were martyred as well.

Malik's dream had told him God would test His most loyal warriors. Malik had the Prophet's threads and scent inside him. He had the Leader of the Faithful's embrace on Earth. He knew Islam led the way.

COMMANDING GOOD and forbidding evil, Malik was proud to be an officer to "promote virtue and prevent vice."

Malik had been chosen by Mullah Omar. By God. And Mullah Qal-amuddin even gave Malik an entire district to run, in charge of investigating all crimes against Islam in Deh Sabz, near Kabul Airport.

As he had learned much of the Holy Qur'an by heart, Malik quickly memorized the prohibitions of Sharia's "heavenly order" to be a good Muslim. He led his men to bring Islam to the city people. He was building a true Islamic state.

Sharia told Malik that all beard shaving, keeping pigeons, kite flying, and British and American hairstyles must be banished. Women must never be allowed to wash clothes along the water streams of the city or have their garments tailored. Music and dance at weddings and the playing of drums were banned, as was gathering at the bazaar at times for prayer.

Every time Malik administered "heavenly order" laid down by the Leader of the Faithful, he touched the Cloak of the Prophet Muhammad; he smelled the camphor and musk of the Holy Prophet and felt the warmth of Mullah Omar's embrace. The Leader of the Faithful's very blood now pumped his own heart. Since Islam prohibited him to think about girls, he willed himself not to.

And Malik acquired a new habit. He noticed now that his eyes would tear up. But he knew that the tears contained the salty sweat from the Leader of the Faithful, infused with the Holy Prophet's scent and threads. The very fiber of his soul now cried with the Holy Prophet's touch.

The Taliban Ministry of Aviation and Transportation was gathering materials for a new wing to the airport. Because the people trusted him, Malik received a tip that six bandits were stealing iron beams. He led his men to the construction site, where they opened fire at the six thieves. Arresting them, Malik and his men blackened their faces with engine oil and tied them on top of their Toyota pickups. Driving through Kabul, honking their horns, they told the thieves to cry through their blackened faces so the whole city could see their oily shame. Since they had only tried to steal government property, their hands were spared. If they had stolen personal property, Sharia provided that their hands would be cut off.

Malik had been in charge of the Deh Sabz district for a year when he was called to battle again. Fighting to liberate Mazar-e-Sharif, Malik and his men honored Mullah Ehsan the Martyr and successfully freed the city from infidels.

Malik was then promoted to be a chief of virtue and vice for Jalalabad and the region extending through Nangarhar Province to the border at Torkham. He was nineteen.

For two years in eastern Afghanistan, Malik enforced the fear of God. For adultery, a married woman would be stoned to death; a single woman would receive one hundred lashes, according to Islam.

"We made drives against vulgarity. Bringing people to the mosques to pray five times a day, beating those who would refuse. Making sure that no one charged too much in the market and no one charged any interest at all. That was *haram*. We brought Islam to the people so that they could live with God," Malik explained.

He was based near his home province, though he had stopped hearing from his father long before. He was also near one of the large camps of the guests of the Taliban: the men from Al Qaeda. He saw Osama bin Laden and other Al Qaeda, but they kept to themselves, as did Malik and his men.

A senior Al Qaeda leader, Abu Mohammad al-Masri, had told Malik that the Taliban were too young and naive.

Malik felt such behavior ran against *melmastia,* the hospitality that must be shown to a guest and the guest must in turn respect, according to Pashtunwali, the Pashtun tribal code of honor, and to Sharia, the Islamic law. But it was equally un-Islamic for him to show anger at this stranger's remarks, so he remained silent. He had no use for Al Qaeda.

When 9/11 happened, he didn't think much of it. Everybody said it was most likely the work of the Americans and Jews to create an excuse to attack Muslims and dominate Afghanistan.

He had heard the senior Taliban leaders held a Loya Jirga to decide whether to turn over bin Laden and Al Qaeda, or the Americans would attack. Some of the leaders wanted to give up bin Laden. Most thought that the Americans would just attack by air and believed the

Great Infidel too cowardly to launch a ground invasion. But Mullah Omar said bin Laden was a good Muslim and Islam forbade them to turn him over to unbelievers.

If Malik had not been a good Muslim, he would've become angry. "To think Al Qaeda thought so little of us Taliban, and here we were protecting them," Malik said. But he never showed the least flash of anger, even though the Americans invaded by land, not even a month after 9/11.

Panic swept through Jalalabad, Torkham, Tora Bora, and Nangarhar Province, all areas under the command of Malik, who just turned twenty-one. He led his Virtue and Vice men on sweeps of Jalalabad to prevent looting and un-Islamic activities.

Kabul quickly fell to the infidel invaders. Malik received no word from Taliban leaders in Kandahar. There was little resistance as Taliban started to flee. Many headed for the mountains and Pakistan. The Al Qaeda leadership first went to Jalalabad and then fled to Tora Bora.

Malik and his loyal men tried to maintain Islamic order. They remained true and would fight until the last man if ordered to.

But there was no order to resist, so Malik led his men, along with other Taliban, back to Pakistan. If there had been resistance, he would have stayed and fought.

Near the Pakistani border at Tora Bora, Malik and other Taliban slept on the side of a mountain. Suddenly, they woke to a sharp order in a foreign accent. Surrounded by Northern Alliance soldiers, who were allied with the infidel Americans, Malik and the Taliban were cornered. There was no way out.

The Northern Alliance men were heavily armed. They took the Taliban weapons.

"But they were very nice," Malik said. "They asked us if we wanted to join and help them. But we said no."

Malik led his men over the Pakistani border he knew well, and each went his own way. He went back to his father in Swabi for the first time in five years.

———

MALIK WAITED FOR a sign from God but had no dreams.

More than a year after fleeing Afghanistan, one of Malik's men finally came to tell him that the Taliban leadership was regrouping in the two largest border cities of Pakistan, Peshawar and Quetta. Malik went to join them.

The first task the leadership gave him was to gather his men inside Pakistan for the resistance in Afghanistan: specifically in Laghman, Jalalabad, Nangarhar, and eastern Afghanistan.

Malik joined the renewed insurgency with orders from Mullah Omar's top deputies: Mullah Baradar, Mullah Usmani, Mullah Ubaidullah, and Mullah Dadullah.

Some months later, Mullah Ubaidullah summoned him to Quetta, saying that Mullah Omar himself needed to see Malik personally "on a matter of great importance."

Malik asked Mullah Ubaidullah if he knew of his previous meeting with Mullah Omar in Kandahar.

"I know, Brother Malik," Mullah Ubaidullah said. "That's why Mullah Muhammad Omar Mujahid, Servant of Islam, Leader of the Faithful, needs to see you now—for the *true dream* of a believer."

As his eyes would tear, Malik now felt his feet sweat. He knew that an audience with Mullah Omar was saved only for the chosen. After the defeat in Afghanistan, Mullah Omar now needed to see him— Malik—of all people. The Leader of the Faithful needed a dream from Malik—of all God's humble servants. Malik surely was touched by the Hand of Allah.

That evening, Mullah Ubaidullah's driver took him in a Land Cruiser. Malik had to be worthy of Allah Almighty before the Leader of the Faithful, Mullah Omar. Jerking back and forth between the high mud-brick walls and narrow lanes of the Pashtunabad area of Quetta, Malik could have thrown up. Instead, he let the rocking motion of the Land Cruiser lull him to sleep in the backseat, so he could be blessed by God with "a true dream."

In man's greatest time of need, Allah the Most High does not disappoint. Turning and twisting in the Land Cruiser, Malik knew that if

Mullah Omar heard his dream, the Taliban would bring peace to the world and Islam to every infidel, even the American invaders. Dizzy and sick, he vowed to himself to rise to the occasion, to serve God at any cost. Give his entire life to the Glory of Allah. Why else had he been put on this dark brown suffering earth?

Driving through the dusty alleyways, they arrived in the evening at a Taliban madrassa. Mullah Ubaidullah led them through its unending students and rooms, through several courtyards, and down a long brown corridor. At the back was a hidden door, through which Mullah Ubaidullah unlocked a large silver padlock with a secret combination, as if he were opening the box to the Holy Prophet's Cloak.

Inside the large windowless room, the highest Shura leaders were sitting cross-legged on brown-and-gold cushions, barefoot. Mullah Omar was in the center. His one good eye quickly spotted Malik.

"This is the boy who dreamed before it happened that you wore the Cloak of the Prophet," Mullah Ubaidullah said loudly to all assembled.

Mullah Omar looked up from his single eye.

"Mullah Omar knows," he said.

Mullah Omar motioned for Malik to sit next to him. Malik could see his holy leader's slight, tender smile within the strong dark beard.

The other mullahs made space for the boy. Mullah Baradar smiled at him and pointed to the spot where he should sit—right next to Mullah Omar.

Now Mullah Omar himself smiled.

"As the great Hadith told us that Allah's Apostle said, when the Day of Resurrection approaches, the dreams of a true believer will never fail to come true," Mullah Baradar said.

As Malik went to sit down, their noble leader rose and embraced him again. Malik was surely blessed.

It felt almost as magical as the first time. Mullah Omar's breath and beard and smile on him, the Holy Prophet's Cloak wrapping the boy in ecstasy once more.

"Time for Isha prayer," Mullah Omar said.

All the mullahs and Malik performed *wudu* in the far end of the room, and, facing Mecca, Mullah Baradar led them in prayer.

Now Malik knew his dream was true. Now he knew he must tell the Leader of the Faithful.

Yet, no sooner than prayer was finished and sweetened green tea served did Mullah Omar himself, the light of faith illuminating his face, ask Malik for his dream. Malik's eyes watered, beads of sweat collecting above them. He even felt one salty drop leave him and fall to the ground.

As once before, his whole life came to this single point, where God called him to stand on the flesh of his feet to bear witness and redeem all that is noble and holy.

"Mullah Muhammad Omar Mujahid, may God protect you, Servant of Islam, Leader of the Faithful, it was a true dream I had while driving to meet you, *Inshallah,*" Malik began, clearing the spit from the back of his throat. He could barely speak. But he had to. If his entire life meant anything, it only meant something now.

Mullah Omar turned his palm over, as he had once turned it through the sleeves of the Holy Prophet's Cloak, the people fainted and proclaimed him the caliph of all Muslims. Malik didn't want to faint now.

"In the dream, my eyes were burned by its force," Malik started. "The vision took me over, Praise be to Allah, the Most High."

All were stone silent. The power of a dream could never be disputed.

Malik was soaked with sweat. He had the fever of his mother and had to stop to wipe his forehead clean. His eyes were so full of water he could barely see.

"I couldn't see," Malik continued. "It's as if the entire sun was fired like a Stinger missile at my eyes, the flash was so powerful and bright. It was you! Oh, my Esteemed Leader of the Faithful, Servant of Islam, it was you." Facing Mullah Omar, Malik was crying as if his mother just died, as if he were reciting from the Holy Book. "Your beard itself," he said, grasping for air, "your very own beard turned a blinding white—for it was now made of the threads of the Holy Prophet's very Cloak, Praise be to Allah the Most High." Malik took a deep breath and tried to steady himself.

"Al-Hamdulillah!" Mullah Usmani was the first to cry, breaking the faithful silence.

"Al-Hamdulillah!" Mullah Omar himself said. "God has spoken. Mullah Omar shall return to jihad with the blessing of Allah, the All-Seeing."

"And live long, Praise be to God the Most High," Mullah Ubaidullah added.

"Allah-u-Akbar," Mullah Baradar led the others. *"Allah-u-Akbar,"* they spoke as one.

Then Mullah Omar, in all his towering height, stood up. Malik rose with him. And the Taliban leader held the boy again.

As Mullah Omar embraced him, Malik saw that his true dream lifted them to the clouds of Heaven. He felt like fainting, the air grew so thin.

Malik knew that God was at work as he now grew as tall as the Leader of the Faithful himself.

MALIK'S "TRUE DREAM told Mullah Omar to lead the jihad against the Americans and Jews," Mullah Ubaidullah explained. And it wasn't too long before Mullah Ubaidullah and Mullah Omar's other deputies gave Malik a key role in the Taliban's jihad. His men were loyal to him and ready to fight in their home territory of Jalalabad and eastern Afghanistan as soon as they got the orders. Malik waited to lead his men against the American Crusaders to the glory of God.

But the Taliban leaders ordered him on a new and more immediate mission. They gave him cash, cameras, weapons, and supplies. Malik, with a select few men, was to travel inside Afghanistan and give the money and goods to Taliban fighters. In turn, he was to report on battles and troop needs to the Taliban leaders back in Pakistan.

He served the critical role of liaison between Taliban commanders in Pakistan and Taliban soldiers on the ground in Afghanistan. He received a regular salary from the Taliban, and its leaders even entrusted him with large sums of cash. He never realized until years later why they'd picked him for this role.

Only when you lose everything can you really know God. The Taliban had brought peace to Afghanistan. It had brought pure Islam—the triumph of good morals—for the first time to the lowest of the low. That is what the movement meant. Taliban rule under Sharia meant that the faithful farmers and believers in the countryside would live under the same divine law as the rich and powerful in the cities. Islam saw all men as equal before God, and each man must give to God and live by His law. No man was better than another. No one could charge another man too much, steal, commit adultery, or covet women.

"We were building a society of Muslims, pure and equal in the sight of God Almighty. And this is what we lost. This is why we were invaded by the Americans, for the greed and power of infidels who do not believe," Malik said.

And only when you've lost everything do you truly face God in all His majesty, in all His compassion. Malik now clung with ever-greater power to his steadfast faith.

It led him over the treacherous mountains and dry valleys, through the hot deserts and deserted villages of Afghanistan. The Taliban fighters he spoke to all fought with the same certain faith, the same determination to do good. This was a jihad of the good against the un-Islamic ways of American invaders and their puppet local slaves. God was on their side.

But when Malik returned with his battle reports, the mullahs complained they needed more money, more victories, and more opium.

Just like alcohol, any kind of drug was un-Islamic. Mullah Baradar, Mullah Omar's right-hand man, said that since the opium was going to the Americans and infidels, it was Islamic for the funds from selling it to come back to the Taliban.

Malik and his men never had any trouble crossing the border. At first they went over back routes, but Mullah Baradar told them just to cross at the official border checkpoints. The Pakistani guards would never stop them.

Malik and his unit traveled in the southern Afghan provinces without problems too. It was the early days of the fighting, and if they met up with any Northern Alliance, they just had to give a small bribe.

Once they ran into some foreign infidels, and after a brief firefight, the sinners quickly fled.

Mostly, Malik and his men went unmolested. Only one time did Fazil, another fighter, get frostbite on his toes, and when they passed through one of the villages, an old man cursed the Virtue and Vice Police.

That hurt Malik. They did not "terrorize" the people. Where did those myths come from? They were administering heavenly order, bringing the blessings of Islam and morality into people's everyday lives. And when the man said that the Taliban ran the country for Al Qaeda and bin Laden had built Mullah Omar a beautiful house in Kandahar, Malik didn't know what he was talking about. It was just more lies from the Americans.

As they were leaving, the old villager cried out, "Why did you kill my son?" Malik didn't know what to say. There must have been a reason.

He heard other complaints like that. But mostly the men he met just wanted the Taliban back. They were waging jihad against the infidels and foreigners. They were fighting for Islam against Hamid Karzai, the corrupt puppet of American Crusaders, and his new Afghan government in Kabul, which operated against the rules of Islam.

"I will never take Washington as my *kibla*," Malik said.

GOD ALMIGHTY'S great light will always reveal the dark sins of men.

It was an abnormally sunny day. God shined clearly in all His glory.

It was during the middle of 2006. Malik had been ferrying supplies and carrying back reports for more than three years. He had been a faithful Taliban commander.

Mullah Ubaidullah now asked him to transport a shipment of arms to the southern front. The mullah, one of Mullah Omar's top deputies, gave him a location in Peshawar as the first stop. The code name was "curious."

Malik arrived at a modern apartment, with unbearded men inside.

They were like women unveiled—like ISI Pakistani army officers. They gave him a map and address in Chaman, at the Pakistani border near Quetta.

He went to the address with Fazil and Jumma and Dost, three of his most trusted companions from the old madrassa days. They had fought together for ten years now. They drove together, walked together, slept together. He loved his men like brothers, and they loved him.

Yet when Malik opened the door to the address in Chaman, he nearly vomited on the spot. There in front of him was a Pakistani army officer, in full uniform, from the ISI. The Pakistani army— worse, its intelligence agency.

Malik hated the government of Pakistan. The so-called Islamic Republic was a joke. The Pakistanis flew the flag of Islam while wrapping themselves in infidel American dollars. They wore Islamic clothes while stealing from the poor. They proclaimed Islam while using Pashtun soldiers like himself and Fazil and Jumma and Dost as pawns to serve the Americans.

The ISI man now addressed him as an equal. Malik looked at Fazil and Jumma and could barely offer the ISI thug a proper greeting. He was just glad that Dost was waiting with the pickups and didn't have to see this.

The officer's manner was rude, like a Westerner's. "What's the matter, cat got your tongue? You simple Afghans are all the same. Strong, silent types," he said, laughing.

Malik felt like saying he had been born in Pakistan too, you fool, but said nothing.

The Pakistani ISI man led him into another room with more ISI officers in full dress uniform. They didn't even feel the need to greet Malik and his men in civilian clothes.

They were drinking. "Want a cigarette?" one of them asked.

Didn't they even know that smoking was *haram*? Malik felt dirty as one of the fattest officers led him in back to three Pak army trucks full of small arms, ammunition, and remote control bomb devices from the ISI.

"We can't drive these," Malik said, morally offended that he would have a Pakistani army vehicle.

"No, you ninny, whaddaya think? I'd let you take our trucks?" the ISI man said, laughing.

It was the vile display of arrogance Malik fully expected from an officer of the un-Islamic *kuffar* rule of Pakistan.

The ISI officers didn't even lower themselves to help Malik and his men load the arms into the Taliban pickups. They went back to smoking, drinking, and playing games of chance.

As he loaded the arms from the infidel *kuffar* onto his trucks, Malik felt unclean but said nothing to Fazil and Jumma and Dost.

Before they left for the border, he washed himself a full two times before Maghrib prayer. Indeed, he performed not the regular ablution, or *wudu,* but the *ghusl* required after sex or another dirty act.

IT WAS ON that evil day Malik began to see.

He must have been traveling with the Devil's jinn, over the border at Spin Boldak, all the way to Helmand Province in southern Afghanistan and back. The Taliban fighters told him they needed more food. They missed their families and wanted leave.

Malik reported to Mullah Ubaidullah in the center of Quetta. The mullah had a nice office and talked on a fancy cell phone. Like the sun, it struck Malik. The top Taliban leaders had no fear of arrest. They moved through the cities of Pakistan free and clear. In Peshawar and Quetta, they lived openly. Brazenly, they used their cell phones. All under the protection of the ISI: any fool could see that. You cannot block out the sun with the palm of your hand.

It broke his heart. Malik was fighting for Islam.

Two months later, Mullah Ubaidullah ordered him to make the same run, only this time he didn't have to stop in Peshawar first.

Passing through the border unmolested—the Pakistanis just waved them through—Malik now knew why. The trip this time seemed endless. It had always given him a sense of adventure before, a sense of purpose to his life that he never questioned. He was on the side of Islam. That's all he needed to know.

Now each turn of the truck's wheel ground into his heart, each belch from its smoky exhaust ate at his empty stomach as if unseen jinn had flown inside. He couldn't eat or sleep much. He couldn't even enjoy the brotherhood of his friends. It was hot and dusty. It was dirty.

Arriving at the outskirts of Lashkar Gah, the capital of Helmand Province, they dropped off the weapons and ammunition and loaded the opium. Drugs were *haram,* like drinking. But the poppies were only to harm the infidel invaders. They were part of the jihad—another kind of jihad.

But when Malik and his men returned, Mullah Ubaidullah ordered them to deliver the drugs to the same ISI safe house—the very same ISI officers.

How is this jihad? Malik thought.

"I will not bow to Islamabad any more than Washington," he vowed to himself.

He knew it wasn't right. As a mujahid, he could never ask a mullah anything. But he had to know whether what he was now fighting for was a lie.

Malik wanted to leave the front and join the Taliban media team.

"My father is sick, and I need to be closer to home," he said, asking Mullah Baradar's permission. The mullah agreed, as long as he continued to make occasional runs inside Afghanistan and kept his men ready. Mullah Baradar also cut his pay by half.

Malik didn't care. He was just relieved not to have to see the faces of those ISI dogs. And he liked the media safe house. He got to read jihadi books and websites and improve his basic Urdu and little bit of English. All he had to do was summarize what everyone was saying so that the Taliban—or the Islamic Emirate of Afghanistan, as the leaders now decided to push that name—could speak in the very best language of jihad.

After a couple of months, he started to work with someone about his own age who called himself a doctor—even a mullah. Malik didn't see how. This so-called mullah had a short beard and never washed thoroughly before prayer. He looked dirty and talked too much.

Malik asked Mullah Ubaidullah if he could see Mullah Omar again. He also asked Mullah Baradar. He tried to find Mullah Dadullah too. He told the mullahs he'd had another dream, although he hadn't. He just supposed that when the time came to see Mullah Omar, he would. But they never took him to Mullah Omar. Some of his madrassa men were even sent to fight. Malik wasn't called.

The so-called Dr. Mullah began to take on a larger role in the Taliban media wing. One night after evening prayer, "Dr. Hanif" even asked him to take dinner together. But Malik was shocked when he arrived at the "doctor's" apartment in Peshawar. It was the same ISI safe house where more than a year before he had picked up the address for the munitions delivery.

Thank God, Malik saw no ISI vermin crawling around, though he could barely eat the dal and kebabs. He didn't like dal anyway. Only meat, like a real Pashtun.

The "doctor" talked on and on. Malik hated any man who talked a lot. He wished he could see Mullah Omar. If only he could see Mullah Omar again and have another dream, or at least a vision, he knew everything would be set right. Mullah Omar, Leader of the Faithful, could not possibly be part of this perfidy with the Pakistanis.

"What makes you think you're better than me?" the so-called Dr. Hanif said.

"I'm just following Islam," Malik said.

"You're saying I'm not?" The pretender almost spat.

"With the ISI?"

"They're loyal Pashtun."

"They're *kuffar*."

"You think you know everything? Where did your arrogance come from? They're an undercover operation of Pashtun officers who truly support our jihad."

Malik said nothing more. It was shameful. He didn't know how he could even appear at the media office again. He just wanted to do God's work. He had fought for jihad too but kept wondering who the real enemies of God were now.

MALIK LEFT THE old Taliban silently. At first he just started showing up less and less. He didn't even pick up his pay. And no one called him. He started writing for a local Pashtun newspaper in Peshawar. It wasn't a lot of money, but he could write about true jihad, what the Taliban had really meant, not what it had now become.

Hamid Karzai, the so-called president of Afghanistan, was a slave to the Americans. That's who they were fighting against. The old-line Taliban leaders were slaves to the Pakistanis. How was that any different from Karzai and his dogs, when the Americans owned the Pakistanis too? Malik could only ask God that Mullah Omar not be part of this unholy alliance.

After he stopped going to the Taliban press office, the "Dr. Mullah" became the mouth organ for the Taliban traitors, constantly talking to Western reporters. It wasn't long before the Americans tracked down his cell and arrested him. "Dr. Hanif" even "confessed" on Afghan TV and said that the ISI was funding the Taliban and protecting Mullah Omar in Quetta.

"I told Mullah Ubaidullah from the very beginning that man talked too much," Malik said.

At least the phony Dr. Mullah told the truth—though not about Mullah Omar, Malik still hoped.

Then it dawned on him why the mullahs had him transport the cash, weapons, and drugs all those times between Afghanistan and Pakistan: the mullahs didn't trust any other senior Taliban leader not to steal some.

It all broke his heart.

Months later, Yahya, his madrassa loyal and true friend, was slaughtered by the Taliban, accused of being an American spy. The truth was that Yahya had told about the corrupt transport trade of the Taliban. Truck drivers from Karachi would bring oil and other supplies to the

Americans. They would siphon off the oil in Pakistan, drive through insurgent territory, steal or blow up the trucks, and share the proceeds with the Taliban leaders—and no doubt the corrupt ISI.

Malik had cut off the hands of thieves for the Virtue and Vice Police: how was this any different? Any different from Karzai and the American dogs that used the so-called Reconciliation Commission in Kabul to bribe former Taliban—even Mullah Rocketi had now betrayed them.

The Taliban had proper Islamic rule, commanding good and forbidding evil. The poor could advance. Now they were used. Evil reigned: Malik wrote in the Pashto newspaper under a fake name.

Only weeks before the Americans killed him in Helmand, Mullah Dadullah came to the newspaper office. He confronted the editor and demanded to know the identity of the reporter who had written the scandalous articles. The editor said they had just come in the mail. He didn't know who. Mullah Dadullah said that if they did not stop printing the articles, the Taliban would blow him and his entire office sky-high.

Mullah Dadullah had arrived in an official Pakistani car. Thank God, several weeks later the Americans showed the world Mullah Dadullah's dead body.

MALIK NOW TURNED toward me. I felt hope. Malik had rejected the moral corruption of the Taliban, as Ahmad ("Bernie") and Abby both had with Al Qaeda. I also felt the same kind of human connection and bridge between us. Indeed, it seemed that out of enmity a bond had been forged.

I began to think that from the very heart of faith, from Islam's most pious, there could be a path to peace. The corruption of the Taliban and Al Qaeda leaders simply had to be exposed for what it was. They were as crooked and ruthless as the worst politicians anywhere. Among the people, we could find common ground. This must be the answer in faith we were all searching for. This must be the answer in virtue that any religious person can understand.

Malik nodded and reached out to hold my right hand—as customary a sign of friendship among Pashtun men as a handshake is in greeting.

I could feel his sweat. I could feel his rough fingers intertwine with mine. A coarse, muscled hand that had seen much struggle held fast to a thin, delicate one that had never wanted for a meal.

His brown eyes fixed on mine, Malik spoke in a soft, consoling whisper: "I want the world now to know the real faces of those who are truly fighting for Islam. We are alive, and we are marching forward. We are the new Taliban."

Still staring at me, his eyes began to tear, as he recited by heart the Holy Qur'an. "The Book always makes a truly pious man cry," he said in a whisper.

The Uncreated Word of Allah flowed through him, as if he were back in madrassa. He even recited the holy verses in Arabic first:

The greatest enemy of the Believers is the Jews.
Twice they will spread corruption on the earth and be full with
mighty arrogance, and twice they will be punished.

"It is so in our times," Malik said, breaking from the Holy verses. "We face now their second arrogance in our homeland, for Americans are the Jews of our times."

"There is a sound Hadith," he continued, "related by both al-Bukhari and Muslim. The Holy Prophet, peace be upon him, told that the Day of Judgment will not come until Muslims kill all the Jews. And when the Jew hides behind stones and trees, even the stones and trees will speak: O Muslims, there is a Jew behind me, come and kill him. Only the gharqad tree will not speak to the believers because it is the tree of the Jews. This is a sound Hadith beyond dispute, and we know today that Americans are the second arrogance who will be punished, for the Americans and Jews are one."

"Now," Malik continued, squeezing my hand even tighter, "we will root up every gharqad tree in the land. Karzai and his puppet Afghan government are under the left hand of the Americans and

Jews. The old Taliban leaders are under the same unclean left hands of the Pakistani ISI and army, beholden to those very same American apes and pigs. And all of them are stealing, committing evil, and blaspheming Islam.

"It is time for a new, true Islamic movement, no longer controlled by foreign infidels. A pure Taliban that will bring peace and God's will back to all of Afghanistan and Pakistan. It is time to attack Pakistan itself and free the Taliban of the near enemy.

"America is the father of all evil. The new Taliban of the Pure must attack the near enemy of Pakistan first. The new Taliban must become the Fedayeen-e-Islam, the Partisans Who Sacrifice their Lives for Islam. Then we will go after the far enemy of America, free Afghanistan and Pakistan from the infidels, live again under God, command good, and forbid evil." "Fedayeen" is an Arabic term the Taliban often use for suicide bombers.

The tears flowed down his cheeks. He still held my hand in a vise. By that point—interview be damned—I just wanted to get away from him. The only thing that finally loosened his grip, and freed me at last, was when I asked if he'd had a dream.

By God, he said, in his dream, he had seen "fire consume the citadel of American greed, the pig trough where the Pakistani generals, politicians, and crooked Jewish apes and swine fed. It was a tall building in Pakistan's corrupt capital, Islamabad. As the American shrine burned to the ground, so the infidels' evil plans for domination burned too."

And he saw Mullah Omar, passing over to him "the Holy Cloak of the Prophet Muhammad, peace be upon him."

I WAS SAFELY at home in Washington, D.C., more than two months later when I saw the news from Islamabad—and remembered Malik's dream.

"The fire has eaten the entire Marriott," Muhammad Ali, an emergency worker, said.

"The explosion has left the building in ruins and a deep crater where the bomb detonated," the news continued. "Yet the deeply blackened structure of the hotel doesn't fall. Inside the lobby, the floor is covered in scattered shards of glass, broken bits of the ceiling, torn carpet, leaves, and small pools of blood. The once blindingly luminous ceiling chandelier now dangles precariously over the reception desk, underneath ashes and bodies everywhere."

The Fedayeen-e-Islam—the new Taliban group Malik had mentioned—claimed credit for the Marriott attack, saying that its purpose was "to kick the American Crusaders out of Pakistan."

Part II

THE JIHADI TRAINER AND "CAPTAIN OF TERROR"

4

THE CONFESSIONS OF ZEDDY

AHMAD, ABBY AND MARYAM, and Malik were true believers. However misguided, they fought for love of faith. Out of a commitment to be good Muslims, they sacrificed themselves for God's Word in the Holy Book and for God above all. Their piety and religious visions, like those of many Taliban and Al Qaeda fighters I interviewed, seemed to define a movement of faith whose actions presumably could be changed by faith as well—though, of course, a vastly more tolerant interpretation.

Zahid ("Zeddy") was different. A colleague of Osama bin Laden in his early days, Zeddy was deeply entwined in the radical Muslim politics of Pakistan. For nearly three decades, he was, in his words, a "career terrorist for Islam." And what motivated him was not simply the faithful world of many of his colleagues. Here is the inside story of faith and raw power, faith and ruthless greed, faith and bloody revenge. Zeddy even became a "professional terrorist" with his finger one step removed from Pakistan's nuclear arsenal: he worked directly for Pakistan's army and its intelligence arm, putative American allies all. Zeddy's story is a chilling warning.

From his conversations with bin Laden, Zeddy also shows why America is the symbolic "Great Tempter" for jihadis. American ideals of freedom, achievement, and individuality all compete with the radical Islamist model of collective identity, personal sublimation, and unquestioning faith. And it's a competition that the jihadis are deeply scared of losing.

I met Zeddy during the summer of 2008 in Pakistan's capital, Islamabad, not too far from the mountains of his home near Abbottabad. We met through three Pakistani journalists, one of whom had almost singular access to both the radicals and the Pakistani army, particularly its intelligence agency, the ISI. Unlike almost all of my other interviews, with Zeddy I had to do very little prodding. His thoughts and feelings came rushing out, as if he were in a long-delayed confessional. And unlike most other jihadis, Zeddy was not a young man in his twenties or thirties either. He had lost most of his hair, and what was left around the bald edges was entirely white. His beard seemed to have faded too, leaving in its place a stubbly gray growth far from the full dark beard of a youthful jihadi. His skin was scarred and wrinkled, his eyes bloodshot. He had even acquired a small but noticeable potbelly. Terrorism as a career seemed to have taken its toll, much as a coal miner or someone with another physically demanding job often visibly shows the wear of his years.

Given Zeddy's desire to share his story, it's best, I feel, to present his life in his own words, as he told it to me. I have corroborated, with independent sources, Zeddy's revelations of working directly for the Pakistani army and its intelligence agency in close support of terrorists. This account adds to the gathering evidence of official Pakistani complicity in terrorist attacks, as well as the ISI providing safe haven to Mullah Omar and the Taliban leaders—and even more surprisingly, to the leaders of Al Qaeda, including Osama bin Laden himself. Bin Laden's refuge in Abbottabad—home to Pakistan's military academy and a garrison town—also confirms Zeddy's account.

While I was able to corroborate much of what Zeddy told me, he spoke for himself—freely and forcefully. And since he spoke in fluent English, there is no intermediary to present the unique and frightening voice of the "Captain of Terror." So what follows are the confessions of Zeddy, "Pakistan's most notorious terrorist," as I took them down.

———

SEVENTY-TWO. Please to excuse, that is the number. There're seventy-two scars across my chest. Scars from seventy-two stitches, just like the seventy-two Virgins in Paradise I was told as a martyr *shaheed* I would meet but never did. Just like the seventy-two nukes my country has, and you trust us to keep safe. I'm sorry, Sahib. I'm getting ahead of myself.

I am Pakistan's most notorious terrorist you never heard of. That's right, Pakistan, you've heard of it, I'm sure, home to Al Qaeda, the Taliban, the entire lot—and me. Yes, I know, that Osama fellow too—never mind that cheeky bugger. I know all about him, of course, and I'll tell you too. It was my Islamic Party, after all, that harbored his top lieutenants following 9/11.

But please. Stop worrying about what you think you know. What you don't know is much more important. Yes, it's about the nukes. No, no, not that Pakistan is the only Muslim country with nuclear weapons. Any fool knows that. But you bloody Americans have no idea about the power and lies of the Muslim Brothers. And our goal has always been to put the nukes in the hands of true Muslims. Maybe not all seventy-two, but it only takes one holy nuke to get loose, pry its way free into the wrong or right hands, God's or the infidels'.

You would see what terrorism really means then, my American friend. We're not so stupid as to leave a return address either. You'll know all about that when you hear my story. A story I tell now for the first time.

You'll see how little you understand about the jihad that will greet you at your front door. You may think you understand, talking about this bin Laden and Al Qaeda or those Taliban. Ha! You will know the day after a nuke is delivered to New York, Washington, or Des Moines, Iowa. The day after, you will know. The day after, you'll first taste the meaning of jihad. The day after, you will know for the first time what terrorism really means.

And why do I tell you? Because my heart is ripped out from inside. I look death straight in the eyes. I want to meet God. I am tired of man. I am Zeddy.

I'm retired now. Imagine that: a retired terrorist! No pension or benefits, though. No retirement home for old terrorists either. Hardly like you retired Americans, living in the sun in Sun City. I'm living in sin in Sin City. My jihad has become a jail, my life a hell.

What, you keep saying, you never heard of me? That's just the point. It's always been. Remember: our purpose was to conduct terrorism secretly; our goal was to work with our hidden friends inside the Pakistani army and ISI under cover. Inter-Services Intelligence. But they never say that: just ISI. If you remember nothing else from my whole story, remember please those three initials: ISI, Pakistan's all-powerful intelligence agency, under army control and filled to the brim with our jihadi friends. Jihadis whose names you never heard of, just like me, terrorists with no return address. What you don't know is what can hurt you the most. The true face of jihad is something you don't see. I told you. With all your fancy reporters, CNN, BBC, you only think you know. But please to excuse, you don't.

How do I know? I was a terrorist, reporting to Aabpara [the ISI headquarters]. I was a jihadi for Pakistan's army, the very generals you Americans fete and proclaim as great democratic allies. They employed yours truly to train jihadis, to kill, wreak terror, and attack the infidel Indians. These selfsame Western-loving generals gave your Zeddy his bread and butter, fed him his salary, and bestowed the secret orders of Noble Jihad, for war in the cause of Allah is not terrorism but divine justice.

I trained, nurtured, you might say even birthed, thousands of recruits—who can keep count? And now, observe most carefully what my wayward offspring do: they bomb the American hotels and restaurants, all mere practice to let loose on your shores, elementary experiments for the next attack on the home of the brave and the land of the free itself. Oh, America, you're way too much on parade not to bring down to size and do the needful, "auld lang syne," as we Pakistanis say.

Of course you've never heard of me, Mr. Ken Sahib. I'm no showman like the tall Arab. I'm what you Americans call the "real deal." I suppose every cause needs its salesmen. I was never after your fifteen seconds, minutes, I don't know which, of fame. I know that's what you Americans will sacrifice everything for. No, for us Muslims, we care not a whit for your fame. It's all about Islam. Making Pakistan Islamic, getting those nukes, and defeating the infidels. If we act like Western democrats so you *kuffar* [infidels] don't see the real threat, so much the better. You'll know us the day after. Oh, yes. Then nobody would even remember the name bin Laden again. Just the holy name of Allah the Almighty, and Allah's only return address is in Heaven. Just try to retaliate against that. You'll have to launch your fancy nukes to the moon. You can blow up the moon, but it won't save you. Its white stones will just fall to Earth like your dead white bodies. You could blow up all of Pakistan, but by then, it's all too late, there'll be nothing left of New York and Washington, so what then?

After all, did not the founder of my Islamic Party, Maulana Maududi, tell us that "Islam seeks a world revolution to *liquidate*"—his word—"all its opponents and rule the whole earth—not just a portion, but the entire planet." That is the only goal. Please, Mr. Ken Sahib, mark his words, for he did not lie: "It is therefore the first duty of all those who aspire to please God to launch an organized struggle, sparing neither life nor property, to secure power for the righteous believers." That's right: "There is *no* other means left to please God."

But I get ahead of myself, don't I? Apologies. That is a most bad habit I have, ever since I was a kid. I'm always ahead of everyone else. Perhaps that's what made me so dangerous. Who knows? I don't. You can tell me when we're done.

I became a waiter, a driver, a guard, a soldier, a bomb maker, a bomber, assassin, and murderer. I killed hundreds, maybe thousands, but that's not the bottom line. What do you Americans say? It's about the economy, stupid? It's about the nukes, stupid. There I go again, getting to the end before you know the beginning.

I washed loos and cleaned latrines. I shoveled shit and slit the throats of infidels. I did whatever jihad demanded, and I did it with full dedication and sincerity for Islam. The hell with suicide bombers. I lived again to kill over and over. That is the true terrorist, the true martyr, the one that keeps killing. I taught my mujahideen that unless one man would kill a hundred enemy soldiers or five colonels or one brigadier general or higher, he was not a true *shaheed*. But once more, my dear Mr. Ken Sahib, I must apologize for getting ahead of my story. You see, I have so much pain buried inside of me that I cannot keep it in, the pain that caused my chest to explode, and by a miracle from God, I was saved in twenty-three hours of open-heart surgery. You see, my family was nothing if not good doctors. Good doctors or good family, they lived to save the life of Pakistan's worst terrorist. I was the king without a crown. In jail, on campus, on the streets or the battlefield, I was the "Captain of Terror," that's what they called me, so I can tell you, tell you right now, without delay, and without getting ahead of myself once again, my story . . . this time I'll try to tell it right. Welcome to my world.

MY GREAT-GRANDFATHER was the very first medical doctor from our part of Pakistan. My extended families were great landholders, the bin Ladens of northwest Pakistan, a big rich family network with unending relatives and money.

My grandfather was also a pioneer medical doctor, my father also a doctor, my brothers and sisters all doctors, one in North Carolina, one in Saudi Arabia, one in England, five brothers and two sisters in all, all doctors like my father, none of whom managed the family land—that vast rich land that I had nothing to do with either, which was left to other relatives to grow and guard the feudal wealth—everything in our part of world is about families, feudal families and tribal ties, stuff you Westerners know nothing of—so much for family land.

My father didn't care about the nitty-gritty of making money either, another high-minded Westernized doctor who dressed in Savile Row suits and loved all things British but hated the British enough to join the Muslim League. See, you could like the English, just not like them ruling you. So, those ironically most English of Muslims, still true Muslims, were the ones who made our Islamic Republic of Pakistan, all the while loyally loving the English. Oh, the proper English!

My father sent me to the very best English school in all of Pakistan, run by the Christian Fathers on the British public model: Burn Hall, the famous English Christian missionary academy in Abbottabad. It's properly called Senior Burn Hall, later taken over by the army to become Army Burn Hall College: from fathers to generals!

While my classmates rose to distinction in the government, business, and armed forces, I did as well—don't forget the ISI. Yes, ISI generals and guardians of the Holy Grail, the Islamic Bomb, those prized nukes—they were my friends and fellow Abbottabad Hallians, because I rose with distinction to the heights of my chosen field too. I followed the great Burn Hall name literally, the college's motto: "*Quo non ascendum,*" i.e., "To what heights can I not rise." Oh, to the very top, my dear alma mater, to the very top!

Oh, yes, I was always first in my class, you see. Never did much work. Didn't have to. I didn't care much for sports too. A lot of games, for what? Though I must candidly admit, fighting with my classmates came easily enough. I was always a powerful boy, a muscular four-square kind who wasn't scared of showing off. No one could touch me. I was a brilliant student and a bully, you could say, but I refused to address any of my teachers or principals as "Father." They even made my own father come in; your boy will not address us properly. That's right, I told them. "You're not my father, so why should I call you father?"

What could they say? I was number one in the class. What could my own father say? I was the sharpest blade. They could say nothing. Fathers. Ha ha! Fathers who replicated the English public school system to make the boys from Burn Hall the very leaders of Pakistan's future made this Burn Hall boy a leader too. Don't you just love those English?

Oh, and little did those fathers know—my own included—what lurked in the depths of the soul of this Burn Hall boy. Yes, in his heart burned a force far different from the other boys or all those bloody fathers, a force from only God knows where.

Okay, just say it, you might as well: from God. Anything unexplained comes from God, doesn't it, though actually it came when I was sixteen and read Maulana Maududi. One read, and I was done.

All the confusions, debates, rivalries of my family and classmates, and all that occurred in my own mind, Maududi neatly tied together and summarily dispensed. I'd search no more, for it was God I was searching for. And God that I had found. Maududi called for God's rule to replace the tyrannical rule of man over man, something I tasted firsthand at Burn Hall, so I was an overnight convert—the worst kind.

I knew I was starkly alone among family and friends—no one around me thought this way—but that's what convinced me, I suppose. It all made the number one student at the number one school in Pakistan really number one. No more mental tricks and intellectual gymnastics, no more arguing a point or thinking it through to the bitter end. I could dispense with it all. No doubts were left since every question was answered. I went only to God Himself. And God in His most pure form. Back to the ways of the Prophet, and the True Jihad. Inquiry was shown the back door, Maududi and his Jamaat was my path. Damned if I were to follow like an ass-sniffing monkey all of my four brothers and father into medicine, even my sisters. Zeddy would choose his own future and not the one the other father and fathers chose for him: medical doctor taught by Christians, British and all that rot. I was a Muslim, and I'd march to the drum of Islam. And Jamaat—that's Jamaat-e-Islami—was the Muslim Brothers of Pakistan, founded by Maududi the great Muslim jihadi teacher: what more did you need? Nothing, I said. Time to dive in the deep end and not come up for air. Time to abandon the ways of the fathers for the way of God.

My new ways indeed made me stand out like a sore thumb at Burn Hall. The secular teachers and students profoundly distrusted my religious garb. And I felt like a fool having to dress in the standard Christian college uniform. I vowed more than ever to become a jihadi in service to God. And like the very first prophet, Abraham, at age sixteen too, leave all the idol worshippers behind.

I never looked back. For a bright boy, you'd think I would have thought some more. I admit: it's kind of amazing to look back now. I studied little Islam, never even read much more than Maududi. I knew about the seventy-two virgins, the rewards of Heaven, and the representatives of Hell on Earth, those followers of Satan who were the godless infidels: the Communists attacking my Muslim brothers and the godless Ahmadiyya, who were my enemy too [a sect considered heretical by fundamentalist Muslims]. I prayed as required and followed His Word in the Holy Book. My mission was to die for God. It was a logic of emotion. I was captured by a feeling, and I let it take me over. I can't tell you it made sense. I can only tell you that's how it happened.

And once devoting myself, I didn't think about it until it was all too late, until I can now barely lift my head and look at the sun, until the pain that eats away at my chest makes it hard to breathe. I'm an old man now at just forty-nine. I could pass for seventy-nine. An old man, hunched over and shriveled, a shell of my former virile self. I won't live to see my children graduate from university; I won't live to see my grandchildren. Would God punish me so if what I did were right? Would God inflict this pain and early death if I had truly followed His path? Swept away by adventure and glory, I never looked back. Now God has reached into my chest and pulled out my heart, squeezed out the very life from me. So I ask you, did I do it for Him or for me?—Apologies, I'm back ahead of myself again.

I COULD NOT wait to leave Burn Hall in Abbottabad and go to the big university, Peshawar, in the capital of the North-West Frontier Province. I knew university was my chance—not to study but to join Jamaat.

Jamaat was Maududi's Muslim political party, the Muslim Brothers, the vanguard of the Muslim revolution, which would create an Islamic utopia for all, everyone on Earth, "not just a portion, but the entire planet." Maududi wrote that his party would be the only one to succeed because it followed nothing but "the highest ethical and religious standards," enjoining each of its members, indeed every Muslim, "to live morally upright and adhere without compromise to the very highest standards of Islam." Jamaat was no mere political party. We were Maududi's "virtuous community" brought down to do God's noble work on Earth.

At last I was in university to be "a foot soldier in the path of vir-tue" for Maududi and Jamaat. For Islam—for to me they were all one and the same. Sure, I had to go through the motions of class. But the right professors would pass you through if you were brothers in arms. That's right. Like what you say about football players in American universities. In the United States, you pass the athletes through class whether they study or not. In Pakistan, we pass the radicals through instead. For university life in Pakistan has little to do with studies and everything to do with which political party you join—and fight for. I started, though, in law, something different from my family's medical curse.

The first day at university, I went to Jamaat. My aunt's husband, he flirted with Jamaat too—well, a lot more than flirt: he was a major player. And he gave me a personal introduction to the leader—we call him the emir—of the student wing of Jamaat at the University of Peshawar. Yes, in fundamentalist jihadi circles, it's about who you know too. That cinched the entire deal. My rebellion was complete.

Immediately, I became part of the student Jamaat's infamous "Thunder Squad" and put in charge of the pressroom. Mind you, not to read any of the Jamaat pamphlets but to guard against attack by Communists, socialists, and other infidels.

This was because God blessed me with an imposing physique. At six foot three and two hundred pounds of pure muscle, I was a fearsome sight. Yes, you're right, like one of your American football players again, linebackers, you say. I have no idea what that is, but if someone strong and menacing, I accept it. That was me. I shelved my brain somewhere else. Put it "in the deep freeze." Thank you. You know, it's most clever to tell my story to an American—an English-man would never come up with all these fanciful expressions you Americans have.

Yes, your Zeddy started as a guard. I was there but three months when a group of infidels arrived past midnight. My fellow brother (he was a real thug, admitted to university solely for his muscle) guarded the door. There was a group of six or eight of them with cricket bats.

We were armed with bats too. But Zeddy did not check his entire brain on the shelf or "in the deep freeze," as you say. I made sure we were armed with daggers, something at that time the students usually shunned.

You can imagine the mayhem. Two of us against the rabble of infidel Communists. We held our own until my fellow brother started to be overcome and unsheathed the knife I had made him carry, cutting the gut of one of our attackers. This stopped the whole lot dead in their tracks. Shocked, they ran to the rescue of their comrade and beat a fast retreat. I cannot tell you whether this fellow lived or died. What I can tell you, since I have sworn to be honest with you, is that your Zeddy got quite a thrill that night. This had taken the lightweight fights at Senior Burn Hall to a whole new level. It was exhilarating. I felt powerful, ruthless; the Jamaat proclaimed us heroes. I realized, why stop at knives? It was time to defend the pious true Muslims with real arms.

I was the first to acquire guns for the Jamaat students. They had always fought with bats, wooden sticks, sometimes knives. Yes, your Zeddy was the first to bring Kalashnikovs to the university campus— what many commentators later called the "Kalashnikov culture" of Pakistani university life. I told you I was an innovator.

The PPP [Pakistan Peoples Party] Communist infidels had beaten us to bloody hell the night we had overturned their record player. They were playing Umm Kalsoum, some Arab lady singing while unveiled. No more, I said. I got an order of Kalashnikovs. We stormed the PPP headquarters and opened fire. I was fast promoted from pressroom guard to the personal guard of our student emir.

Then in 1979, the Russian Communists attacked Afghanistan, and I knew why my life was chosen for jihad. Our Pakistani Muslim student body overnight allied with our Muslim brothers in next-door Afghanistan. We were invaded by infidels. The meaning of jihad, a Holy War in defense of our homeland, was brought home. No debate or pamphlets to guard: this was it. The year before I was to take the civil service exam, I switched to medical college so that my father could continue to support my jihadi activities. I remained eight years in medicine fighting for jihad.

I was in medical school for jihad. On campus, shutting down parties, smashing alcohol, destroying music, beating Communists. But I always refused when it came to women. Some of the Jamaat would beat women without purdah, without the veil. But to me, I would never strike and harm a woman. In all my years, and in all the people I killed, I never once harmed a woman.

Soon after, as the Afghan jihad raged, a real opportunity came my way. My uncle-in-law, rising fast in the ranks of Jamaat, set up a dinner for me with the great Muslim fighter and leader, Gulbuddin Hekmatyar [a principal of the Afghan mujahideen and now of the Taliban alliance.]

There was no greater Afghan mujahid than Gulbuddin Hekmatyar. I shared *naan* and lamb kebob with the great mujahid hero. I was completely smitten, you might say.

Hekmatyar had it all: twelve of the most fearsome bearded bodyguards you could imagine, shiny black Land Cruisers courtesy of the ISI, all the latest Kalashnikovs: oh, the man had it all! The legends of his battlefield prowess swept the dinner conversation. He could recite the entire Qur'an by heart. All kind of overwhelming for this country boy from the mountains! Spot on, I offered to become his personal driver to show him around the byways of Peshawar, soon to become the capital in exile for the mujahideen.

It was an honor to be his driver. My mission was to die for Islam. Soon enough I drove with Hekmatyar wherever he led and went for jihadi training myself at the military camp in Khost, just across the border in Afghanistan. A natural jihadi, I took to training and then fighting against the Russian Communists. I was number one in both, in truth my heart becoming stronger the more I killed. I told my father, "You have four sons left, whatever you do or say, I will fight in Afghanistan for jihad." My father called all my brothers to stop me until I said, "I am free with God," and the calls stopped.

But I get ahead myself once more, noble brave mujahid fighting in Afghanistan. What of my progress in university, where I was supposed to excel and become a bloody doctor?

It turned out that we needed to bomb the Peshawar police head-quarters, as there was an order to arrest one of our members. The plan was to have our men plant bombs coming from different directions. I was walking fully armed from the north side when the police stopped me.

When Zeddy had a mission, he would do it. That's the long and the short of this story. When the police stopped and tried to arrest me, I told them to back away, as I had a bomb on me that would take me out along with everyone around us. (You see, I'm telling the truth when I say I was an innovator in the arts of terror. I must've numbered among one of the very first suicide bombers, as such a thing was unheard of back then.)

I sat down in the middle of the road, as the police backed off and hundreds of people gathered round. "If Zeddy is surrendering today, it'll be big news. The world will know," I proclaimed. "Those who bear witness with me come forward," I shouted. And hundreds of bystanders joined the jihad, surrounding me to stop a police marksman from taking me off like a fly.

The police sent their captain to negotiate. I asked for a judge. When the judge came, I asked my brothers around me, "How many of you will testify against Zeddy in court?" None volunteered. "I asked the judge, 'You see, I'm a hero to my brother Muslims. What sentence do you want to inflict to make me a greater hero?'"

The judge understood, and I only served ninety days in jail for firing an unauthorized weapon. With all that I did—murder, bombings, smuggling, you name it—those ninety days were the only time I ever spent in jail. Jail hardly mattered either, as there were always plenty of police sympathetic to Jamaat, jihad, and Islam. We were everywhere.

WITH MY TIME in jail came another promotion in jihad.

My street protest came to the attention of the onetime emir of Jamaat for the entire North-West Frontier Province (and the party's new secretary-general), Qazi Hussain Ahmed, and I became his personal driver and bodyguard. The emir came from the University of

Peshawar and was close to my uncle-in-law too; we traveled in the same circles.

I was the only person the emir ever grew to trust enough to leave his daughter with alone. The emir would always say, "When my daughter Khowla is with Zeddy, my only concern is if Zeddy drops dead."

You see, I was ready, willing, and able to drop dead. The party was everything. That was jihad, and we were the party of God.

The first order I received from the party leaders was to take care of a PPP Communist. This "friend of the Jews," as he was called, had been a prominent political science professor and Communist to the bone. Our leaders had to walk next to, breathe the same air, and compete with this Commie. So the party gave your Zeddy the order to do the needful.

I waited outside the Commie's home in my jeep. Another jihadi was on a walkie-talkie telling me when the good professor would leave on his scooter. As soon as I got the word, I took off at full speed to strike the infidel and make it look like an accident.

The professor went flying in the air, and even though I kept flooring my open-roof jeep at full speed, the force of the hit sent the professor in my direction. His body hurled through the air like a Stinger missile, and somehow he landed direct in the jeep on the front seat next to me.

I see your face, Mr. Ken Sahib. You question the good professor's flight path or Zeddy's knowledge of basic physics. But I recount this man's peculiar aerial acrobatics because it should have stopped me dead in my tracks. It should have woken my deadened soul from the dark fanatical fog I lived in; it should have roused me to life.

"Are you okay, my son?" he asked before he died. Only he wasn't completely dead. I was a medical student. I could tell there was still a pulse, though he'd lost consciousness. I took the good professor to Lady Reading Hospital, where he remained at hospital for years, never to recover.

I remember his question to this day, his glassy brown eyes fixed on mine. I tell you this story because I executed hundreds of people for jihad. Most were killed by bombs I left, so I never saw their faces. I never knew who they were. Or like the good professor, they were killed from afar. But I can never forget the professor's question.

Or Lady Reading. If our esteemed leader Maududi Sahib could go to the Great Satan's hospital in Buffalo, New York, to get the latest in medical treatment, I could go back to Lady Reading. Alas, like our beloved founder who died in the hands of Buffalo's medical miracle workers, my poor Commie bugger was decked out as a corpse on a white hospital bed, looking at me with his eyes wide open, frozen in a coma—those eyes which had asked me if *I,* his assassin, were okay.

You see now why my heart hangs out of my body in pain, why my own eyes eat a hole in my head, why I must face my Maker as a middle-aged man wearing the mask of death.

So I followed my emir, and so the emir soon rose to become not only secretary-general but emir of all of Pakistan. Imagine that! My personal emir became the leader of the largest Muslim political party in Pakistan. Please do not mistake Qazi Hussain Ahmed for any of his religious rivals. The great "Qazi Sahib," as we called him, was a cultured, well-traveled intellectual Muslim who always spoke in the measured voice of a university professor, with all due seriousness. I never once heard him raise his voice.

Oh, contrast that with the crude leaders of Pakistan's other Muslim parties: Maulana Fazlur Rahman, wearing his crass golden robes, the head of our main Islamic competitor, the JUI-F [the Jamiat-ul-Ulama-i-Islam]. "Mullah Diesel," they say, earned his moniker after becoming rich by trading in permits for exporting diesel to Afghanistan during the jihad. Or the famous Maulana Sami ul-Haq, head of another JUI faction and the "mullah factory" of the Haqqania madrassa, which churned out most of the Taliban leadership. Poor "Sandwich Sammy" achieved his illustrious nickname after he was photographed in quite a novel position in between two bedmates.

Qazi Sahib was different. He headed the intellectual party founded by Maulana Maududi, the most profound Muslim scholar in South Asia. Qazi Sahib led Pakistan's most important democratic Islamic party—indeed the world's. The Jamaat would purify Pakistan by

peace and democracy. The Pakistani people, convinced of the righteousness of true believers, would elect us to power. But first we had
to take care of anyone who stood in our way.

Mullah Diesel's protégé Hafiz Habib from Quetta was a short, fat,
bald-turbaned "long beard" who never shut up and never ceased trying to cause trouble for us—the Jamaat Islami—or to our friends JI
for short. This stunted small-minded cleric ran a JUI madrassa that
churned out mujahideen by the thousands for the Afghan war—mind
you, under J-*U*-I, not JI. Remember the "U." Like in "Fuck *U*." Yes,
the fucking J*U*I, run by Mullah Diesel, our bitter brother in arms. The
two radical Islamic parties hated each other like two twin sons, who
both sought greater favor in their father's eyes.

Hafiz Habib came from a long line of radical Deobandi clerics.
At Binori Town in Karachi, the other famous madrassa factory for
jihadis, Habib excelled at leading anti-American demonstrations,
while gathering women like trophies, each one blessed by clerics who
looked the other way as long as he didn't incite riots against them.

But what made Habib "the JUI whiz kid" dangerous was his official marriage to the daughter of one of the leading feudals in Sindh
and the wealth that now allowed him to build up a formidable real
estate empire to challenge JI strongholds. Besides, it was an open
secret he was cutting behind the scenes deals with the Americans: why
else when his wife became sick did she fly first class to the Mayo Clinic
for VIP treatment? At the same time he's busy leading anti-American
demonstrations, he's getting a visa for his wife. How cute is that?

The fat boy wore his radical clothes to extort money and visas from
the Americans. This is a game played by many of them—especially
now after 9/11. They'll come down from their radical perch long
enough to preach at you in brotherhood, take the money, and then
mount back on up to preach hatred so you give them more money all
over again. You Americans fall for this every time! It's one of the easi-
est ways to make more than a few dollars in Pakistan today. And if
the radicals-cum-moderates don't milk the U.S. government, they go
after your even sappier NGOs, those do-gooders who are the biggest
suckers of all for the sweet talk of brotherhood!

But the buggery was that our JUI competitor was busy using his radical real estate empire to challenge JI candidates. He was too clever for us by half—hence the order to do the needful.

We followed his bullet-proof Mercedes from a Shura brotherhood meeting in Quetta to make peace among rivals. As he pulled into his luxury wing at the madrassa, one motorcycle lobbed a grenade in front, the other shot an explosive from behind, and a third opened fire with automatic weapons, as the fat one with his bodyguards tried to fight their way out from the Mercedes death trap.

We didn't kill him, only one or two of his bodyguards. He never challenged JI again.

Years later, well after 9/11, I saw that long beard on TV. He was holding forth on how he was in charge of a delegation of pious clerics, which fearlessly braved the perilous Afghan frontier to convince the Taliban who had seized those South Korean women—you know, the Christian missionaries—to release them on Islamic principles. "You don't kill women, it's un-Islamic" was his line. He basked in the television glow, claiming full credit for saving the lives of those poor Korean women hostages.

Please to excuse, that fat cleric fuck must've saved instead a shitload of dollars from you Americans, busy convincing you of his religious bona fides, fighting for mankind, freeing innocent Christian women, and so on and so forth. Do you know how much you Americans bloody paid him? Your very own *Newsweek* quoted a Taliban leader himself as saying that the only reason they released the South Korean girls was a secret four-million-dollar ransom from Korean intelligence. Yet you paid the long beard plenty to "save the girls," or maybe just to feel good about yourselves for supporting "moderate Muslims." Oh, yes, there's a fortune to be made in the jihadi business, playing all sorts of angles. Playing the Americans and other do-gooder foreign types being one of the most amusing.

Let's face it. In our part of the world, your friends can be your enemies and your enemies can be, well, less of an enemy than you might think. You really have little clue who is friend or foe. Sometimes the ones you think are your mortal enemies, if only you just sat down and talked with them (or bribed them), they'd be ripe pickings for a deal. Sometimes they are indeed your mortal enemies—no matter what you dangle in front of them. But ah, watch your "friends." They're the ones who'll pick your pockets, play a double game, until it's all too late and explodes in your face—and often blows back on them just as viciously. This is a playing field where everyone's being played. But I digress once more! With apologies, back to my story.

THE PARTY CHOSE Zeddy to be the captain of our secret "terror squad." That was what they called it, Ken Sahib, not me. Anyone they told me to eliminate, I obeyed. Any bombing or killing or beating, I obeyed. The leading Islamic party in Pakistan presented a peaceful, democratic image to the world, but we had a dark, covert side. We were true believers. And in the name of jihad, we used terror. As bin Laden's number two man [Ayman al-Zawahiri] once said: we are Muslims who believe in terrorism. For isn't that the meaning of Islam, when you believe you are on the right side in a Holy War? For then it's simple: you believe in terror. You are justified in any act, for you are fighting a war on the side of God Himself. Did He not tell us in the Holy Book that He will cast "terror in the hearts of the infidels, so strike off their heads, strike off their fingertips!" I just followed the command of God.

Ah, there you go, back to bin Laden again. Don't you understand that this is not about the word of one man, but the Word of God Almighty? Still, you Americans will not stop with this bin Laden! Your obsession with him is enough to drive you to distraction. Yes, I know, I promised to tell you about him, just as I promised to tell you how some in the army who guard Pakistan's nuclear weapons are sympathetic to Al Qaeda and the radicals. But here I just told you that one of the leading Muslim political parties in the world—indeed the most important one in nuclear-armed Pakistan—has a secret terror squad to assassinate opponents, and you want to hear about bin Laden! Don't you understand that some day this party may be elected to power, have control over our nuclear weapons, and then what? If they resort to terror covertly now, do you trust them when they accede to power overtly? What about all their loyal members hidden but firmly ensconced in the high ranks of the army, the ISI? I just showed you the true face of these true believers, the danger you face from educated people who talk the Queen's English, who walk the democratic walk, who sit down with you across the table in international conferences, who take billions in American aid smiling nicely, and are willing to cut your throat from ear to ear, and you, you want to hear about bin Laden? Oh, please!

Very well, then. Don't say that I haven't warned you, though. Bury your head in the sand, and think only of the outlaws like bin Laden. When the day comes that the nuclear weapons are in their hands and delivered to your front door by the generals and politicians you now know, you can look back at this account and know you were duly and most properly warned. Don't talk to me of state deterrence. The only state these true-believing ISI generals live in is the state of God. I would have thought that when the father of our atomic bomb, Mr. A. Q. Khan, had given its secrets to the Iranians, you would have then realized the truth of what I tell you. How can you possibly believe General Musharraf's denial that the army and ISI didn't know about that? I will tell you about the leader of the ISI, and about Musharraf too. And after I tell you later, if you can then say to me with a straight face that they didn't know all about what Mr. A. Q. Khan was up to, I will don a dress right before your eyes.

I was General Hameed Gul's driver, guide, and servant. That's right: General Gul, head of the ISI. My order was to take him inside the camps in Jalalabad. We waited at the safe house in Pakistan before we crossed to Afghanistan. I was with the general on JI orders from my emir. I knew the camps inside out. I had helped build the secret tunnels from which the Taliban and Al Qaeda later escaped. I knew Tora Bora like the back of my bloody hand. Who General Gul met with or what he did, I cannot say. That was not my mission, though the battle against the Afghan Communists was not General Gul's finest hour. But when Benazir Bhutto later sacked him from the ISI, I was assigned to guard him. We spent one month together, sleeping, eating, shitting, and praying in the same house. That's General Gul, once in charge of Pakistan's Inter-Services Intelligence, our CIA and military intelligence all wrapped in one, the most powerful arm of our government who in time would control our nuclear codes. And General Gul and I were together because he is a true believer who supported the Jamaat and jihad. And you think that they didn't know about Mr. A.Q. giving the nuclear bomb secrets to Iran?

Wait a minute. How do you think the Taliban have been able to build up their fighting forces inside Pakistan and grow in strength after 9/11? I can drive you myself right to their front door in Quetta where they operate with ISI protection, and their boys cross the border with ISI intelligence and fire on you Americans with ISI weapons. Oh, I know they tell you it's just some "rogue" ISI generals who have set up their own deal. But you cannot get those kinds of weapons and intelligence from rogues—unless they're the real rogues of the official sort.

Yes, didn't General Ahmed Shujaa Pasha, stationed for years in Quetta and now in charge of the ISI, even admit so much himself, brazenly telling a German newsmagazine that the Taliban leadership could launch jihad from Quetta because of their "freedom of opinion"? These ISI generals indeed are true champions of democratic rights!

Oh, my dear Americans, how you've been played. Let me count the ways. Do you suppose it sheer accident that Khalid Sheikh Mohammed, Mr. KSM, the mastermind of the 9/11 attacks and a Pakistani from Balochistan, was arrested at a JI safe house? Was it also just further happenstance that the Jamaat safe house happened itself to be inside a secure ISI housing estate in Rawalpindi [the headquarters for the Pakistani army]? I would've thought you might have gotten a clue when, the day after Mr. KSM was arrested from a JI safe house, the spokesman for Jamaat, Ameerul Azeem, told your *New York Times* that the mastermind of 9/11 was really "a hero of Islam."

But of course, Mr. KSM wasn't the only one: Al Qaeda militants were arrested in Jamaat safe houses in Karachi and Lahore too, all while Jamaat officially denied that Al Qaeda even existed. How about that? At the same time, the ISI dutifully defended Jamaat, holding a press conference to tell the world that Jamaat had no links with Al

Qaeda. My, do you Americans believe in the power of coincidence over conspiracy!

You see, the ISI, with Jamaat's help, was happy to turn over several loose Al Qaeda ends—pure bait—while they were busy propping up the Taliban and furthering the cause of their blessed nukes. Let me give you a quiz: how many Taliban leaders has Pakistan turned over to the Americans since 9/11, even though they're all here? I know, not that it makes a whit of difference, I am most certain, because you want to hear about that skinny Arab! You Americans!

See what your narrow obsession has cost you. Did you really think the ISI would ever willingly give you bin Laden? Remember how I told you that there's real money in the jihadi business? That goes for the Pakistani army and ISI. They got $10 billion from the U.S. government to be your partner in the grand "war on terror," in turn handing up a half-dozen foreign Al Qaeda types and not a single Taliban who mattered, of course. And the last thing they'd ever imagine doing in their wildest dreams would be to turn over bin Laden on their own and lose their meal ticket.

That's right. Just as the ISI provides Mullah Omar and the entire Taliban leadership sanctuary in Quetta and Peshawar to fight against you Americans in Afghanistan, these self-same ISI generals who happily take your American dollars look the other way and allow Osama bin Laden and the Al Qaeda leaders safe haven inside Pakistan too. How do I know? Long after 9/11, I met with a senior ISI Wing officer, together with bin Laden's top operations man, near Abbottabad. General Gul, one-time head of the ISI, radical-to-the-bone and my long-time colleague, explained that while Mullah Omar is under direct ISI protection, with bin Laden, the ISI only "keeps tabs" on the Arab and his friends: the difference between "an informal alliance with the Taliban and off-the-shelf surveillance of Al Qaeda." Comes down to the same deal for you Americans, except that Mullah Omar is fighting you from Quetta and bin Laden, at least as of a year ago, is leading the war from northwest Pakistan.

In any event, that's what General Gul told me. Only I don't believe it. Mr. Ken Sahib, please to note: I've trained many Al Qaeda recruits, under the direct command of the ISI. More: I've had meetings with Al Qaeda operatives chaperoned by high-level ISI Wing officers no less. It sure looks like an alliance to me. This "keeping tabs" and "off-the-shelf" stuff sounds like more ISI nonsense. And why wouldn't the ISI be sleeping with Mr. Osama? Never mind their radical sympathies, the skinny Arab's worth at least ten billion in U.S. dollars to them so far, and billions more to come. You don't have to take my word for it. Just inquire of your famous journalist friend, who's close to the Taliban, Al Qaeda and the ISI too: he'll tell you what General Gul has said. [The reporter, who indeed has unique access to both the radicals and the ISI, confirmed to me that General Gul had also told him that former and current ISI officers were aware of bin Laden's safe haven inside northwest Pakistan.]

You Americans are funding both sides in the war on terror. Sending your young men to fight in Afghanistan at the same time you pay the generals who run Pakistan billions while they covertly harbor the Taliban and Al Qaeda leaders—right under your nose. This is the Pakistani version of the "Great Game." Oh, I know these freedom-loving generals also let you drop bombs from drones on some wayward radicals—but only those militants that Pak generals consider a threat to them, not to you. I have a question for you: Do you ever think about what might happen if the U.S. suddenly stops giving the generals—at least the more secular ones—all those billions? Would they then still protect bin Laden, Al Qaeda, or the Taliban when there's no money in it for them?

I think at heart you pay the Pakistani government simply to feel good about yourselves and say, see, Muslims don't really hate Americans. Ah, but the ones who consider themselves most pure do hate you. To Al Qaeda, the Taliban, Jamaat, all of the Muslim Brothers and even their secret supporters like Gul among the generals and the ISI, you'll never be more than base infidels. It doesn't matter how much you shower Muslims with riches or attack us with bombs. You'll always be infidels, deserving of only one fate decreed by the Holy Book itself: death and Hell.

Yes, I was a driver and guide for Osama too. I received the order from JI, and I obeyed like always. Please Ken Sahib, no more whys.

The answer's always going to be exactly and precisely the same: because I received an order. This is jihad. Holy War. You obey orders. That's the way it works. Although my emir did say that just like the Wahhabi sheikhs in Saudi Arabia once welcomed Maududi's people as brothers-in-arms, it was our turn to throw down the welcome mat for this Saudi Wahhabi. Now, do you want to hear about the skinny Arab at last?

Bin Laden was living in Peshawar at the time in 1985 and wanted to find a good location for a camp. I knew the language. I knew the terrain. Bin Laden did not. We spoke in English. Imagine that: the great jihadi terrorists conversed in the language of the colonial Crusaders!

Bin Laden was like me. From a wealthy family and well educated in his own right, but without deep religious knowledge. He said he attended the best high school in Arabia. Not that I believed him there. The best Arabian high school could be nothing like the very top high school in Pakistan. The proof: this Osama could not for the life of him converse to you in near-perfect English the way I can now. But like yours truly, he came from wealth and privilege. He needed none of that. He was on jihad.

I took him around Peshawar and we even crossed into Afghanistan, for I knew the terrain near Khost too. I had helped to build many of the tunnels that bin Laden would later use to his advantage to elude you Americans. You have to remember, these were the early days of the Afghan jihad. I knew bin Laden's mentor Professor Abdullah Azzam as well—this was all before bin Laden really got going.

Anyway, you could say we really hit it off. Privileged wealthy educated jihadis; we were even the same age. You could say we spoke the same language, though of course, we didn't—we spoke in English! And over the course of several weeks leading bin Laden by the nose, he confided in me his dreams, his plans. To tell you the truth, while I liked the guy—he never raised his voice and was perfectly punctual in prayer—still, who is this bin Laden with his big dreams? I was jihad. I cleaned latrines, guarded underground presses, killed our enemies with one shot, fought with my bare knuckles, fought with my Kalashnikov. I was a mujahid; he was a dreamer. But his dream was big.

He told me of America's big dream, its big lie, the double game it played, and the power it had against Muslims. He truly hated the Americans for funding the mujahideen and the Pakistanis for taking that money.

Coming from the wealth and privilege that I had denounced too, the wealth and privilege America offered had to be denounced as well. We Muslims were like children. Our father was America, who we loved like our own fathers but who smothered us with all that they had. Osama and I both knew that story firsthand.

Here's the rub: our jihad looked inward. That's right: the jihad of the Afghans and Pakistanis was all about us. Bin Laden's big dream was about them. To look out across the ocean at the America we knew all too well—the rich relative we expected much from and loved. And held in equal if not greater hate for all he could do and did, and all he could do and did not, and most of all for the dream he offered us but that we had to spurn to be ourselves. To be Muslims. To be free.

Bin Laden, with his riches-to-rags tale to serve his fellow Muslims, was an intoxicating brew. From his own family struggle, like me, he also felt on a visceral level the draw of the American myth and how, if he could turn that myth on its head, the jihad would have a whole new meaning.

I hear all this rot coming from your fancy commentators that Zawahiri, the Egyptian, is really the brains behind Osama. I never met the Egyptian. Wouldn't know him if I ran over his corpse in the bazaar. But bin Laden understood all this long before the Egyptian ever arrived on the scene. He told me as much. Osama knew that the love and hate you had for your rich father was more powerful than just the hate. Welcome to our world.

One other thing this skinny Arab knew: the power of hating the Jew. He could quote from the Holy Book chapter and verse the perfidy of Jews. He could show the dagger of Israel stuck in the soul of Jerusalem where Prophet Muhammad ascended to Heaven. And this son of Islam's most holy places could wrap it all up in a tidy little conspiracy, the Jews in New York controlling America, the Great Satan, launching their crusades against Muslims everywhere. See, we Muslims are nursed on the mother's milk of conspiracies. And unless you have a conspiracy to explain everything in one neat package, we simply won't believe you.

You're right. I never met an American before—or a Jew.

You're also right; it's most good to meet you, Ken Sahib.

My very own father indeed knew the Jew who helped Iqbal found Pakistan, Asad Sahib. Maybe I should have met him too, but I was too busy rebelling, too busy trying to see the enemy, so I wouldn't look at my own face. I'm not saying bin Laden or Maududi or Qazi Sahib or any of them was right. I'm simply saying that the conspiracies they spun in the name of God struck a deep note.

I never saw bin Laden after those weeks. He was on a different path, and I followed mine. More to the point, I followed the orders of my emir, which didn't have me cross paths with bin Laden again— except when I met one of his operatives after the 9/11 attacks, who was after the suitcase nukes, but I'll get to that. I know, Americans are always impatient for the punch line. Don't you understand that unless you know what really makes us tick, the bottom line becomes incomprehensible?

Now please, Ken Sahib, don't ask me about every single killing, every last bombing: please know my pain. My red-face shame. I gave my soul over to these people. It was a love jihad, don't you see? I was caught up in a passionate swirl and never grew up until it was all too late. An overgrown 222-pound smitten adolescent, drunk on power and violence, like a rush from heroin. Yes, apart from targeting opponents and rivals, we blew up a JUI madrassa, a voting stronghold for the PPP in the NWFP [North West Frontier Province], and a press for the ANP [the Pashtun Nationalist Party]. Innovators in the arts of bombing mayhem, designed to wreak electoral havoc or advantage. Sometimes at the bidding of the ISI—well, mostly at their bidding, if it was not some kind of act of personal intimidation or revenge. No more whys. I cannot talk about these things. When I was looking for true Islam, they gave me faith, so why should I doubt?

Qazi Hussain Ahmad was my emir. I was his protector and guard. I sat at the right hand of power, the leader of the most important Islamic party in Pakistan, and I was entrusted with their most important secret mission. Heady stuff. Find that kind of thrill in medicine. I foreswore the simple pleasures of healing to be at the vanguard of the Islamic Party. Yes, I went from reading one small ten-page book by the founder himself to be at the center of power of the party he founded, and I never looked back.

I was fortunate, you might say. Qazi Hussain was the emir of my province, but within several years, he was promoted (and yours truly by extension) to be secretary-general and emir of all of Pakistan. By the side of Qazi Hussain Ahmad, the "Architect of the Silent Revolution," we'd say, the man responsible for the Islamic renaissance of Pakistan, "Qazi Sahib," as we addressed him, peaceful and pious and the leader of the future.

BUT POWER ONCE gained becomes petty. I heard all the high-flowing phrases, and I followed unquestioningly, as was my lot. Yet these so-called holy men, up close, quickly turned into men. There's nothing like a bath in the hot oil of exercising political power to burn your flesh and even wake up a dead mind like mine.

As if they could sense something I didn't even know at the time, I was unceremoniously relieved of my duties as captain of the terror squad. Not that they said anything specific; I just began receiving other assignments in quick succession.

The Jamaat, with the ISI, had a central role in smuggling arms to the Afghan mujahideen. First against the Russians and later, after 9/11 and the American invasion, to the Taliban. At first I didn't know why the ISI used Jamaat to smuggle arms from Pakistan.

I did three runs for Jamaat from the ISI garrison depot in Rawalpindi, across the border to the Afghan camps. I was told, "If you're caught, we'll disavow any knowledge of you" in a press conference. I felt strangely wounded by that remark. After all that I've done and if I were caught, they wouldn't even acknowledge me? But why would

I be caught if the ISI was supplying the arms? I thought. Of course, I never dared ask.

The first run, I led a convoy of ten trucks of weapons and ammunition. Well, we started out with ten. By the time we passed through various Jamaat checkpoints, the various JI leaders ordering me to leave one truck "for Islam," I arrived in Afghanistan with just six on the first trip, seven on the next, and five on the last. Those arms "for Islam" were no doubt sold on the black market for Jamaat and the ISI officers at great profit—that was the kind of relationship they had. The last mission, when I asked the JI operative which truck is "for Islam," he just stared at me. They never asked me to lead the convoys again.

We fought jihad on two fronts—Afghanistan and Kashmir—and sent young men to each as noble *shaheed,* martyrs to jihad. The next task Jamaat gave to your jack-of-all-trades—you may say I drew the short straw. No, really, I was a tool, or more precisely, please to excuse, the condom you'd discard after using your tool. I could've been a doctor but chose to be a terrorist jihadi. Islam was my father and mother. I was the bastard son.

Jamaat assigned me the duty of notifying families when their real sons became martyred. Looking into the eyes of brothers, sisters, mothers, and fathers, jihad turned quite personal. Oh, I knew the drill: "Your son is in Heaven, reserving a special place for you" (when he's all finished with those seventy-two virgins, of course). Some parents talked about God's will; others just broke down in tears. The hell with the seventy-two virgins, I delivered the news for forty-three dead boys.

One young mujahid fighter I knew well. The boy was a cousin from Mardan. He'd been killed fighting in Afghanistan, and we rushed his body home to the NWFP (because a *shaheed* had to be buried quickly to ascend to Heaven). The boy had entrusted his lockbox with the will inside to me, so I read the will in front of his grieving parents.

The boy had nothing to leave in his will, only his love. But he asked Jamaat for one simple thing. It seemed that his uncle, who lived next door, continually siphoned electricity from his parents, leaving his father with an electric bill that he couldn't afford to pay. In his will, the boy asked Jamaat to do a jihad on the government power bureaucracy and install a simple meter box for his parents. I went straight to the top and asked the emir himself to fulfill this young martyr's single last request. Instead, the emir couldn't be bothered and referred me to a countless stream of other JI officials in a nonstop game of bureaucratic Russian roulette. At the end of the day, the boy went to Heaven, seventy-two virgins and all, but his family had to remember their son living it up in the heights of Heaven while they sat in the dark. Jamaat never got the meter box.

The Jamaat leaders also excelled at celebrating the martyrdom of other people's sons. Disobeying his father, the son of one of Jamaat's naib emirs [deputy leaders] went to a jihadi camp on the Kashmir front. First the mother called me frantically: my dearest firstborn will go into battle tomorrow; you must do something and save him. Then, as night follows day, the third in command of Jamaat himself called me to help him "rescue" his "cherished eldest." We flew together by army helicopter to the camp. Another armed military helicopter accompanied us as well. No expense was spared. Armed with my Kalashnikov, I led the naib emir to the Kashmiri commander. The Jamaat official demanded the boy because his mother was ill. Our show of force made it clear to the Kashmiri militants that the boy was more important than their blood. The moral of this little tale? The boy now owns a dental supply company in Kansas City, in the heartland of the good old U.S.A.

It went both ways. Another naib emir's son went to the Afghan front as a battle tourist. This was quite common among the more well-off students at the time. These Gucci jihadis would take summer vacations or holidays at the front as tourists so they could wear it as a badge of honor to their friends, a jihadi souvenir, so to speak. Watching the battle from what should have been a safe distance, the naib emir's son had the misfortune of being in the path of a wayward missile. I was sent on "emergency highest priority" of bringing the scattered remains back for full *shaheed* honors. The boy had died fighting bravely and went nonstop to Heaven. The father and great naib emir Jamaat leader was so distraught with grief he soon suffered a heart attack.

My uncle-in-law told me there was an opening in our home district. Wouldn't you be interested in standing for election as a Jamaat candidate? I never seriously entertained the idea—then again, it might be a nice change of pace. Why not? It's not like any of the Jamaat men were any more qualified to sit in Parliament than me. Ah, but it turns out the Jamaat had their own deal on the table. Jamaat was supporting their dreaded adversary's candidate from the leftist, Communist, infidel PPP in return for a secret bargain: the PPP would back another Jamaat candidate, who Jamaat wanted to win, in a different parliamentary district. I never ran.

And I saw how the emirs lived. I never took one penny from Jamaat. Not one red cent, as you Americans say. The monthly stipend the ISI funneled to me from the army in the last few years wasn't JI money, and it was hardly enough to support me. I had my father support me through school, and then I sold off parcels of family land to support myself, living with my wife and children over time at the ancestral family home and later at the Multan Road Jamaat commune in Lahore, before my brothers chipped in to support the great wayward family jihadi, and then the ISI army stipend kicked in.

Our honored founder, even though martyred in Buffalo, said that a Muslim leader "can never draw a half penny more than the minimum needed for a Muslim of average means." But our emir sahibs had an entirely different definition of "average." The party leaders took anything they wanted from Jamaat, treating the party's funds as their personal piggy bank, charging phone calls, cars, vacations, hotels, meals, clothes, massages, marriage ceremonies, you name it. All these little perks were on top of their fat salaries, of course. Oh yes, respecting Maududi's solemn edicts, some Jamaat leaders nobly refused to take official salaries (though some managed to take salaries in positions other than officers, so they only looked as if they served unpaid). Remember that son of the naib emir who died by accident in Afghanistan but we presented as a heroic *shaheed* to the world? Well, the entire elaborate funeral celebration, I mean "religious ceremony," was paid for by the party.

It did not stop with the emirs themselves. Even if they covered in public and wouldn't be caught dead with makeup, the wives of the emirs had to be all dolled up in private. The charges to Jamaat for jewelry, shoes, and beauty salons would rival any Parisian woman. All was charged to the party, from funds collected from poor people who could barely afford the naan to feed their families. Sure, they skimmed from arms smuggling and ISI payments, but that was for their personal accounts. When it came to party funds—or should I say "partying" funds—they made sure the party faithful footed the bill.

My last straw was the phone calls to Switzerland. Don't ask me why this irked me so. I saw in the office a phone bill of some 540,000 rupees, I guess around $7,000, in calls to Switzerland from a naib emir's line. What the bloody hell was he calling Switzerland for? There's no jihad there—they've never even seen a living Muslim.

I called the numbers myself. They'd never notice a couple more calls to Switzerland. They were to the Commerzbank in Zurich and mostly Credit Suisse in Geneva. I took it upon myself to go and ask the naib emir what this was about. He didn't look at me, feigning to shuffle the papers on his desk (probably bank statements!). I cleared my throat. He said nothing. Not a word. The bugger didn't even justify it as Jamaat business or tell me I was way out of line to ask. He did not dignify my presence. He wouldn't even look at me, who had sacrificed nearly two decades of my life to these people, their cause, which I thought was mine, God's. I no longer knew.

When I think today of the gall of that fat little swine who charged to the party *even the phone calls* he'd made to Swiss banks to hide the funds he stole from jihad, and these are the men from God! It makes me sick. This is what I killed for; this is what forty-three boys—and God only knows how many more—died for. Years later, I heard this stunted pig became a purveyor of "flights of delight" [fizzy drinks] in Pakistan. At least he pumped part of what he stole back to Pakistani boys drinking Pepsi, burping up sweet little bubbles of jihad!

Did I address the emir? Talk directly to the great Qazi Sahib himself? No, I was a coward. Have you worked for a powerful leader? No one ever is the messenger of honest confrontation. When you serve, you become part of the aura that surrounds the leader and makes him immune. Telling him he's wrong is like telling yourself that your life's work is worthless. Unless you've been close to power, you cannot understand the feeling of entitlement and immunity that clings all around it—more so when clothed in religious garb.

You can fault me; you can criticize me. I deserve it. Caught in the swirl of my own self-importance, the adventure of living a grander-than-normal life, being the rebel king without crown, the captain without troops, it all went to my head. I was dizzy, and today, I can no longer see straight. I have migraines, ministrokes, pain in my chest, pain in my butt. Let's face it: I am my own continual pain in the ass. I have no peace. Unless God is a *goonda* [goon] paying for hits, He could've never been calling for this jihad.

JAMAAT THEN SENT me to run their training camp. In some dim part of my unthinking brain, I somehow divined it was to be my final assignment for Jamaat too.

I was in charge of training mujahideen at the famous Mansehra camp, near Abbottabad. Trained them to fight in Afghanistan. Trained them for Kashmir. Bosnia. Chechnya. Wherever. We always had plenty of men. From all over Pakistan, Kashmir, Afghanistan, then Uzbekistan, Saudi Arabia, Egypt, Morocco, and even a few from England and America. One I remember well. He was a pilot in your air force and never went back to Seattle, I think it was. Killed in Kashmir instead.

Yes, that's right; I trained your friend "Shaheed." He was at my final camp, with Jamaat, Al Qaeda, Jaish-e-Mohammed [an Islamist terrorist group], and other green recruits. Did you know that your friend's name, Shaheed, means "martyr"? Hmmm—an ironic jihadi! How can I forget him? He was one of the last jihadis I ever trained, around the time of your 9/11.

Ding dong! Good, you're writing about him too! [He's profiled next in chapter 5.] He was indeed tall, bright-eyed, and fearless, just the type these boys follow, filled to the brim with dreams and what-all. Jihadis always praise Allah with visions. And your friend's head was well stuck in the clouds, though he was a first-class boy—with a "white face," the other jihadis said, who hung on every last word of his dreams and jinn fairies. Not that I have a problem with that sort of thing. Made the boys stronger in battle, willing to die for one another, so I had no issue at all. What I could not stomach were the young boys.

In the first years, we took kids as young as eight or nine, but I put a stop to that. Give me credit, Ken Sahib, for one decent thing. Unless you needed living land-mine detectors, these kids were useless as real soldiers. Slaughtering innocent boys was not my idea of jihad. Then again, what exactly was my idea?

So, at least at my camp, we upped the age to sixteen, the rite of Prophet Abraham's passage. Didn't stop the kids from pouring in, like the arms, ammunition, and cash. First from the Saudis and other Gulf Arabs. Then plenty of rich Pakistanis. And from the ISI. Always the ISI.

How many times did General Hameed Gul, onetime ISI head, stay in my house? How many terrorists did I train to make bombs, slit people's throats from end to end, and shoot straight from more than 250 meters with a Kalashnikov? How many people did I kill from bombs, so-called accidents, assassinations, just damn right cut off their heads?

Could you keep count? They all ran through my fingers—through my now old, knotted arthritic fingers. Like blood, an open wound that never ends.

First eighteen days, we'd lose a quarter of the boys. Next three months, another half. Only the strong would survive to fight jihad. I did not care who. We had mill owners' sons. Sons of industrialists, generals. Didn't matter to me. If they could not survive my training, let them find another jihadi camp. I trained five thousand boys for jihad in one year. From shit to sugar: ammunition, weapons, and all the elements of basic training. My greatest innovation was the first aid course I made the boys master. I was trained as a doctor from a family of doctors, after all. Came in handy at last.

And these boys knew nothing of Islam, jihad, except what they were told, what they were led by the nose to believe, seventy-two virgins, Heaven, Hell. It all just boiled down to avoiding harsh punishments and reaping sweet rewards; loving your brother Muslims and hating your enemy infidels. We defined ourselves by our enemies, above all the Americans. Our open-season bloodlust couldn't be cured by rational medical treatment.

Since the ISI, in reality, supplied, controlled, and commanded the camp, breaking with Jamaat at last came all too easily. JI had little to do with what was really happening at the camp anyway. I wrote the emir a letter. Yes, a faceless coward's letter. Didn't even have the guts to go eyeball to eyeball. The first letter detailed everything that was wrong: the killing of rivals, the intimidation of opponents, the secret collusion with the ISI and army, the petty politics, the graft, corruption, and power plays—all made so much worse by being clothed as the work of Islam.

I never sent the letter. I just wrote the emir a simple question: why do you still want Zeddy to be in Jamaat? He never answered. Twenty-two years in Jamaat, and no answer. I don't know, maybe the emir was visiting Boston, as his son Asif was at Boston University. Maybe the letter got lost in the post.

The ISI switched me to another jihadi camp. I didn't miss a step. I continued to train jihadis for the ISI and the Kashmir front, now the so-called Al Badr, until the ISI asked me to lead a contingent of my Al Badr mujahideen to Kashmir in 1999.

For a decade or more, jihadi militants were crossing from Pakistan into Indian-occupied Kashmir and fighting in small numbers. But for the first time, I had the honor of leading jihadi fighters under the direct command of the Pakistani army itself. My mujahideen were no more than a thinly disguised ruse so that the army could officially deny it attacked Indian positions.

The ISI and army commanders took us to the front, and showed us where and how to cross the Line of Control. The Al Badr mujahideen were to be the "shock troops," or more accurately the cover for the army's Northern Light Infantry, who we fought under and saluted. Major General Javed Hassan, who led the assault, told me the whole shebang was the brainchild of the new army chief of staff, Pervez Musharraf [and subsequent President of Pakistan]. All I know is that we were to occupy the heights on the Indian side as "brave mujahideen" so that the Pakistani army could formally deny they provoked a war with India.

Ah, for once they'd give us credit. Of course, that was a complete lie. Indeed, Musharraf proudly and publicly claimed that the jihadis under my command had achieved a great victory at Kargil, even though we later withdrew and Pakistan nearly came to nuclear blows with India for nothing. Nothing but a vain general's pride and an entire ISI operation dressed in jihadi clothes, like so much else that really happened in the name of pure Islam.

I was used, nothing more than a Donald Decoy Duck. Done up in the dress of Islam, I was simply an ISI, Jamaat, or another man's whore.

Some people wanted some power. That's the sum total of it all.

Indeed, the Kargil conflict brought Pakistan to the brink of nuclear war, masterminded by these same ISI and army generals who claimed they had nothing to do with us jihadi mujahideen.

THANK GOD FOR 9/11! Oh, thank God!

The Americans made the ISI finally shut down our camp, and we closed it in November 2001. After lifetimes of this shit, I finally had to find some honest work. Yes, I'm bitter. Yes, I regret every second of what I did, every lousy second.

Not long after, leave it to the ISI, they asked me to start another camp in the FATA [the Pakistani tribal region bordering Afghanistan] to train the Taliban who escaped from you Americans after Afghanistan fell. These camels don't change their stripes. While Musharraf was busy taking ten billion dollars from you to hand over a few stray Al Qaeda cats, the Taliban dogs were being trained, supplied, and armed with the latest intelligence by the ISI itself inside Pakistan. I know because they asked me to help.

And what do you Americans say, from the mouths of babes come pearls of wisdom or pearls before swine? You tell me.

Well, if it wasn't for my seven-year-old son: "I want to be muja-hid," begging to become a great jihadi mujahid hero like his daddy, I probably would've just taken that Taliban training post and not be here talking to you now. It was just too much to take to hear my little boy, my Mustafa, saying he wanted to be a jihadi, a mujahid, like his dear old dad! That was it. Ken Sahib, my mind was fucked; for the God's honest truth is, I would've kept doing it if my boy hadn't asked to be just like me.

Oh, I forgot. One last thing. A well-placed ISI Wing man—I couldn't dare name him, Ken Sahib, or they'd slit my neck within minutes. Not like dear old General Gul, I can sing in the shower about him. Everybody knows: Hameed Gul helping the Taliban and Al Qaeda is an open book. I understand you want me to name the ISI officer and I would, Ken Sahib, but I have family. I can only tell you this much because the ISI's role with Al Qaeda is hardly a state secret. I'm not the only one who knows. Let me just say that the ISI man is no low-level snot-nose. And we met next to Abbottabad with one of bin Laden's top-level lieutenants too. Mark my words. This senior ISI officer wanted me to help an Arab bin Laden man go to the Russian Federation in search of loose nukes for a suitcase bomb. Imagine that. The Al Qaeda man even said, "If we had the nukes for America before, we would have had a much better 9/11."

By then I was spent. This is no real jihad against the Americans, I said. If I came and killed one of your family members, would you spare me? If Americans had come instead and flew two jets into the Holy Mosque of Mecca, we'd launch a jihad against them, so why does it surprise you now that they attack us? It's like when the rain pours at the same time the sun shines bright—no one can see the other side. If there were no 9/11 and the Americans were beating on our door, now there's a real jihad, so stop talking to me about jihad against the Americans.

These are all the things I am taking out of my mind. One by one in painful succession, like a gruesome comedy of errors, a jihadi Jekyll and Mr. Hide-and-seek.

I was powerful. I was important. Now I am nothing. I was always nothing.

Today, I work in the jails, starting again as a medical assistant. They're desperate for anyone medical in our godforsaken prisons. Worse conditions you cannot imagine, unless it's at your Abu Ghraib or Guantánamo.

I work in the jails to escape. I work in the jails to make all those young boys who want to go to jihad get a job.

Heaven, oh Heaven! If I die for Islam, I will go straight nonstop direct to Heaven. But no one told me about the hell we'd create first here on Earth.

My fellow "old boys" from Burn Hall are General Mahmud Ali Durrani, ambassador to the United States and top national security man, and General Tariq Khan, and on and on—businessmen, lawyers, doctors, but of course, doctors.

My heart broken—I had open-heart surgery.

My soul broken—there's no operation we doctors can perform to save that.

Yes, my little boy, my Mustafa, asked me if he could be a mujahid like his father. Ken Sahib, my seven-year-old son! These are all the things that I am taking out of my mind.

I now work in jails to forget. I see suffering. It cannot change my own. I see men go hungry. I am still empty. I go every day to jail to escape. I cannot. My mind is fucked up.

I talk to all those kids in jail. What jihad do you want? I show them my old shriveled white-haired chest, all seventy-two scars, one for each virgin in Heaven I never had.

I don't change many minds. Maybe one or two. Slowly, slowly. It's quick to go to jihad. It's an exciting shortcut to life. Not the hard work of plowing ahead in our part of the world, where there are few jobs, little excitement, much drudgery.

If I died for Islam, I could welcome my whole family to Heaven. I could welcome my father I betrayed, my sons I neglected. That's right. I could welcome them all to the shining, blinding light of Heaven. But all I see now when I look back is darkness.

Yes, I understand, if I killed one of your family, you'd kill one of mine. I know that's how America feels after 9/11. It's not jihad for these young boys to now fight America when America itself was attacked. But America, listen please: one of bin Laden's men told me that they were trying to get a briefcase bomb, a nuclear one, from the Russian Federation, or from one of their own in the ISI, or maybe more likely through one of Jamaat's many friends in the military. And then, America, who are you going to kill here? What will it matter then?

Please to excuse. I didn't mean to hug you like that. I hope you're not embarrassed. I'm glad you're not. I don't know where that urge came from. You seem like a good man. A good American and good Jew too.

A good soul.

I am sorry.

AFTER INTERVIEWING ZEDDY, I later assured him that I would disguise his identity.

"Mark my words, Ken Sahib, it may not be enough. Once your book is published, my mortal days will tick-tick away. The ISI will never let one of their franchise terrorists 'under Wing' speak truth to power, no, truth to righteousness, for the ISI true believers must now 'strike off my head, every one of my fingertips,' as God commands. I just worry about my sons and daughters; my family—and you, Ken Sahib. They shall wantonly go after you. Tear you and this account down with the Jihad of the Tongue: the lies, rumors and gossipy muck they spread is only to defend God and ISI. If I were you Americans, I'd worry more about these ISI Wing men and Generals who harbor bin Laden and the Taliban than that wayward Arab and his ilk. And I wouldn't be taking holiday any time soon among our scenic and stately mountains. In Pakistan, accidents happen, even if coincidences seldom do."

Part III

LEADERS OF THE NEW JIHAD

5

THE SECRET SHAHEED

AHMAD ("BERNIE") and Abby witnessed the moral—indeed, religious—corruption of Al Qaeda and turned away. Malik, Mullah Omar's seer, became disillusioned too, but his alienation made him in the end an even more radical and violent extremist. Zeddy directly embodied the corruption that changed these men and turned away himself.

After so many interviews of jihadis, I began to feel the confidence of someone struck with singular insight. What other Westerner had gotten this up close and personal with jihadis?

So when in June 2008 I first met Shaheed, I thought he would simply follow the path of Ahmad and Abby and turn from violence or follow Malik's example and become even more radical. (The jihadis who never questioned their lives were either not insightful or not truthful with me or with themselves.) I never imagined there could be an entirely different path. And I never dreamed that I would personally play a part, however small, in Shaheed's taking that path.

Shaheed was different in other respects too. If Malik and Mullah Omar were guided by dreams, Shaheed exposed the meaning of nighttime dreams as divine prophecy on an even deeper level. More, the conflict between traditional beliefs, such as in mystical jinn (unseen spirits described at great length in the Qur'an), and the modern secular world played themselves out with great force and deadly consequences inside Shaheed himself. He was once part of the Fedayeen-e-Islam Taliban cell Malik had mentioned, which claimed responsibility for the suicide attack against the Marriott Hotel.

Over the course of my lengthy interviews, Shaheed indeed emerged as the unusual person Zeddy had trained and described—a mystical and enigmatic man whom other jihadis would follow. Shaheed also revealed to me the intimate details of his childhood, which added a wholly unexpected psychological view of his rise as a jihadi. As had occurred with Malik and Zeddy, three Pakistani journalists and a Pakistani radical cleric with close ties to the Taliban made the initial connections.

While Batoor was his given name, I'll call him by his at first secret nickname, "Shaheed." It was the talismanic moniker his beloved grandmother bestowed and that he devoted his life to earn. "Shaheed" in Arabic means a martyr for Islam.

THE FOLLOWING news bulletin flashed over the BBC on September 22, 2008, two days after the bombing of the Marriott:

> A little known Pakistani militant group, Fedayeen-e-Islam, says it carried out Saturday's devastating attack on the Islamabad Marriott. . . . The suicide bomb devastated the hotel, killing at least 53 people and injuring more than 266. . . . The BBC Urdu service in Islamabad received a call from the Fedayeen-e-Islam group, which gave instructions to call another number. That number played out a recorded message in English.
> It said the aim of the Marriott attack was to kick the "American crusaders" out of Pakistan. . . .

NEARLY THREE MONTHS earlier, "Shaheed" Batoor Khan Khattak got into a Peshawar Motor Cab taxi for the drive to the Marriott Hotel in Islamabad.

Riding to the Marriott in Pakistan's capital, he thought of how he had once dreamed the prophecy of the fall of America's Twin Towers. It was his "true night dream," which none other than Sheikh Osama bin Laden had spoken of after 9/11.

Shaheed couldn't help but feel a little pride—an emotion that as a true believer following in the footsteps of the Prophet Muhammad had to be denied. Shaheed simply wanted to do right by God. He strove to do only good deeds and fight evil ones for Allah the Beneficent and never wanted to act for worldly praise or human pride. Yet he knew that it was his dream that had changed the world.

Having dreamed the prophecy recounted by Sheikh Osama, Shaheed was forever changed too. His bond with Osama bin Laden was from Allah the Most High.

And, he thought, Allah knows best: Pakistan was now on fire from His will. Throughout 2008, the headquarters of the Taliban and Al Qaeda inside Pakistan had given birth to a new army of holy warriors. From the assassination of Prime Minister Benazir Bhutto to attacks on the Luna Caprese Italian restaurant and the Danish Embassy in Islamabad, the Pakistani Taliban had become a powerful force in the only Muslim nation with nuclear weapons.

Yet the bombing of the American Marriott in the capital would shortly become the turning point. And the Marriott attack would soon be carried out by members of Shaheed's cell.

Like bin Laden, Shaheed came from a family of privilege. His grandfather, a wealthy landowner, had helped to lead the fight for an independent Muslim Pakistan, while his father had become a Pakistani army officer responsible for securing the country's nuclear arsenal.

Educated in the very best schools, to his colleagues Shaheed could be another Osama. And while more than two decades younger, Shaheed indeed had the same height as the "noble sheikh" (over six feet, three inches), the same flowing brown beard (only no gray), the same billowing white robes and turban, the same penetrating, pure brown eyes and distinct aquiline nose. Most of all, like the "noble sheikh," Shaheed was a mujahid, a soldier to jihad. He even came from bin Laden's second homeland, the Pashtun tribal belt of Afghanistan and

Pakistan, whose "false border" meant nothing to the proud and faithful Pashtun who lived there.

Riding to the Marriott now, Shaheed waited for the word from God once more. Would Allah command the fall of America's hotel?

As the taxi belched its way along the M1 motorway to Islamabad, Shaheed knew he must be on the way of God in jihad when his motor cab passed a six-wheel Hinopak. On the driver's side of the Pakistani-made Japanese truck, he saw the neon painted figure of Buraq, the winged steed of Prophet Muhammad. The Holy Prophet flew atop the lightning-mount Buraq to Jerusalem on his way to Heaven. Shaheed could see Buraq rising now. The magical steed's wings were painted emerald green, his mane a fiery amber, his tail the rainbow colors of a peacock, and his torso the brightest blinding white. In the truck's dense exhaust, Shaheed's taxi cab flew past as if Heaven bound as well.

For Shaheed was Allah's undying vessel, like Buraq's winged truck pulling him to the Marriott or toward Heaven itself: there was no difference now in the Almighty's eyes. If the American Zionist hotel had to be bombed, God alone would tell him.

Shaheed was on jihad in the Way of God.

JIHAD BEGAN with jinn.

As a boy, Shaheed loved his grandparents' sugarcane and "sweet Virginia tobacco" farm in the so-called Valley of Latter-Day Saints in northwest Pakistan. The leafy green tobacco moved with the wind toward the great mountains in the distance, calling Shaheed to dream of high places. Grandfather would take him, along with his many dogs, to the sugarcane and tobacco fields, and even sometimes toward the mountains themselves, though the old man was by then too feeble to climb. Yet it was Shaheed's loving and "different" Yousafzai grandmother who made the valley saintly.

Grandmother had dark, leathery skin and was taller than any woman Shaheed had ever known. But he could always see her knotted brown, gray-speckled hair, as she kept herself uncovered, and her large brown eyes that grew wider as she talked and the jinn entered inside.

Grandmother knew all about the jinn. Created by God from smokeless fire, jinn were unseen to the normal eye, but not to Grandmother. As the Noble Qur'an told her, jinn moved through the world as the wind, taking any form they pleased, even appearing in human shapes. And her mountain jinn were righteous in the sight of Allah the Most High. For both male and female jinn were equal in every respect, one no greater than the other. In fact, the male jinn would stay at home and take care of the child jinn while the female jinn flew invisible with the wind and visited the valley below.

Many said that the Lund Khwar area was called the Valley of Saints because it was a great center of Islamic tradition, home to many religious scholars. But Grandmother said that Lund Khwar was called the Valley of Latter-Day Saints because of its saintly jinn.

Sometimes Shaheed would hear Grandfather say that the jinn possessed Grandmother and that he should contact a *mirasin* to direct a consort of women to hold a *baithak* session to exorcise the jinn inside her. But Grandmother kept saying that the jinn that visited her were good; as the Glorious Qur'an says in the seventy-second surah, devoted to jinn, "Al-Jinn," there are good jinn and evil jinn, believers and nonbelievers, just as with humans. And she drank only the good jinn's milk.

Grandmother knew because the female jinn would visit her, one in particular. Helly was her name, Grandmother whispered. "Don't say her name in full voice," she said. "That would bring ill." Helly, that strange name Shaheed had never heard before, the secret talisman— like his own nickname—that could never be said out loud.

"Keep the toilet lid covered" was Grandmother's other command, as evil jinn came from its water. Grandmother wanted nothing to disturb Helly's peaceful visits.

For each night before final Isha prayer and *wudu* (ablution), Grandmother would drink a small sacrifice of her own warm urine brewed with a healthy dose of sweet green tea, so Helly would come to her bed and spend the night.

Lying still as a corpse, Grandmother waited for the cool air to drift through the splintered wooden windows, underneath her mahogany door and around her two serpent bed posts. Grandmother's skin knew: the air seeping in wasn't a calming moist cool; it was a biting mountaintop cold, until Helly's unseen fire would take hold of her without letting go. Grandmother saw in Helly's eyes pure green—the color of Islam. And the jinn's narrow fingers were topped with nails like the *hilal,* Islam's new crescent moon.

Shaheed wanted to go to the mountains and see the jinn for himself. But he could dream of Helly too, coming to him at night, the same way she came as a smokeless flame in the shape of the most beautiful of girls for his grandmother.

Every night Grandmother put Shaheed to bed with stories of the jinn. She would cuddle next to him and, with her long right forefinger, draw the triangular shapes of the wings of the jinn on his smooth young back. Falling asleep to her touch, Shaheed felt the warmth of his newly drawn invisible wings lifting him to Heaven in his dreams.

Grandmother always told him that she loved him "as the wind," kissing each of the toes on his right foot (never the left). She would tell him how he had a "white face" infused with God's light, how he was her special "Shaheed" and one day, his feet too would grow unseen jinn wings as he ascended to Heaven, a martyr for God's love.

SHAHEED'S FATHER would have none of such "stuff and nonsense." He was a soldier in Pakistan's "Army of the Pure." No, that would be an insult. He wasn't just a soldier, or a lowly officer, but a lieutenant colonel, who in time rose to become privy to the special Army Strategic Force Command (Strategic Plans Division), entrusted with protecting Pakistan's God-given nuclear weapons.

Shaheed, dream carrier to bin Laden and martyr to sacred jinn, always honored his father, if only in one respect: Colonel Tahseen Khan Khattak was a guardian of "the Islamic Bomb."

But "the right colonel" thought himself anything but Islamic. A staunch nationalist for Pakistan, he was a "Pak man true" at a time when the Pakistani army prided itself on its British heritage of military discipline and protocol. Indeed, Colonel Tahseen loved all things English and was an "enlightened humanist" at heart. An athletic six foot one, with deep-set black eyes, oiled black hair and matching shiny eyebrows, he even sported the colonial-style waxed handlebar mustache, de rigueur for distinguished spit-and-polish English army officers and their Pakistani fellow travelers.

Shaheed proudly wore the short, trimmed mustache and full beard, following the example of the Holy Prophet.

Shaheed's father, colonel and guardian of the Islamic Bomb, wanted nothing to do with "bird-nest beards" and "lamp genies." Graduating from Pakistan's elite military school, the Pakistan Military Academy in Abbottabad, even taking the officers' course at Washington's National Defense University and claiming the famed Royal Military Academy Sandhurst too, the colonel came from one of the leading families of Lund Khwar. And in his mind, his father had made only one mistake in his entire life: marrying his jinn-drunk mother.

Their marriage began almost in sin. Shortly before Pakistan was born in 1947, the family—from the Khattak tribe of Pashtuns—arranged for their eldest son (and Tahseen's father) to marry a Yousafzai Pashtun bride outside the family tribe. No longer clannish, they represented "the new Pakistan." The mixed marriage joined sugarcane and sweet Virginia tobacco as well, making them quite successful upper-crust landholders, even approaching the kind of power that feudal families exercised over traditional Pakistani life.

Raising his son in privilege, Grandfather decided in turn that his eldest son, Tahseen, should help the rising Pakistani nation by attending the best military schools, joining the army, and likewise marrying a Yousafzai. Tahseen obeyed but really decided to marry the Pak army instead.

Absent from home far more than he was there, the future colonel slept with his wife barely long enough to sire Shaheed and his brother, Asif. Colonel Tahseen Khan Khattak indeed followed in the footsteps of the legendary General Khan (Ayub or even Yahya), cultivating the English-speaking society ladies of Lahore, though over time he came to settle mostly in the Strategic Plans Division at the Chaklala Garrison, near the Islamabad Airport in Rawalpindi, where, he said, "A man could be a man." Of course, that left his wife without a man.

Bitter and alone with only a few servants to help her, Shaheed's mother farmed her kids out from the Cantonment in Peshawar to Lund Khwar whenever she could, and certainly every summer and possible holiday or weekend.

At Lund Khwar, Shaheed found peace from the wailing of his mother, left alone so much of the time in dusty Peshawar. Peace from his little brother, Asif, who constantly squabbled with him. And peace from whenever his father was at home, telling his mother no table was ever set right, raising his deep voice in perfectly crisp colonial English (for he always spoke in English when he was mad, and he always was mad): "How do you bloody well expect me to live? All you do is lap up my money like a womanly rag, not that you can properly supervise the cook like a Lady Lahore. Thank God we've got the army batman to watch over. What I wouldn't give for Lady-made *korma* and *halwa*. Why were you chosen for me—what was Father thinking? My God, must've been drinking from *I Dream of Jeannie*'s tit!"

But Shaheed knew what Grandfather was thinking, even if his father didn't. He knew what Grandmother was thinking. Righteous jinn lived with them. Carried by the breath of God, they flew from the snowy mountain tops to your bed after Isha prayer. Softly, they held you through the night in their magical embrace, warm as the invisible fire that burned your nocturnal dreams.

Shaheed hated Peshawar. In school, the other boys teased him. He was "farthead" and "big booger eyes." They would hold their eyes wide open every time they passed him in the hall, and start cracking up. They were from Peshawar and called him "tobacco breath" from "No Luck Khwar." Worse, the teachers called him "Batoor." Yes, that was his given name, but Grandmother gave him his true name.

And his "English are civilized" father said their Peshawar house in the Cantonment area was "not even fit for an unclean mongrel." Shaheed wanted nothing more than a dog of his own. He would even sneak out with whatever naan and food he could to feed the stray dogs in the Cantt.

Shaheed longed for Lund Khwar. Grandfather loved dogs, and in the Valley of Latter-Day Saints, he could love them too. One even became his pet. With the large, strong body of a wolf, he had huge sharp teeth, powerful jaws, and a deep bark that could be heard across the entire valley. But the German shepherd's fur was completely jinn-white. "Buraq," as Shaheed called him, became his best friend.

EVERYTHING CHANGED when Shaheed turned eleven.

It happened in Arab class, where they taught the Holy Book.

Though Mr. Arab Teacher was the youngest teacher in the school, he was the most sickly. His cheeks sank toward his teeth; his skin was oily and covered with acne craters. He coughed when he spoke in an Afghan accent. From TB, they said, but Mr. A.T. said nonsense, he had been cured long ago. And even though he was a tall man, he taught hunched over. At least that way the coughs were directed to the ground and not the boys, who constantly made fun of "Airhead"—for he always wanted to open the window for "fresh air." There was nothing fresh about the stale air surrounding the Government Primary School for Boys in Peshawar.

Then Mr. A.T. told the boys the story of Isa (Jesus), the last great prophet before the Chosen One. He read from the Holy Qur'an how Maryam gave birth to Isa "when no man had touched her."

"That might have worked for Maryam," Mr. A.T. coughed, "but I wouldn't count on it working for you. You boys know what you have to do?"

The question hung in the air like a balloon.

"You, baby-face Aimal!" Mr. A.T. shouted between coughs.

Aimal was sitting next to Shaheed. Aimal was always stone silent.

"You, Kashif. How are babies really made?"

Kashif, the class bully, no longer looked so tough.

"Well, Kashif, what's the matter, cat got your tongue? What do you think, boys? The cat's got Kashif's slippery tongue?"

Shaheed's thoughts had drifted outside the window. They flew on his beloved Buraq's invisible wings, out of muddy Peshawar, on the road to the Lund Khwar farm, over the green tobacco plants, and up the great black-and-white mountains in the distance.

"Batoor, snap to!" For a moment, Shaheed didn't realize the shout was directed at him. He had long since stopped listening. He knew the Word of God from Grandmother and her jinn. He knew from mosque when Grandfather took him and felt somehow that Mr. A.T. must be of the same ilk as his own father, the colonel, who never set foot at mosque.

When Shaheed left Arab class that day, he couldn't look the teacher in the eye. How could he set foot in that hellish classroom ever again? He wished he could fly to the mountains like one of Grandmother's righteous jinn. But justice would be his, or so he thought. He didn't have to wait long.

Only three days later, the school director, Mr. Headmaster, came to the classroom.

"Boys, it's my turn now to quiz you on the Book, not Mr. Arab Teacher," the headmaster bellowed. He was a short man, with a thin black mustache and quite light skin, who wouldn't be caught dead in the traditional Pakistani *shalwar kameez,* always a Western coat and tie for him.

"Tell me how babies are made." He stared at the class. You would have thought he didn't need to ask, as his belly was so full he looked pregnant himself.

"Speak, mute devils!" he shouted, now brandishing the thin wooden rod he had carefully concealed when first entering the classroom. The headmaster even carried his own special punishment rod, with his initials, MAK, in English letters carved at the head of its bulbous end.

In the silence that ensued, Mr. Headmaster began slowly to tap the special "MAK-rod" in rhythm against his fat leg.

Not that being hit with the rod was any big deal.

"A firm hand yields a bright child" could have been the motto of the Government Primary School for Boys, as it was of any good Pakistani school. The rod came out for any transgression; none was too minor: talking out loud in class, failing a test (or, for a good student like Shaheed, getting only a passing grade), farting out loud (or even silently, if the teacher smelled it), looking out the window, dreaming of jinn. Any of these merited a spot in the front of the class. If it were just a minor offense, you had to hold out the palms of your hands and the teacher would take the cane and whack them several times. If a more serious transgression, you had to turn your palms over and have the back of your hands whacked again. If you then cried or had committed a grave crime like laughing at something the teacher said, you would have to turn your face toward the blackboard. And the teacher would take the cane and beat you across the fleshy cheeks of your tan bottom till they burned bright red underneath. But the worst punishment was reserved for anyone who dared talk back, which would earn you a quick trip to the headmaster's office for "personal punishment" with his uniquely carved MAK-rod.

For Shaheed, going to school was like going to prison.

Mr. Headmaster now tapped the MAK-rod against the blackboard louder and louder. "Come, pretty boys," he bleated, beating out a devilish rhythm with the MAK, the grin on his fat lips getting wider.

"You, Aimal, speak! What did Mr. Arab Teacher tell your sweet little face?"

"Don't know sir, Mr. Headmaster Sahib."

"Whoever doesn't know will get three whacks across the back of their girlie hands."

"Kashif, ugly mug, answer me quick."

"Sir Headmaster, my esteemed Director Sahib, Mr. Arab Teacher told us . . ."

"Out with it, boy, or be whacked across your yellow teeth." The headmaster was now clutching the discipline rod so tightly in his fleshy right hand that his knuckles looked almost white.

"Mr. Arab Teacher said that you must take your stick and put it inside a woman and—"

The headmaster didn't wait for the bully Kashif to finish his disgusting drivel before the rod between his fingers flew out like a Stinger missile, striking the bully dead on across his lying lips.

"Is that what Mr. Arab Teacher taught you filthy dogs? You smelling arseholes!"

"Move!" Mr. Headmaster shouted. "Up front with your pants dropped and your stinking arseholes out!"

All twenty-seven boys lined up in front. Turning to the blackboard, they untied their pants on command, letting them fall to the floor.

Shaheed felt a breeze coming from the east. His bottom felt cold. Why should he be hit when he never believed Mr. Arab Teacher one whit? He never believed Mr. A.T.'s lies like the other boys, like Kashif, Abrar, and Siddiq, who always teased him, who called him "boogie eyes" and "*naswar* breath."

The boy standing two boys away from him, Shaheed couldn't tell who it was, yelped. Buraq never yelped. He was no ordinary dog: he never even whimpered. Shaheed would refuse to whimper too.

The headmaster's stick hit Shaheed's back. He had once heard the sound of a drum when his father took him to the army base to watch a marching band in full Pak army dress. His father had been so proud; Shaheed had hated it.

Something now rose inside him instead. Like a righteous jinn who visited his grandmother late at night, it seemed to come from nowhere. Still, it came—powerful and mysterious—before involuntarily passing through his lips in the form of actual words:

"I never believed it, sir!" Shaheed said, "The Word of God is true."

It is the greatest sin of all to speak when you're being punished. And you could never say anything out loud to the headmaster. He was the school's "father."

"Shut it, swine." Mr. Headmaster struck harder. "How dare you open your mouth?" He hit again. "Report your name."

"Shahee—," he was so scared he began to say, before quickly correcting himself, "I mean Batoor, sir."

The other boys all starting laughing, even though their bottoms were "bare to the rod."

"A boy who pretends not to know his own name? What a cheeky dirty mouth. What a talk-back devil."

Mr. Headmaster grabbed the waist of Shaheed's pants and jerked up. He didn't let go and pulled him by the pants to the head office for "personal caning." Shaheed walked along. The headmaster didn't have to pull.

Arriving at the office, he sent Mr. Assistant Headmaster to continue the collective punishment of the class and locked the door so that the Government Primary School's "father" was alone with the "back-talk boy."

Mr. Headmaster released his grip on Shaheed's pants, letting them drop again to the floor below. He ordered him to bend over "all the way."

"More, Batoor!" he shouted. "Till the tippy tips of your pretty little fingers reach your toes."

Shaheed wasn't sure exactly what the headmaster meant, as he had on the shiny shoes his father made him wear, but he dared not talk back again and touched the tips of his shoes instead.

Even though he was bent over, he could still see Mr. Headmaster holding the specially carved MAK-rod in his right hand, even waving it in a circle above his head.

The foul rod suddenly struck his calves. Shaheed didn't whimper. The MAK-rod struck the back of his knees. Shaheed was strong as his loyal Buraq. Mr. Headmaster's carved rod blistered the cheeks of his bare bottom. Buraq would never whimper. The drum kept beating, in cadence with the headmaster's words.

"I'll teach you to be a smart-arse with me, Batoor." The headmaster wouldn't stop shouting "Batoor" over and over again.

But Shaheed wouldn't answer. Not that it didn't take every fiber of his strength not to speak out again, for why would Mr. Headmaster strike *him* when all he was doing was dreaming of jinn and his beloved snow-white companion Buraq? And why would the headmaster take him to the office for "personal punishment" and cane him more than any other boy, when Shaheed had simply said that the Word of God is true?

But the rod wouldn't stop its devilish beat; the headmaster wouldn't stop shouting in rhythm: *"Ba-toor, Ba-toor!"* Every time the MAK rod struck his bottom, the pain felt even deeper because it was so senseless.

WHAT HAPPENED NEXT, Shaheed could never forget. Although God knew his secret, he said that I was the first person he told. He would suffer *sharam*—the highest shame and dishonor among fellow Pashtuns—if he ever told another Pashtun. Indeed, I was the first American and Jew he had met. Shaheed said only God could have brought us together, before he told me what he will always remember "until the moment he leaves Earth."

After striking his bare cheeks without end, Mr. Headmaster threw his thick left arm around Shaheed to hold him tight. Shaheed felt squeezed to death. The headmaster's fat left hand—the one he used to clean himself—without any warning then grabbed the boy's "privates." And before he knew what hit him, the MAK-rod was shoved hard all the way up his eleven-year-old bottom.

Shaheed still dreams of the rod from Hell burning a new hole deep and red and bloody inside him.

But he never cried or whimpered, even though the pain was unlike any he had known before. Instead, the force inside that made Shaheed speak out against his beating wasn't finished, indeed couldn't be stopped, and now blurted out even more, only this time directly from his bottom onto the headmaster's foul hands. The headmaster was so stunned, he stopped pushing on his fiendish rod.

Wiping the back of his hand across the boy's shirt, Mr. Headmaster yanked out "the rod from Hell" and just as quickly jerked up the soiled pants from those blackened feet and legs, ordering him to wash.

Shaheed knew that only God could've saved him from the unjust punishment and punished the headmaster instead. As Shaheed cleaned his feet, hands, bottom, and pants in the basin the boys used to wash for prayer, he vowed never again to answer to "Batoor." What had happened to him had happened to Batoor. Batoor had been MAK-rodded, and Batoor was buried with the MAK. That boy was dead. He would no longer go by that name, at least not in his heart. From that moment, he vowed one day to live up to the meaning of his true name from Grandmother. He swore to be worthy of Shaheed: a good Muslim and martyr for God alone. His name would now determine his fate.

TWO YEARS LATER, life stopped.

Grandmother told him that the moment you wait for is when life stops and God speaks. That is the moment when your suffering ends and you become a servant of God.

Shaheed matured by growing straight up, six feet tall at just thirteen years old. When his father was promoted, he moved Shaheed from government school to Peshawar's elite private Army Public School and Degree College. The son of an army officer couldn't be seen at a lowly government school. Shaheed didn't see much difference, especially since his classmate Aimal and the bully Kashif had followed him.

Yet towering above his classmates at the Army Public School and Degree College gave him a certain authority he never had before. Though he remained quiet and shy, his height alone seemed to cause a cease-fire in the teasing that had been the daily bane of his school days for so many years.

Shaheed was walking alone, as was his habit, through a dusty, grassy field in Defence Park near the Army Public School. Here the boys kept vigil, trying to spy a girl to "Eve-tease." Boys would taunt the neighborhood girls, much as they'd used to tease him, behavior that he abhorred. Led by the notorious bully Kashif, "Eve teasing" was a game the boys always planned in advance, picking out the "tightest" girls and teasing them as they crossed through the no-man's-land of Defence Park.

Laila would often walk with her friends through the park. Some girls wore a partial covering, a *hijab* or head scarf, but few were covered so that you could only make out the eyes. Since they were Afghan refugees, Laila's father insisted she cover herself in full.

The dress didn't matter. Shaheed had seen that her eyes bore the same flecks of green that marked Grandmother's loving eyes, so despite the covering around them—or perhaps because of it—they stood out like liquid jade to entice the boys and make them ask for more.

But when Shaheed saw her that day, he was the one chosen to see so much more: her eyes indeed had the pure green of the miraculous Helly. The blessed jinn was now brought down to Earth by God Himself, in Defence Park, close to the Army Public School and Degree College!

Kashif began the crude Eve-teasing talk, followed by Husain and Salman. Sometimes when the boys started their teasing, the girls would flirt back. But not Laila. She was pure, which only seemed to provoke Kashif and his sinner friends even more.

"C'mon, Lay-la baby, whacha gots behind de veil?"

"Hey Lay-lay, lemme kiss them lips, ha ha."

"Lemme see wha' ya hidin' in there, sweetheart."

It was shameful. Laila held her head high and kept walking. Shaheed burned red.

Then Kashif did the unthinkable. He crossed into her path. She turned to walk around him, but Kashif was determined to put on a show for the other boys—even the girls. First he licked his lips and let out a vile grin. His loyal band of followers started to laugh, hoot, and cheer, as if Kashif had hit the winning shot at cricket.

Shaheed was just on the other side from Laila, but he could see in her eyes. It looked as though those most beautiful green eyes in the world, from his grandmother's saintly Helly, no less, would soon be covered in tears.

As God had come to Shaheed when Mr. Headmaster had MAK-rodded him, answered his prayers, and made the hellish rodding stop, so God came now. Shaheed leapt like his loyal Buraq catching a flying squirrel. And with a force neither he nor anyone else knew he possessed, planted himself in front of Laila, directly in Kashif's way.

"If it isn't big-eyed Batoor, playing the Prophet Muhammad to save his girlfriend Aisha," Kashif spat out the words, before laughing like an evil jinn or the devil Shaytan himself.

Shaheed swung at the sinner with all his force. His right fist met Kashif squarely in the jaw. Shaheed "hit middle stump," as the boys would say in cricket (and he was a fine cricketer).

The blood dribbled from the sinner's broken lips as he propped himself up from the dusty ground.

Shaheed kicked the dirt straight into the swine's mouth, so that Kashif now began to spit out black blood. All the boys and girls moved aside, but Shaheed quickly turned to see Laila's eyes instead and smiled.

It was a small smile, just the upturned corners of the end of his shaking lips. But he smiled at this wondrous girl with the jinn's eyes and felt all the blood leave his head, just like it was leaving the mouth of the sinner below.

"Thank you, dear Batoor," she sang. For the first time since he was eleven, he didn't mind his name.

He couldn't move, let alone talk. He was awed by her heavenly beauty. He felt his soul leave him, travel with his grandmother and Helly high in the mountains, to the white clouds of Heaven above.

From that magical moment, he knew he would marry Laila.

SHAHEED WAS EATING at the Cantt house. It was one of those rare dinners when besides naan and dal they were served spring tandoor lamb because the Great Colonel actually deigned to partake of a meal with his wife and kids. He even had his new army batman join them— "not be a servant." The colonel disdained rigid traditional Pakistani hierarchies.

Not that Shaheed, his younger brother, Asif, his mother or even the batman could breathe a word. When the colonel talked, you shut up. A father's at the top of the Pashtun family order. You could never oppose him outright.

"*You,*" the colonel began. The colonel always addressed his eldest as "you." At least that was better than Batoor, Shaheed thought.

"Sir, Colonel Sahib," Shaheed said.

The boys were never allowed to address him as "Abba" or "Father" either. That suited Shaheed just fine. The colonel was anything but a father to him.

"It's about that damn school I send *you* to. Not to be believed. An army public school, indeed. The only bloody reason I send *you* is their pedigree. Not like the rest of these backward superstitious Muslim ninnies. This fucking town is crawling with 'em. Give me Lahore—or Islamabad, the Chaklala Garrison and 'Pindi even better. Oh, Chaklala! Where a man can be a man in Strategic Plans! Why do you think I never like staying in this godforsaken bloody hellhole?"

Shaheed hated the colonel's words. He felt they were directed at him, his mother, his brother. Maybe it was all just to show the army batman what a great man the colonel was. Shaheed wondered if the batman even understood his father's colonial English.

"When will Pakistan leave the Dark Ages and finally enter the light of the twentieth century at last?" the colonel asked no one in particular, certainly not Shaheed.

"Even at your school, my God. They expelled that boy Kashif Ali for blasphemy, 'taking the name of Prophet Muhammad in vain.' It seems *you* hit him after he blasphemed, or perhaps something to do with the girl. Imagine, a son of mine part of this stuff and nonsense! Now the father of that poor girl wants to punish *you*. See what *you* get for mucking around in religion! It's not enough for this Afghan mullah-mullah to have his own daughter lashed with a leather whip in the twentieth century yet. Imagine, lashing of ladies! Figure the religious bastard felt virtuous in not having her stoned to death. Islamic justice, Sharia. Ha! Now it's your turn. I told him that I want nothing to do with the lot of this Pashtun *wali-wali* honor bugaboo. I'm an army man. Bloody Pak army! Why the hell did I bother to

The father's large hand went down and started to pull at Shaheed's shirt—pulled at him while he prayed! What kind of a man of God could this be? As when the foul Mr. Headmaster ripped at his pants, Shaheed felt the foul brown rising in him as it had once before and recited *"Allah-umma inni a'udhu bika minal khubthi wal khaba'ith"*: O Allah, I seek Refuge with You from all offensive and wicked brown things, male evil jinn and evil doers," as Grandmother had taught him to say whenever he went to the toilet.

Shaheed could only ask God to be worthy of Grandmother's name and die as a martyr.

He didn't know how long he prayed on the cold, splintered floor. He didn't know how long the father was above him, the wooden punishment rod in his giant hand. It all felt like a dream from Shaytan. But God indeed protected him, as the father just walked out without saying a word. Leaving Shaheed untouched on the floor half naked, the father never spoke a single word—not even a *salaam* in greeting.

God had saved him again. Now to thank God and serve no other but Him, every day after school for the next five years and, of course, without his father's knowledge, let alone permission, Shaheed went to mosque and learned the Holy Qur'an, surah by surah. He was so endowed by God that in one year he could learn by heart 33 of 114 chapters and in three years all 114 chapters, the entire Uncreated Word of Allah.

His remarkable ability to become the most exalted student of the faith—a *hafiz* who memorized His Holy Word—told him, and all those at mosque, that the boy could only be touched by the Hand of God Himself.

When Shaheed asked his father if he could attend madrassa full-time, his father struck him across the mouth. The Great Colonel who loved humanity hit him like Mr. Headmaster, another one who worshipped at the unclean feet of the idol of "Western reason." It didn't matter. One day, Shaheed would be worthy of his true name. Besides, he spent almost all weekends and holidays and vacations at Lund Khwar. God had His ways. Shaheed's lot was to submit and not to question. In time God would reveal why, as He always did.

And soon Shaheed would be gone. Away from the "enlightened humanity" of the Army Public School and Degree College. Away from Colonel English-waxed Mustache, who insisted on being called colonel when he wasn't even a full colonel, just a lieutenant colonel. Away from his long-suffering-in-silence mother, his sad-sack mother who never dared talk back either. Away from headmasters with MAK-rods and silent Afghan fathers with kohl eyeliners. The only ones he'd miss would be his grandfather and his beloved grandmother. It didn't matter that his father refused to send him to madrassa and demanded the University of Peshawar instead. If Shaheed had found God at the Army Public School and Degree College, he could find God anywhere, Praise be to Allah and His Prophet Muhammad, peace be upon him.

THE FIRST DAY at university, Shaheed did not shave.

Saying good-bye to his parents, he didn't even bring a razor. Saying good-bye to Grandmother the weekend before, he had perfectly clipped the nails on his toes—the toes Grandmother had so often kissed—so that he could now wear only open-toe sandals. The shiny black Army Public School patent-leather shoes belonged to the devil Shaytan. Shaheed prepared himself for God instead.

He didn't prepare himself for how the students would be just like the boys from Army Public School—in fact, many were. Only now, at university, they bullied others according to which party they belonged to: secular, Islamic, socialist, Pakistani nationalist, Pashtun nationalist, and everything in between. This was the taunting of Army Public School elevated to an entirely new level. One student party would shun, mock, spit at, or even beat the other. Forget childish teasing; these boys had brass knuckles. Yet they still Eve-teased the girls with the same childish vigor they had at Army Public School. That much didn't change.

Nominally, Shaheed was admitted to study agriculture. The important thing was that he could excel with very little effort, so he could devote his true energy to the Holy Qur'an, prayer, and dreams.

Not dreams of his future success, marriage, or politics, but dreams at night. They were the "true dreams" that gave him a sign and told him the way.

Shaheed went through the motions of going to class, passing exams, eating his meals, saying as little as possible to his classmates, praying five times a day, going to mosque, but he lived in his dreams. He lived for God.

That was why God put him on Earth, and why he joined Jamaat.

Jamaat-e-Islami was the party of Maulana Maududi, back to the ways of Allah the Almighty and His Chosen One. It was the leading Islamist political party of Pakistan, its "Muslim Brotherhood."

He now devoured the writings of Jamaat's great founder Maududi, as well as other teachers of jihad, such as Sayyid Qutb and the medieval scholar, Ibn Taymiyyah.

Above all, Shaheed wanted to be a good Muslim.

SUMMER VACATION MEANT camp—jihadi training camp. Three months, from June to September 2001, for the new Jamaat student recruits to learn not just the ideas but the practice. It was time for Shaheed to become a soldier of God.

He thanked God that the Jamaat training camp was in the mountains. Indeed, the camp was in the mountains Grandmother had always dreamed of, home to her beloved jinn. It was the first time Shaheed had ever entered these mountains.

The camp was near Mansehra. Captain Zeddy was in command. The famous captain moved with such force that even the air followed behind him. A stocky, muscular man with tough, leathery skin, Captain Zeddy had no beard, just a grizzled mustache and slight, wispy goatee. Captain Zeddy and Shaheed's father the colonel were both military commanders of the same generation, even went to school in the same town (Abbottabad), but there was no mistaking the captain's true jihadi credentials.

Unlike his father, Captain Zeddy had an unquestioning faith and did the needful to make every man "a direct sergeant" on his own.

The "Captain of Terror," as he was called, continually quoted the noble Maulana Maududi: "The establishment of an Islamic state *requires the whole earth*—not just a portion, but the entire planet. It is therefore the first duty of all men who aspire to please God to launch an organized struggle to liquidate all infidels and secure power for the righteous believers. There is no other means left to please Him."

Training the best young mujahideen to become foot soldiers in the path of virtue, Captain Zeddy gave no lift. Following morning prayer, they learned everything needed to be true soldiers of God: from handling Kalashnikovs and grenades to cutting barbed wire, crossing borders at night, making bombs, practicing dispersion and infiltration tactics, and more. The physical rigor was like nothing Shaheed had felt before, even when training for the championship cricket match at the Army Public School and Degree College. He was exhausted after last prayers. He slept in a bunk with other students from Peshawar University and even Aimal from Army Public School too.

Then Shaheed had a dream. In the mountainous home of the jinn, he had waited patiently for more than two months for a true night vision to carry God's voice directly to him.

A mighty green bird, larger than an eagle or hawk, flew overhead. To say it was large would be silly. It was the size of a great airplane, dominating the sky. Jinn were in command, Helly was the flight attendant, and the pilot was a very young Captain Zeddy. The great bird darkened the sky. Everything was black until a blinding fireball lit up the entire sky with a blazing white fluorescent light, and Shaheed woke up.

Only a few days later, Captain Zeddy ordered the recruits into mess following evening prayer. Gathering around the warm glow of the commander's old TV, Shaheed could not believe what he saw. It was his dream: first one great bird struck, then another followed, before a fireball lit the screen, and the towering twin symbols of the infidel empire's dominance fell to dust.

One of the recruits, Shaheed didn't know who, let out a yell, *"Allah-u-Akbar,"* until others joined in, whooping and hollering in unison.

Shaheed didn't join, nor for that matter did the great "Captain of

Terror" Zeddy. Oh yes, Shaheed knew it was his dream; he saw his prophecy live on the screen. But was this the jihad that God ordered— it seemed so from his dream—or was it the act of man? The recruits had no right to celebrate, he thought, unless they knew it was God's will. It wasn't like when God shakes the earth and an earthquake follows or God delivers water in overabundance and the plains are flooded.

Shaheed was right, for the honored Zeddy then spoke. "Do not celebrate the defeat of others unless God has commanded," he said sternly.

The boys were quiet. Shaheed felt he now had the right, indeed the duty, to speak.

"Mr. Camp Commander," Shaheed said softly. He always spoke softly, as the Noble Qur'an told him to speak in a low voice—unless he invoked God's wrath.

Captain Zeddy turned toward him, his kind brown eyes shining from his leathered face.

"I was visited by a dream last night."

"Pray tell," the camp commander encouraged him.

"A massive bird covered the sky, and you, sir, were in the cockpit, piloting the enormous airplane eagle. The great bird-plane darkened the sky. Everything was black until a blinding fireball lit up the entire sky with a blazing white fluorescent light."

Now the cries of *"Allah-u-Akbar!"* resumed in full-throated glory. Shaheed wasn't sure what his dream really meant, but everyone else seemed to know. Even Captain Zeddy now seemed to voice approval.

That evening, Shaheed became something of a hero, the star oracle at Camp Mansehra. For no one could dispute the power of a true night dream.

When Shaheed, Aimal, and the others soon returned to university, Aimal told all of the Jamaat students Shaheed's dream. As the students demonstrated in the streets of Peshawar and at the U.S. Consulate, Syed Hassan, the head of the university Jamaat, spoke to the crowd and recounted the dream.

At every speech now, believers spoke of Shaheed's dream as the prophecy behind the 9/11 attacks. The newspapers even picked it up, and Shaheed wondered whether the colonel would read about it in his beloved *Dawn*.

Months later, one of the Jamaat students even said he had heard the blessed Sheikh Osama mention the dream on a video tape. When Shaheed and the other Jamaat students finally watched the famous video, they witnessed firsthand the power of dreams. They lived in the divine breath of God as Sheikh Osama retold Shaheed's dream to the world. (Although by then many students had started to question whether Sheikh Osama had really directed the attacks or the Crusader Americans and Zionist Jews had staged them as an excuse to attack the students' brother Pashtun Muslims in Afghanistan.)

Shaheed felt himself walking in the path of God. When he had class, he paid attention enough to pass, but the university was frequently shut down. The Jamaat would attack any gathering where music was played or the sexes mingled. If a boy held the hand of a girl, the Jamaat would beat the boy bloody and taunt the girl into fleeing. Clashes among Jamaat students, PPP gangs, and ANP (Pashtun nationalist) boys grew so violent that the authorities would have to impose curfew and lock down the entire university.

Shaheed prayed instead. He lived in his dream with God.

THE NEXT SUMMER vacation, Shaheed went with Aimal and other holy warriors to fight in the glorious mountains of Kashmir. It was a God-given mission of jihad to liberate Muslim brothers from the idol-worshipping Indians and their infidel American masters.

In the Kashmiri mountains, Shaheed fought alongside Aimal as they were ordered from safe house to safe house, living among the tribal families of Azad Kashmir and fighting for brethren Muslims for the glory of God. Shaheed shot rockets, threw grenades, fired his Kalashnikov, and wondered whether he'd no longer be "Secret Shaheed" but become the real thing.

Fifty-six days later a blow hit him greater than any he could imagine, no matter how many bombs and bullets were fired back.

He got word that the devil Shaytan had struck the left side of his grandmother's head. Her face half frozen, the words came out as satanic grunts no one could understand. Shaheed could only pray until, eight days later, he dreamed that his front teeth fell out. Immediately he left the jihad, as everyone knew that the dream was a sign of death. He had to see her face one more time before she was buried.

Grandmother's body was lying peacefully on a cot at the farm near Lund Khwar. Her face was turned toward Mecca, her eyes closed and toes tied together, ready for burial in the Pashtun way.

Shaheed kneeled beside her and prayed that she was now with Helly on her way to Heaven. Then he untied her toes. He kissed each of her right foot's toes, from the smallest to the largest, before he heard the colonel shout, "That's enough, boy."

How dare his father snap at him as he lovingly kissed his dear grandmother good-bye? Kissed her right foot with the same love she'd always given him, with the same devotion he'd heard that even Sheikh Osama had kissed his own mother's feet. He wished it were his father lying there instead of his beloved grandmother.

What would it be like to get the secret code to the nuclear weapons his father guarded, he thought, and deliver the Islamic Bomb into the hands of real believers—true mujahideen, like Captain Zeddy—instead of the colonel and other pretenders to Muslim honor? If the 9/11 fireball were large, imagine what one of Lieutenant Colonel Khattak's nukes would do. It would light up not just lower New York but most of the United States, if God so willed. As the lieutenant colonel's son, he felt there must be a way. He just didn't know how. But if it were meant to happen, God would lead him, so that the so-called Islamic Bomb would at last be truly Islamic.

He knew there was a reason God had made him this miserable man's son by blood. When Allah the Almighty was ready, he would be His humble servant.

Shaheed wept for Grandmother for an entire week. And when he at last woke up with his snow-shepherd jinn Buraq beside him in bed, he knew Grandmother was now in Heaven.

———

BACK AT UNIVERSITY, things did not feel the same. Shaheed became more pious, reciting the Glorious Qur'an throughout every day, even defying his father and taking religious courses at Islamia College.

Shaheed listed his official residence as Chaklala in Rawalpindi so he could stay in a university hostel and share a room with Aimal. Each hostel usually had about a hundred boarders with most rooms having four students, some two. Shaheed was blessed to have a double with Aimal.

Every night following Isha prayer at mosque, they would pray together again right before bed. They'd first perform *wudu,* washing their hands, neck, nose, face, and feet. Then, inside their room, they would put down the prayer rugs facing Mecca and pray together as one. Shaheed would usually recite the prayers as they moved in unison, not missing a single movement shoulder to shoulder.

They always performed the Jumu'ah prayers together at mosque too, and, of course, each of the five daily prayers. Now the two took almost all the same classes and ate every meal with each other as well.

Aimal had a classmate from engineering who sometimes joined them at mosque. His name was Tariq, from a noble Pashtun tribe in Afghanistan. His father was a noted mullah and holy warrior, leading the Taliban now from Quetta against the infidel American invaders. Tariq was quiet and kept to himself, which made Shaheed and Aimal suitable companions for the honorable Afghan son of a top Taliban commander.

The three bonded and started to hold study sessions on Islam, *da'wah,* jihad, the Qur'an, Hadith, and the great thinkers such as Sayyid Qutb.

There were 13 million Pashtun on the Afghan side of the "false border" and 26 million on the Pakistani side. The Taliban were Pashtun from southern Afghanistan. Shaheed, Aimal and Tariq were Pashtun too. The American invasion of Afghanistan had attacked their Pashtun, Muslim brothers. And the boys now wanted nothing to do with parties like Jamaat that cooperated in any way with the Pakistani government, whose president, General Musharraf, now allied himself with the United States.

Eschewing Jamaat and other established Islamist political parties that were not radical enough, the small "study group" began to attract Muslim students who were truly pure of heart, mind, and spirit. Boys who forswore girls, gambling, music, and the corrupted politics of the existing Muslim political parties. Boys who would fight for their brothers in God.

Shaheed's group was of the most pious. The other kids began to call them "the holy rollers." Such teasing only made him feel prouder.

By their fifth year in University, they had some eleven loyal members. As the year ended, Nadeem, who Aimal had befriended, became their youngest member at age nineteen—a number Shaheed knew from the Holy Book meant God-blessed change was at hand.

Nadeem had long black hair down to his ear lobes and chocolate skin that made his snowy teeth shine. Most of all, his unusually thin fingers ended in perfectly arched, uncut nails—the bright crescent moons of Islam that Grandmother had always said Helly wore. Baby-face Nadeem didn't even have a single beard hair. Just starting at university, the boy looked no more than sixteen. Perhaps because his father was an important Muslim League feudal from Islamabad, Tariq tried to win him over.

Following in his father's Taliban footsteps, Tariq had become the group's clear manager, shrewdly balancing personalities, cash, activities, and anything they needed to function. And if Tariq was the undisputed Ayman al-Zawahiri of this close-knit band, Shaheed had to be its Osama bin Laden. Soft-spoken, clean, with a calm spirituality and unquestioning faith, he became a spiritual force—at least among this group of outcast pious students at the University of Peshawar, during a time of increasing radicalization in the Pashtun areas of Pakistan. And of course, the boys knew his fateful dream at Camp Mansehra.

Funded by their families, the leaders and even some followers of this most devout circle extended their time at university so that they could continue their radical discussions, pious study, and scrupulous practice of their faith.

———

WHEN TARIQ TOLD his father about the group of his "student brothers," the Taliban leader offered to finance them. It was at that moment that Shaheed and his companions forever left the realm of radical students—even if students who had fought in Kashmir. They would now go down the path, as so many of their fellow students did, of becoming radical terrorists instead.

A famous old-line mullah of the original Islamic Emirate of Afghanistan and now a leading Taliban commander against the Americans, Tariq's father saw the importance of the rise of a new generation of Taliban fighters. They'd appeal to the global jihad and Al Qaeda way of thinking. Cultivating these mujahideen inside Pakistan would open a whole new front in the Afghan war.

Even after the Taliban was defeated in Afghanistan in the fall of 2001 and its leadership took up exile inside Pakistan, it continued to receive covert support from Inter-Services Intelligence—the infamous ISI—Pakistan's intelligence agency and part of the Pakistani army. While officially allied with the United States, the ISI secretly provided safe haven for the Taliban leadership in Quetta, logistical intelligence for border crossings inside Afghanistan, advanced weaponry, and unstinting funding. The Taliban was flush with cash not only from the ISI but from wealthy Saudi and Gulf Arabs as well. Still, there was a growing distance between the older Taliban Emirate leaders led by Mullah Omar and a younger generation of more militant, globally oriented jihadis, particularly inside Pakistan. Many of the young jihadis wanted nothing to do with the duplicitous Pakistani government.

Tariq's father thought it wise to play both sides and keep one foot in the new camp. Just as the ISI hedged its bets and supported both the Taliban and the Americans at the same time, so would some leaders of the Emirate Taliban (principally the Quetta Shura) covertly support the new Taliban, who were directly attacking the Emirate Taliban's putative allies in the Pakistani government, even the ISI-led military.

But as Tariq's group finished their university studies and his father provided living expenses and military training, the great mullah became disappointed with the results. Even though Shaheed, Aimal, and most of the others had fought in battle as true soldiers of God, the group now seemed just to talk. Lacking even a fighting name, all they did was pray. Tariq's father felt he might be wasting his money on his son and his "touchy-feely brothers."

Throughout 2007, attacks in Pakistan gathered force and the cadres of the Tehrik-i-Taliban—among the new Pakistani Taliban—grew. And as 2008 opened with parliamentary elections and more chaos, the militancy of the younger Pashtun generation inside Pakistan increased, freeing the Taliban to further its success across the border in Afghanistan. But where was Tariq's band?

They lived simply, to be sure, on two floors of a house in the University Town area of Peshawar. They ate plain foods and took no worldly pleasure. Some of the men still followed the strong tribal Pashtun traditions: they had arranged marriages with first cousins and kept close clan ties in their home villages. But for Shaheed and the leaders, as his grandfather had once broken strict tribal custom to help lead the new secular Pakistan to independence, they broke with tribal tradition too. Islam now became their family. Earthly relations did not matter. Heaven was their goal. And though Shaheed cut off his family, he retained a relationship with the keeper of the nuclear codes in case one day God asked.

Shaheed, Aimal, Nadeem, Tariq, and the others prayed, recited the Holy Qur'an, Hadith, studied great texts, followed the news, and waited for a sign from God. Shaheed told the group that Allah the All-Knowing must be their only guide.

"As the Book says in the eighteenth verse of the eighteenth surah, when all mankind rejected them, Allah Almighty gave his young followers and their loyal dog peace—until the right time came," he said.

Shaheed hated the ways of man and the politics of radicalism, which he saw firsthand had corrupted the leaders of Jamaat and so many other so-called Islamists inside Pakistan. And the more he studied, he thought that politics corrupted Muslims not just in Pakistan but around the world. The true path of a Muslim was about God, not man.

But Tariq grew impatient. His father took him to meet other Taliban and Al Qaeda fighters, first in Quetta, then North Waziristan, and once in Chitral. Tariq returned knowing how to build a bomb. Before long, he also had a new friend visit, "from Al Qaeda the base itself."

It was March 2008. The Pakistani elections had been held, General Musharraf still clung to power, and Luna Caprese, the Italian restaurant in the capital occupied by foreigners, had just been blown to bits.

"Osama," as the visitor from Al Qaeda even called himself, had large, arching eyebrows but just the hint of a faint mustache on his smooth face. Although he was Arab by birth, he spoke near-fluent Pashto and dressed as a born-again Pashtun. Still, Shaheed could tell that this so-called Osama from Al Qaeda wasn't a real Pashtun—though not from the way he looked or even sounded. After Tariq told the story of Shaheed being chosen with the dream of 9/11, Osama wouldn't stop talking. Babbling without end how God had connected them in prophecy, the Al Qaeda warrior spoke of the new dream Shaheed must now have, a night dream for their struggle against the Crusaders and Jews, who would not rest until they killed every last Muslim. No Pashtun would chatter endlessly like that.

"Allah the Well-Acquainted let us see the true evil of the American Crusaders and their Danish pigs when they mocked the Holy Prophet, *Sallallahu 'alayhi wa sallam* (may the peace and blessings of Allah be upon him). We must avenge the Crusaders and Jews," the talkative mujahid from Yemen told Tariq, Shaheed, and the other men, "for, as the very Word of Almighty Allah tells us in the Book, 'they are the worst of all creatures.'"

Aimal was the first to announce to the group that he would give his "very last breath" to the glory of God. Nadeem nodded in agreement, raising his delicate right hand and pushing aside his thick black hair, shiny as Army Public School patent-leather shoes. And all could bear witness to the white scar in the center of Nadeem's smooth brown forehead: it was the mark of Islam, in the distinct shape of a crescent.

By God, it wasn't Aimal who soon left with Osama the Al Qaeda fighter. It was young Nadeem, the one with Laila's smile, the glowing eyes of Grandmother's jinn, the long hair of the Prophet Muhammad, and the mark of the Islamic crescent. Shaheed knew because the Holy Book told him: the one who carried the number nineteen would bring God's change.

Throughout the spring, with Nadeem now gone to Al Qaeda, Shaheed prayed and waited for God to speak.

In June, Tariq reported, "the Danes, servants of the infidel Americans and apes, pigs, and Jews, who laugh like Shaytan at the Apostle of God," found swift justice brought against them when their embassy in Islamabad was bombed. Tariq said that the mujahideen nearby could even smell the sweet air rise from the martyrs who had given their lives for the glory of God.

"Soon we'll be blessed to breathe the fragrance of musk coming from Nadeem's fresh body too," Tariq said.

The Americans, in turn, responded by slaughtering more innocent Pashtuns, dropping their bombs from the Devil's drones. "If the Americans are not fighting a Christian Crusade, why else would they be massacring millions of Muslims?" Tariq concluded.

Shaheed waited for God. He thought maybe he would have to ascend in the mountains like the Prophet at the Cave of Hiraa, but waited in Peshawar.

Waited while the Americans attacked, the Pakistani army and Frontier Corps attacked, and the Tehrik-i-Taliban fought back to defend themselves.

Suddenly, Shaheed heard from his mother. His father, the Great Colonel, wasn't telling his sons but had been operated on for melanoma. The cancer had spread throughout his body.

Shaheed felt that the poison eating his father's body was God's punishment for the poison the so-called colonel had spewed his entire life. But Tariq saw an opportunity. "Maybe on his deathbed, he'll repent to God and reveal to you the nuclear codes," he told Shaheed.

———

THE KHYBER TEACHING Hospital was the one that always treated university students injured in party and sectarian feuds. Some called it the "Hayat Shaheed" hospital, but Shaheed refused to use any religious name for a hospital that housed his father by blood.

The lead paint from the pale blue-green walls had begun to peel, ammonia disinfectant reeked in the halls, and the black and white linoleum floor tiles were curling from their corners. Walking to his father's room on the second floor, Shaheed thought Allah in His wisdom might have an American-trained doctor "cure" his father.

Shaheed was sorry he'd listened to Tariq. With no sign from God, Shaheed shouldn't be here, and certainly not for his cursed father, whose cancerous insides had finally caught up with his cancerous soul.

The ammonia caught the back of Shaheed's throat. His stomach turned and needed Zamzam water from the holy well in Mecca to settle a growing nausea. He wanted to perform *wudu*. He needed to cleanse the hospital sickness of his blood father.

With Dawn TV News shouting in the background, the colonel was propped up on a white metal hospital bed. Why would his father now repent to God, or even to Shaheed? Why would he ever give up his intelligence, the nuclear code, and the secret to the Islamic Bomb when he had never been a true Muslim to begin with?

Tariq's idea was foolish, and it made Shaheed furious. He should turn around and walk out of this death trap, filled with God's sick patients waiting to be cured by American-trained doctors or die. There was no difference.

"Hello, Dad," he said. Maybe his father would repent on his deathbed and find God. Maybe Shaheed would finally find peace with him before he died. Pashtun tradition—more, the Holy Qur'an—commanded that a son honor his father. But the Book also said that a father should only be honored if he didn't push the son to serve others besides God. Now was Shaheed's chance to honor his father and serve God at the same time.

"It's *you*. Who told *you* I was here? Your damn mother." His father's voice sounded different, almost raw, though he still refused to speak to his son in anything but English.

"How are you feeling, Father?" Shaheed answered in Pashto.

"Colonel," his father corrected him.

Shaheed stared blankly for a moment. The truth was that he wasn't even a colonel, just a lieutenant colonel, before his half-dead father said, "Why the bloody hell? I'm dying in pain, and I'm fucking around with you. You're still my son," he said, coughing up blood.

"I came to make my *salat*," Shaheed said, "pray with you."

His father the lieutenant colonel couldn't stop coughing. No doubt a tubercular cough ripped his guts out, like the blasphemous Mr. Arab Teacher. But Shaheed was much wiser now, watching the yellow spittle hanging from his dying father's cracked lips. Shaheed saw the lieutenant colonel cough even deeper, hacking away until clots of blood came up, and he knew God had a reason for everything.

"You ... better ... pray ... hard." His father coughed up the words.

Shaheed looked out the window and around the room for the *kibla* sign. He went to the bathroom to perform *wudu* and returned cleansed. He kneeled down to pray as his father coughed uncontrollably.

"That's all you could ever do for me," his father muttered between coughs.

Shaheed continued to pray but felt like bolting up from the ground and wringing his father's neck to stop the infernal coughing. He immediately banished the worldly thought in sacred prayer.

As he finished praying, his father's coughing calmed, until the lieutenant colonel said, "What do you want from me, Son?"

It was the first time Shaheed could remember that his father had called him "Son."

Shaheed looked around the peeling blue, ammonia-soaked hospital room, towering over his father on the metal bed below. "To help us," he said. He could hardly get the words out.

His father struggled to raise himself from the sinking bed, to calm himself long enough to speak without coughing. At first Shaheed thought he saw him smile. Then the lieutenant colonel steadied his thin, dry lips, and his eyes didn't move, as if frozen in a death mask. "Why the bloody hell?" he finally said under his raspy breath.

"For the glory of Allah the Almighty, the Most Gracious, the Most Generous, the Most Merciful."

"Where's your humanity? I'm your father, I'm bloody dying." He coughed and spat again.

"Where's your love? I mean, to God?" Shaheed said.

His father now put his uniform back on. "I mean, what would you do with my help?" The colonel was interrogating his own son, on his deathbed loyal to Pakistan and not God.

"I love God," Shaheed said.

His father let out the Devil's laugh. He began to cough more. Shaytan was eating him from the inside. He would never go to Heaven unless he repented—why couldn't he finally see that? Must he remain the same hollow, loveless, and angry man without God until his death, until his body was wrapped in a white linen shroud and buried in the ground without *tawbah*?

"I came here to help you repent before your Lord," Shaheed said, trying to find his father in the sick coughing laughing man dying right before his eyes. Trying to find the father he'd never had, the father who had never loved him. If he wouldn't love him now, maybe he'd finally love his Lord, and if he wouldn't love God, maybe he'd finally just love his son.

His father spat blood. "Just get the fucking nurse." He coughed, short of breath.

Shaheed left and found the nurse, obeying his father for the last time. He knew he shouldn't have come, done Tariq's bidding, listened to man and not God. How could he expect his blood father the colonel to ever change, to really repent, when his whole life was just filled with contempt and hatred for him and all he held sacred?

Shaheed remembered Grandmother, how much she loved him, singing to him the miraculous tales of Helly and the unseen, burning warmth of the smokeless jinn. And he remembered how he had been on jihad and hadn't even had the chance to say good-bye to her. Where had the jihad left him then? Was it a war of God or man?

Shaheed now doubted Tariq for the first time too. Was it just the son of a Taliban commander who had sent young Nadeem to die, or was it jihad from God? Now his blood father, another decorated soldier—the Pak army always said it was fighting a jihad too—was on his deathbed and didn't even want to say good-bye to his own son.

Shaheed vowed to find God's voice. He would no longer look for man's—whether it was Mr. Headmaster's, his blood father's, or even Tariq's. God alone mattered.

BUT GOD WAS silent. Three days later, his mother called with the news, and Shaheed refused to go to the burial. He didn't even tell Tariq that he went to the hospital. He should never have gone in the first place.

Shaheed now felt tired of men's hatred toward other men, for wearing the clothes of God when all they had were human thoughts, for disrespecting God by creating their own wars and calling them jihad. Everything his blood father stood for reminded him of that. He felt that if Tariq asked him in that same raspy voice if he'd seen the colonel before he died, he'd just spit in his face, as his blood father had spat blood at him.

Then something happened that shook Shaheed in his heart. They were watching the news—Geo TV News, as the colonel had been watching Dawn TV News. It was just Aimal and Shaheed.

The noise of the TV filled the room, as it had filled his blood father's deathbed. Hamid Mir, the reporter who had once interviewed bin Laden, was talking. It was the one-year anniversary of the Lal Masjid (Red Mosque) martyrdom, where the colonel's superior officer had ordered the slaughter of the holy warriors inside the mosque. Mir was reporting how a new suicide attack had killed eighteen soldiers when Aimal suddenly said, "Tariq wanted me to ask if you ever got any help from your father."

Shaheed couldn't believe that his one true friend was now doing Tariq's bidding instead of the bidding of the one and only God.

Shaheed said nothing. He felt the dagger of betrayal, its hard steel eating a crater in his chest, as had the cancer in the center of his father's heart.

He turned up the volume on the remote. The two friends didn't speak. When Tariq returned with the other men, Shaheed couldn't look him in the eye.

He began to pray: not only the required five daily prayers, but all of the voluntary prayers to God. He searched for God's voice. He even slept more in the hope of a dream. He was calling God from the pain of his heart. Calling in his prayers, in his dreams, in every clean waking moment God gave him the gift to wait and listen.

He knew God would answer. His blood father was dead, his mother left to live with his younger brother, and soon they would go to America. Tariq wouldn't talk to him, and he wouldn't even look at Tariq. Aimal was now doing Tariq's bidding, not God's but man's—and not even for him but for Tariq.

Whenever Shaheed needed God the most, He was there. God would not betray him.

It wasn't but a couple of days, a week at most, *mash'Allah*.

God spoke.

It wasn't from a mountaintop. It wasn't from a dream, as so often before. It wasn't from a vision, prayer, or supplication to God (*dua*). But from a phone call. Yes, Tariq's cell.

In His infinite wisdom, God always answers those deserving of being answered, and He did not fail His devoted supplicant now.

It came from Tariq's colleague Malik, an Afghan Taliban [and dream seer to Taliban leader Mullah Omar, profiled in Chapter 3]. Malik was in his mid- to late twenties too. He had been a Taliban fighter and commander of the Virtue and Vice Police in Afghanistan when the Taliban ruled. He had even fought under the command of Tariq's father to liberate Afghanistan from the invading infidel Americans.

Now Malik was among the new generation of Taliban leaders fighting the infidels inside Pakistan. Malik and his men sometimes prayed with Shaheed and his men. Malik distrusted most Pakistani militants but knew Tariq's friend Shaheed was a true and pious man of God, uncorrupted by the ISI and other false, ungodly parasites.

———

MALIK HAD JUST spoken to me, whom he referred to as "an American reporter." Malik now said to Tariq that it was time to tell the world what the new Taliban meant. It was time to tell God's truth, even to the infidels. When I had asked Malik for another voice of their new movement, he'd thought of Shaheed and called.

Malik told the men that I wouldn't come to Peshawar due to the security situation and Shaheed would have to travel to Islamabad. Shaheed had visited the capital as a boy with his father, who had a Pak army house in its sister garrison town of Rawalpindi.

Malik also said that Shaheed had to meet me at the American fortress of imperial decadence itself, the five-star Marriott Hotel, near the Pakistani Parliament.

"Bought and paid for by the American corrupters." Tariq said, "It figures that the godless infidel would be holding court there."

Tariq had been telling the group they needed to act. They'd waited long enough. Only weeks earlier, Tariq had even given the men a name: Fedayeen-e-Islam (Partisans Who Sacrifice Their Lives for Islam).

But Shaheed would go to the Marriott only if God told him.

IT WASN'T LONG before Tariq Googled "Ken Ballen" on the Internet: not only an American, but a Jew!

"Like Daniel Pearl," Tariq said. Daniel Pearl was the American Jewish reporter sacrificed in Pakistan by the mujahideen for jihad.

Shaheed would no longer listen to Tariq or even Aimal. Shaheed's father was dead. He no longer had to obey what any man told him. He only had to obey God.

And that night, Shaheed had his long-awaited true dream, *subhan'Allah*. He saw the first prophet, Ibrahim, his blade raised to sacrifice his son Ishmael at Allah's command. Until Allah revealed to him that Ibrahim had already fulfilled his "sacrifice" by his love for his Lord alone and Ibrahim did not have to sacrifice his son.

Except now, in the dream, Shaheed was holding the blade dripping with blood, the blood coming out of the mouth of a coughing American. And the blood kept coming out of the coughing mouth until he could see that the American sported his father's very own English-gentleman waxed mustache, until the severed head was no longer the American's. Instead, in the center of the white hospital bed, floating on top of a deep pool of dark blood, he saw Nadeem's Islamic crescent head, all alone.

Shaheed wasn't sure what the dream meant. He knew that for Tariq it could only mean that the American Jew must be sacrificed "like Daniel Pearl." Indeed, Tariq now said that he'd had a dream too: His skin was black, covered in hard metal. His eyes were calibrated heat sensors. A plastic pipe led from his throat through his stomach, and inside his mouth was a wired fuse.

All Shaheed knew with certainty was that God alone, when He was ready, would tell him the meaning of his dream. Shaheed only had to make the journey to find out.

FOLLOWING MORNING PRAYER the next day, Shaheed took a taxi to the Marriott in Islamabad. During the two-hour ride on the M1 motorway, in between reciting Qur'anic surahs, he waited for God's voice. He felt calm. He'd heard from God before: his task now was to just keep listening. And after seeing the Hinopak truck with Prophet Muhammad's noble steed, Buraq, boldly painted on the way to Heaven, he knew he must be on the way of God in jihad.

The taxi dropped him on the road in front of the Marriott's security gate. But when Shaheed called on his cell and asked for my room, the front desk said that there was no Ken Ballen. Shaheed didn't know what to do. What part of God's intricate plan did he miss?

He always had to be most alert to what God really wanted. You always have to train yourself to listen, watch and be receptive to discern God's true way. He tried calling the Marriott again. Perhaps it was simply human error and not God's plan. The front desk indeed told him to try the Serena instead.

Apart from the Marriott, the Serena is the capital's leading luxury five-star hotel, just a short taxi ride away. Yet unlike the Marriott, the

Serena stands atop a steep green hill, far removed from the road below and the potential of suicide attack. It's said to be the most secure hotel in Islamabad and, given its unusual geography, probably among the most secure of any building in Pakistan. Even a ton of explosives set off in front would send the security center and gates below sky-high, and shatter the windows in the majestic hotel above, no doubt, but leave its privileged citizens largely unharmed.

Shaheed had no problem passing through the hotel's lower security perimeter. This time I answered the call and said I would meet him in the Serena's lobby, under the great chandelier.

Leaving the security center below and climbing the green slope to the Serena, Shaheed could see in the distance the Margalla Hills. They were the foothills of the Himalaya Mountains, where he had once gone to fight, only to be called back to see his beloved grandmother's face before she was buried.

At the second security gate, to the hotel lobby itself, he went through the same security routine without incident.

Arriving in flowing robes and long dark beard, Shaheed was something of a sight. With his pure white cotton robe worn just above the ankles, he revealed sandaled feet, in the style of the Salafi Islamists who sought to emulate the Prophet Muhammad's seventh-century companions, the *salaf*.

Under a bright crystal chandelier, the tan-and-gold Serena lobby was decked out in a profusion of yellow and white daisies, like the sparkling field below the "Guide Map of the University of Peshawar." There were almost as many flowers as smartly dressed attendants, all in matching tan uniforms. Tariq had warned him that the hotel porters and waiters were really ISI agents. Still, nothing prepared Shaheed for the sight that confronted him. Like a white jinn from the clouds of Heaven was something—someone—far different from his vision.

In the eyes that Shaheed now looked into, he saw Grandmother: the same brown with faint flecks of green, perhaps even the pure green of his bride-to-be, Laila, and the jinn Helly. What was God now telling him? He felt the spirit of jinn secretly encircling him inside the lobby of the Serena Hotel in Pakistan's capital, inhabiting his core, or those of others, even inside an American, the eyes of his Grandmother-Laila-Helly entering his own eyes, unseen as the smokeless flame.

"MR. BATOOR," I said to him, "pleased to meet you." If ever I thought I could've met Osama bin Laden, this man would be it. The Pashtun jihadi was a dead ringer for his Saudi Arab hero.

"Ya' Allah," he muttered under his breath, staring down at the ground.

Hearing that name "Batoor" at first made him want to flee. Instead, Shaheed later told me, he had another "Grandmother moment" when life stopped. Strange that, in the infidel hotel lobby of Western decadence, Pakistani colonial opulence, home to all the foreigners who oppressed poor ordinary Muslims, in this shrine to exploitation and oppression, God would come to him. But the Almighty did. And He in all His infinite wisdom reflected Himself back from the American's—yes, the infidel's, the Jew's—eyes. God truly speaks to us in mysterious ways. But if you listen, you will hear. God had never failed him before. And besides, Shaheed thought, the Noble Qur'an tells us always to return a greeting with at least as good a greeting.

He extended his long, tan right hand, each finger perfectly portioned, each nail precisely trimmed and cleaned, the hands—just like his feet—always clean from *wudu* to Allah the Most Compassionate and Merciful.

He was touching a Jew, an American, an infidel, and I was touching a Muslim, a Pashtun, and jihadi dedicated to killing Americans and Jews.

"'Sometimes you love a thing, and it may be the worst for you—and sometimes you hate a thing, and it may be the best for you. Only God knows.' So spoke the All-Knowing in His Noble Book," he said.

"It is very nice to meet you too," I said.

He spoke in clear English, all those years first in Government Primary School and then Army Public School English class now flooding back.

But his eyes still did not meet mine.

I wanted a private place to talk and led him up a mirrored elevator to my room on the second floor. A hotel security guard ("another ISI agent," Shaheed later said) was at a desk outside.

When the door to Room 128 shut behind us, Shaheed still didn't say another word. He immediately took off his leather open-toed sandals. I wore sandals as well but kept them on.

Traditional Pakistani fabrics concealed American appliances and furniture, with an American-style king-size bed in the center. By the large sliding glass windows was a small seating area with three soft green chairs, which Shaheed arranged in the shape of an Islamic crescent. Sitting at the crescent's end, he stared out the window at the Margalla Hills.

I called on the phone to room service for tea. As soon as I hung up, Shaheed shot up from the window chair and grabbed the phone.

"ISI" was the first word he said. He unplugged the phone, and took it to the bathtub.

"ISI might put an insect in it," he said.

"Right, a bug," I said, trying not to laugh.

"I must make my *salat*."

He looked out the window again to figure the sun's angle and the direction of Mecca. He found the *kibla* sign on the wall and slowly, almost tenderly, lay down his prayer rug near the window. He then went to the bathroom for *wudu,* washing his hands, face, neck, and feet before returning to the room to pray.

He told me later that all he could do was pray. Pray in front of a Jewish American *kafir* whose eyes had the green of his grandmother's and the spirit of jinn inside. Or maybe it was the spirit of the devil Shaytan himself. Only God could answer him.

The tea arrived, carried by "an ISI agent dressed as a waiter." He carefully checked the cups, saucers, milk, and sugar for insects.

"Bugs," I corrected him again.

There were none.

We began to drink tea together. It was weak and too sweet.

On the soft chair by the window, Shaheed folded his white robes underneath and let his bare feet hang free above the green-checkered carpet. He felt the edge of his neatly trimmed mustache and ran his long fingers through his even longer, full beard.

Shaheed knew that God wanted him to talk. For during his prayer, he'd had a vision. A sharp pain attacked him between the eyes and in the back of the neck. He saw a silver dagger coming toward him, and then a great hand from the clouds above reaching down and grabbing the dagger away, saying, "Remember Ibrahim's true sacrifice." Of course, he remembered from the Holy Qur'an that God had spared Ibrahim's son Ishmael from the physical sacrifice. Ibrahim's faith alone was all the sacrifice that God ever wanted; now reciting God's words freely is what Allah Almighty asked from him, a testament to true faith—a faith that no American, no Jew, no infidel could ever shake.

We talked for hours, Shaheed chewing on his bitter-tasting *miswak* stick. He was a good Pashtun host, following the tribal honor code of Pashtunwali by showing unstinting hospitality and grace.

His English flowed surprisingly freely. While he'd never stopped listening to his father's English, he hadn't spoken a single word himself in at least ten years.

I finally retrieved the phone from the bathtub, plugged it into the jack, and ordered a late-afternoon lunch, delivered by "more ISI waiters."

I ate with silver utensils food made to be eaten with naan and hands. I thought I could even see Shaheed begin to smile, so I smiled at him. He just nodded back.

The talk continued, his life unfolding.

"Just call me Ken," I said.

He couldn't say my name out loud, for, as his grandmother had taught him (and he later told me), what if I really had inside me a jinn from the mountains instead? Yet as God continued to let his words come out in miraculously free English, he followed His will and let everything come out in turn: his dreams, the colonel's nuclear secrets, Grandmother's jinn and especially Helly, his secret white German shepherd jinn Buraq with its deep bark and invisible wings, Mr. Arab Teacher's infernal cough, the headmaster's "MAK-rod," defending the Prophet's holy name from the sinner Kashif's blasphemy, the rescue of his bride-to-be, Laila, her father's kohl Afghan eyes, his blood father's death, Nadeem's sacred Islamic crescent scar. Grandmother was for love, he said. He never had the chance to love Laila.

It was time for evening prayer; the sun was setting. "Do you want to pray with me?" Shaheed asked. But he didn't wait for an answer before he went to the bathroom to perform *wudu*.

As I sat next to him, Shaheed spoke the *salat,* bowing toward Mecca before Allah Almighty, as if he were in the mountains fighting jihad or welcoming mountain jinn from Grandmother's spirits. It didn't matter that I was old, could have been as old as his father, or that I was American, Jew, CIA, ISI, or only-God-knows-who, he prayed from his deepest heart.

"La ilaha illa Allah" . . . "There is no God but God," Shaheed prayed before Almighty Allah: this son of Abraham would witness a son of Muhammad.

After prayer, I suggested we have dinner in the lobby below. He wanted to wait until he could perform Isha, the fifth and last prayer of the day. But this time he didn't ask me to pray. "Be with me" was all he said before turning to the bathroom again to wash.

Cleansed in *wudu,* Shaheed prayed the final prayer of the day, as he had so often prayed, though never before in front of an American or Jew.

THE PAKISTANI RESTAURANT Zamana in the Serena's lobby was full, so we had to eat at the Lebanese restaurant Al Maghreb, next door.

Shaheed didn't want to eat until first the waiter and then the cook personally assured him that the food was halal. I felt like asking if the food was kosher too, but told Shaheed instead how much I loved Arab food. He let me order a variety of appetizers, or *mezze,* to sample before the tables turned and he was asking the questions.

"Tell me, why have the Americans attacked us? Why do the Americans continue to kill Muslims? Is your president really fighting a Crusade against us, as he says?"

This was the standard jihadi question I had faced many times, but never found an answer that convinced my jihadi inquisitors.

"Americans don't understand. Pakistanis don't understand either. We don't talk to each other the way we're talking now," I said in between mouthfuls of hummus, tabbouleh, and other *mezze* before asking "Have you ever had Lebanese food before?"

"Meat is all a good Pashtun eats," he said, laughing.

"The two of us here together struck me like déjà vu," I said, "like the dream I had this morning."

At the mention of a dream, Shaheed began to stare at me intently.

"It was the kind you have when you're waking up," I said, just then remembering my early-morning dream. "I couldn't stop eating hummus, like we're eating now. But I'd never eaten hummus like this. It was the best-tasting hummus I ever had. It was here at Al Maghreb, before it kept switching back to the Jerusalem Restaurant in Falls Church. The time was blurred, like a dream. And I couldn't tell who I was eating with either. All the different *mezze* kept coming: baba ghanouj, foul mudammas, kibbeh, vine leaves, shawerma, you get the idea, before—" I stopped.

Shaheed's mouth opened wide, as if to breathe in each word.

"Before the dream suddenly switched from the Jerusalem's non-stop food and I looked up to see a figure dressed in long white robes, riding a white horse, which flew up from where I was eating, inside the clouds over the Margalla Hills outside the Serena, except now it switched back again to the Jerusalem Restaurant in Virginia."

His eyes didn't blink.

"The Jerusalem Restaurant is my favorite spot for Arab food, though my daughter prefers Bacchus," I explained.

"You had the dream I've been waiting for, praying for every day," Shaheed said so softly I could barely hear him. "I live for that dream. For whoever sees Prophet Muhammad, peace be upon him, in a dream surely sees him and not the Devil. Whoever sees the Prophet atop the noble Buraq ascending to Jerusalem on his way to Heaven cannot see Shaytan. The Devil can never take the form of the Prophet, peace be upon him, in a true night dream." He paused, before asking, in a whisper, "Did you see his face?"

"No. Just what I told you," I said, not really sure what he was asking me or what I had unleashed.

"Are you sure you never saw his face?" Shaheed asked again. He later said he was testing me. For he had to know if I'd had "a true night dream."

"That's the whole dream," I replied, surprised I had remembered as much as I had.

"It is right," he now said. "Whenever the Holy Prophet, peace be upon him, appears in dreams to a non-Muslim, or someone like you who will one day be a true believer, his face cannot be seen," he continued to whisper, before almost shouting "*Allah-u-Akbar!* God is greater! Greater than man can imagine. In dreams, we see what we cannot know. This is the greater jihad to which God has called, the *Jihad al-Akbar.*"

Shaheed now answered with the words he heard from God, that every American, every Jew, can submit to Him in all His glory. If God had wanted us the same, He would have created us one. As the Noble Book says, He created different tribes and nations so that we can know one another and exceed the other in love of good deeds.

"For it also says in a sound Hadith that two Jews kissed the Holy Prophet's large feet," Shaheed concluded, "like your dream. Just another proof of the miracle Almighty Allah performed today, here in the Al Maghreb or Jerusalem Restaurant in the Serena Hotel, in a Jew's dream seeing the Prophet, peace be upon him, though not seeing his face—the sign of a true dream."

So much for being a Pashto-speaking jihadi; Shaheed was speaking now to the world in perfect English.

"If that is not a miracle of God talking, then tell me, what is? And so much for just being an American Jewish reporter like Daniel Pearl, if you could see in this dream—a dream that can only be from God."

He got up forcefully, taking my right hand. The waiters tried to stop me to sign the bill, but Shaheed kept leading me forward.

"Room 128," I had to shout past the Al Maghreb's door.

The elevator was waiting, and Shaheed led the way. With its small chandelier lights and bright mirrors reflecting behind us, the elevator quickly sped to the second floor. Not letting go, Shaheed ran down the green carpeted hall, past another hotel security guard, into Room 128.

Shaheed explained the vision he had. First, his blood father lying on the Khyber Hospital's deathbed, only he was buried among the nuclear codes of Chaklala, where "a man can be a man in Strategic Plans." Then Nadeem's Islamic crescent head, all alone, cut off by Tariq and his Taliban commander father to sacrifice at the altar of Taliban tribal honor. "No different from Pak army power." All trying to make God serve man. To die at their human hands—Taliban, Qaeda, Pakistan— is not to die a *shaheed*. He now knew what his dream meant. Only God could make him worthy of Grandmother's blessing name.

"As Allah commanded Ibrahim to save his son, so He commands the son to stop killing the fathers, even his own father," he then told me.

I didn't know how to respond. Instead, I just mindlessly repeated the first non sequitur to pop into my head, the flight attendant's peculiar instructions on Qatar Airways to Islamabad.

"Secure your own oxygen mask before helping your son or father," I said, beginning to laugh.

Shaheed started to laugh too. And before I knew it, we were laughing together.

"That's just like when Tariq's father first went to a Western hotel like the Serena or Marriott," he said. "Well, the famous Taliban mullah from Kandahar, who always wore the kohl black eyeliner, had never seen an American toilet before. He thought you just squatted on it, like his holes in the ground back in Afghanistan. So Tariq's father, the great Taliban commander who leads the fight against the Americans, who everyone must bow before and no one can ever question, now squatted on top of the toilet seat, pushing and pushing to get his, you know, out of his bottom. He pushed so hard that the toilet broke and the pieces went right up. He was bleeding so much the hotel had to rush him to hospital." Shaheed kept laughing. "I know it's not funny," he said, "but maybe God's sending us a message."

Shaheed had laughed so much he collapsed on a chair, before he could finally call me by name and tell me more, nothing now held back: all about the Fedayeen-e-Islam, his cell of Aimal, Tariq, Nadeem, and their followers. He told how the Serena was the symbol of domination and oppression, of the West over Pakistan, of Pakistan's secular rulers over Muslims.

"But the Marriott, that's the real temple. Not only of the Pakistani elites, the West, but America itself," he said.

"Good thing I'm not staying there," I said.

Shaheed put his right hand over his heart. "We're together now, Ken." He could at last say my name.

We were sitting next to each other on the soft green chairs, which Shaheed had arranged in the shape of an Islamic crescent by the window to the Margalla Hills and "the home of jinn." Shaheed had taken off his sandals, and I was barefoot too, sitting cross-legged. He had even left the window slightly open "for Helly."

Looking me in the eye, Shaheed held my right hand and said, "No more sacrifices. No more killing."

Reaching down, he took my right foot in his hand and, as with his grandmother, kissed my foot. "No more Daniel Pearls," he said.

THE NEXT DAY, Shaheed did not return to Peshawar. He didn't even call Aimal or Tariq. Instead, he took the train to Lahore.

It was the start of his greater jihad. God told him no less. He went to the headquarters of the Tablighi, the Islamic missionary movement. He knew it from university. He even had read and remembered the *Six Fundamentals* written by the Tablighi's founder, Maulana Aashiq Ilaahi. He now knew he must join. For Tablighi, the greater jihad is the struggle to change our human souls, submit fully to Islam, and love God in peace—that's what will change the world.

A week later, Shaheed finally called Aimal.

"We thought you were dead," Aimal said.

"Reborn, Aimal."

He asked Aimal to come to Islamabad—he would not return to Peshawar—and meet at the Serena.

The next day, Shaheed was waiting in the Serena lobby, just as he had waited some nine days ago for me. But Aimal didn't show. Finally Shaheed's cell rang from a number he had never seen before. It was Aimal.

"I'm at the Marriott, where you met that infidel American," Aimal said, nearly choking on the word. "That *kafir* Jew."

"Without Tariq?"

"Alone, I listened to you."

Shaheed went down from the mountain of the Serena. His life now felt so different from just nine days before. He caught a cab on the street below for the short ride to the Marriott. He didn't know why Aimal was there when they were supposed to meet at the Serena. Waiting in front of the security gate, Aimal barely greeted his former friend, could barely look him in the eye. He didn't even want to go through the lobby door.

It didn't matter. Shaheed couldn't wait to tell his friend what had changed his life forever. And he couldn't contain all that came gushing out from inside him—from God. He told Aimal almost everything: the first look, his vision, Ibrahim's true sacrifice, the end of blood, most of all, my dream in the restaurant. The truth was, Shaheed later told me, he'd felt freer to open his heart to me in a way that he couldn't dream of doing with another Pashtun. He finally finished by telling Aimal all about the Tablighi—that was the group they were looking for, not Tariq's Fedayeen-e-Islam.

But Aimal was dead silent.

"Come with me, Aimal."

Aimal looked down.

"Aimal, we can do this together."

"When you didn't call—" Aimal finally said, still looking down. He wouldn't explain. All he'd say was that the Fedayeen—"the Partisans Who Sacrifice Their Lives for Islam"—were "close."

Shaheed wished Aimal would just look him in the eye at least. But Aimal turned his back and walked to a waiting taxi.

"Aimal," he called.

Aimal never answered as he slammed the cab door behind him. "Close" was the last word he said.

During the next month, Shaheed called him a number of times, though Aimal would hardly say a word. Still he kept calling his cell. After Shaheed told him that he had now married a girl he had met through the Tablighi, Aimal never took his call again.

His new wife, Asma, had a degree in forestry, and she worked for the inspector general of forests, headquartered in Islamabad. So he joined her, working to save the mountains together.

Every weekend, Shaheed and Asma climbed the Margalla Hills with their new German shepherd puppy, Buraq. Shaheed could have been climbing with Grandmother's jinn, with Helly, even with me. "One day, you should come back, Ken, so we can all climb the mountains together," he told me over the phone.

Most of all, he devoted himself to none other than God Almighty, every day sharing Islam through *da'wah* (peaceful teaching) and *khurooj* (spiritual travels), renouncing the violence of the Taliban and Al Qaeda. He submitted to God as never before, waiting for the true dream, working with all the faith of his heart for the Greater Jihad of Peace—the Jihad of Love—he had found through God that hot June evening in the Serena Hotel, as if he had dreamed it himself some two months before.

He'd be "Secret Shaheed" no more.

And at the end of those two and a half months, the worst suicide bombing attack in Pakistan's history struck the Marriott Hotel in Islamabad.

Fifty-three people were killed and more than 266 wounded. The BBC said that it was "a message sent from hell." CNN quoted the Pakistani interior minister, who said it was the "biggest attack in Pakistan" in seven years. Called "Pakistan's 9/11," Muhammad Sultan, a hotel employee, cried out, "It is like the world was finished."

The message that came over the BBC from a previously unknown Taliban group, the Fedayeen-e-Islam, said that "the purpose of the Marriott attack was to kick the 'American crusaders' out of Pakistan."

EIGHT MONTHS LATER, I received the following e-mail:

Dear Ken:

Salaam. I have great blessings for u. I am now a father. A son. It's Mubarak. It's our future of love.

I pray for ur success in this life along with the success of ur eternal life.

Ur Shaheed to Only Allah the Most High.

6

KAMAL: HEIR TO THE JIHADI THRONE AND FORTUNE

UNLIKE CHRISTIANITY—notably Catholicism—Islam does not have a clerical hierarchy. This is particularly true of Sunni Islam, which is practiced by close to 90 percent of the world's Muslims and followed by Al Qaeda and the Taliban. The closest Sunni Islam comes to clerical authority resides in the Wahhab family of Saudi Arabia. Kamal is a Wahhab heir.

Kamal is a man who by birthright alone is afforded profound respect among many devout Muslims. If he were to side with Al Qaeda and radical Islamist groups, their credibility among many Muslims would soar. He is also a person with vast financial resources—significantly more than bin Laden ever had. Donors in Saudi Arabia continue to provide most of the funding to Al Qaeda, the Taliban, and other Islamist radical groups. Our future would be bleak if Kamal devoted his resources, as many in Saudi Arabia do, to fund extremist Islamists and terrorism.

Kamal stands at the fault line between the radical, Al Qaeda interpretation of his faith, and a more tolerant version, which could be revolutionary in the Muslim world. The path Kamal chooses will help determine the future of Islam. But Kamal is not the leader—in his behavior, language, beliefs, or sense of humor—that you might expect.

I met Kamal through his friend Jamil, another jihadi inmate patiently waiting to be rehabilitated at the Saudi Ministry of Interior (MOI) Care Center near Riyadh.

Jamil was twenty-three, slight and thin, his face beardless. He had been a student at Al Imam Muhammad ibn Saud Islamic University, or Imam U. for short, Riyadh's famous Islamic university. He was from Asir, the province in the far south of Saudi Arabia and home of many of the Saudi "muscle" hijackers on 9/11.

Jamil had served three years, four months, two weeks, four days, and seven hours in jail (I didn't ask how many minutes). He had condemned a friend for "his Takfiri ideology" of wanting to fight the infidels in Europe or America. "These are not Muslim lands under attack like Iraq," which Jamil thought gives rise to "the only accepted Qur'anic definition of a real jihad." But after his friend was arrested, he turned Jamil in to the MOI as well. During the interview, I asked Jamil about Ahmad, Abby, Kamal, and other jihadis held at the Care Center prison. While acknowledging that he knew them, he didn't offer any details.

At the end of the interview, Jamil followed me to the bathroom. When I was washing my hands, he thanked me, first in Arabic and then English. As I reached for the paper towels, Jamil reached as well. Grasping my hand, he surreptitiously slipped a piece of torn paper in my palm before whispering in English, "You call my friend Kamal."

As we finished drying our hands, he told me that Kamal was his "special friend" who had "graduated" from the Care Center and now lived in Riyadh.

That night when I called Kamal, I had no idea what to expect. Of course, I knew that he was a friend of Jamil from the Saudi prison for reforming jihadi militants. I knew that Abby and Kamal had been friends at the Care Center too.

What Abby had told me was intriguing. Describing Kamal, he said, "Kamal has a white face"—the highest jihadi compliment—"the light of faith shining through. He'll be our next Osama, the leader of our new jihad."

Abby saw in Kamal someone blessed by God: "Kamal has the

same long black eyelashes and black eyes tinged with red as Prophet Muhammad, peace be upon him," he said.

Unlike the other Saudis you've read about, I met Kamal through unofficial channels. I never even told my MOI hosts about him. It turned out I didn't have to. Kamal came from a family as powerful in Saudi Arabia as the MOI prince who had first invited me.

I came to know Kamal well over three years. During that time, he took me behind the closed walls of the kingdom so I could see for myself—inside the palaces of the royal family, which few Americans have seen firsthand. He also revealed secrets that he'd never share with fellow Saudis and, more particularly, his own family.

Yes, Kamal is a member of Saudi Arabia's ruling aristocracy. And, like bin Laden, heir to an unimaginable fortune. But he is not simply from the proper royal family. Rather, he hails from its elite religious branch—the family of the "Sheikh of Islam."

Most outsiders mistakenly believe there is only one royal family in Saudi Arabia. While the country takes its name from the ruling Al Saud, perhaps no less important are the descendents of Sheikh Muhammad ibn Abd al-Wahhab—called the Al al-Sheikh, or Family (or House) of the Sheikh—who gave the country its interpretation of Islam. For many in the Arabian Peninsula, the bloodlines of the Sheikh of Islam make them Saudi Arabia's true "first family"—the greatest religious family not only in Saudi Arabia but in all of Islam. In fact, even though the Al Sheikh family was thoroughly intermarried with the ruling Al Saud family, they were the ones who gave the royals invaluable religious legitimacy. Without the Islamic sanction afforded by the descendants of Wahhab, the Saudi royal family could easily become yet another domino in the failed line of so many ossified Middle East monarchies and brittle autocrats waiting to fall. From their exalted holy position, the Al Sheikh stood above mere tribal royalty and disdained any earthly titles such as Prince or His Highness. Their authority was only from God. Simply to be called a Sheikh from the Family of the Sheikh was enough to convey their unique and revered place. It is, after all, by following in the path of their sacred faith that Osama bin Laden and so many others turned to jihad.

Kamal Abd al-Rahman ibn Hasan ibn Abdullah Al al-Sheikh was heir to jihad as none other. Among all men, his bloodline gave him the right to render *tawheed* and the meaning of Islam. His illustrious forefather was the most important religious teacher since the Prophet Muhammad. A *sheikh* is a revered Islamic teacher. Kamal was the great-great-great-great-great grandson of the Sheikh himself.

More: Kamal was a direct descendant of the Shiekh's grandson and one of Osama bin Laden's favorite thinkers and role models. Bin Laden instructed all Muslims to read Kamal's ancestor's "most important book," *The Victory of the Glorious*. Kamal even bore its author's name.

Kamal is a leader many Islamist radicals would follow, particularly those who, like bin Laden, adhere to the Wahhabi creed. In a culture that reveres family ancestry, Kamal's lineage as the direct descendant of Wahhab gives him a commanding influence over the future of jihad. As Abby told me, Kamal could be "the next Osama."

LESS THAN TWO days after Kamal and I first talked, a late-model, dark green BMW X5 was waiting for me in front of Riyadh's Inter-Continental Hotel, with a Bangladeshi driver in tow. Kamal, in flowing white *thobe* and free white and red checkered headdress unsecured by the ubiquitous black *igal* cord, was sprawled, almost prone, over the tan leather seats.

As the hotel porter opened the green BMW's door, Kamal rose from the backseat. His loose robes fluttering as if a flag caught by the wind, he greeted me with a soft handshake. Widely grinning, he returned to the rear seat, moving over to sit behind the driver. Yet, instead of sitting forward, he faced me, his back against the window and his legs stretched over the leather seat. I had long since discovered that the Saudi concept of personal space was far different from our Western sense.

Without a word, we left the circular driveway of the hotel where I was staying. We drove around past its florist shop, gym, and mosque, to one side, and out the security gate, with the massive inverted pyramid of the MOI headquarters directly across the street. Just a couple blocks away, the driver eased the "newest X5 from Muhammad Yousuf Naghi Motors," he said, onto of one Riyadh's many teeming superhighways.

As the BMW SUV accelerated, Kamal, still quiet, wouldn't stop smiling. I had no clue what Arab or Muslim custom this represented (or whether it was simply more of his unorthodox behavior), but willing myself not to be a Western snob, I weakly smiled at him in turn. Thankfully, the Bangladeshi driver, "from Chittagong," he kept saying, didn't floor the late-model BMW at more than 100 miles per hour—something I continually dreaded from my MOI escorts. But as we passed 80, which I gathered was a leisurely pace for latter-day Bedouins, my smile quickly faded.

Speeding through Riyadh's beltways, we soon left the modern concrete and shining steel and glass and, in less than thirty minutes, entered a deep valley, where reddish tan cliffs rose dramatically around us. It reminded me of the breathtaking canyons in Sedona, Arizona.

Kamal now explained that by the beginning of the twenty-first century, one of the few remaining unspoiled areas around Riyadh, the booming Saudi capital of some five million, was the sandstone canyons of the Wadi Hanifah. Kamal's father, Minister Sheikh Abdullah, and a select few of some of the most important Saudi princes, decided to partake of the Wadi Hanifah's stunning natural beauty and build grandiose royal palaces "to rival nature's grandeur," Kamal said. He spoke fluent English too.

While I looked upward at the splashy Disney castles on the great cliffs that belonged to his royal cousins, Kamal told me how his father had built their home at the bottom of the canyon instead, in the thick palms of an ancient date farm.

"Not far from here, the soldiers of God, under the command of Khalid and following the first Companion of the Prophet, Abu Bakr, peace be upon him, defeated the first false prophet, Musaylimah the Liar. Now we must defeat the false prophets again," Kamal said. "Slay the liars of today."

Whether from the speeding BMW, having downed way too much *gahwa* waiting in the hotel lobby, or the jarring realization that I was in the hands of a man who had been imprisoned for his radical activities, I felt carsick.

We suddenly turned off the canyon's narrow, freshly paved asphalt road. The dusty palm trees surrounded us in an ocean of pale green. On either side of the even smaller dirt road, all I could see was the unending grove of date palms, until a rough-hewn sandstone series of large, single-story houses suddenly emerged.

Before he led me inside, Kamal gave me precise instructions on how to address his more than ninety-year-old father (Saudis of his father's generation didn't keep track of their exact age). Sheikh Abdullah was not only one of the most powerful members of the ruling Saudi aristocracy but had been one of the kingdom's most conservative and important clerical officials as well.

"Just say *'Inshallah'* to everything," Kamal instructed.

I nodded, hanging on each of his words, and determined again not to be the Ugly American insensitive to cultural differences.

"*'Inshallah,'* you got it, Kenny?" Kamal said. He took to calling me the nickname I hadn't used in thirty-five years, since I'd first left for college.

"Nothing but *'Inshallah,'*" he commanded.

I nodded again, having already heard the word repeated after almost every phrase or sentence spoken in Saudi Arabia.

"Whether the old man says all Christians should have their hoods cut off and the Jews their balls, you say?"

"*Inshallah,*" I repeated.

"In God's Hands," Kamal continued. "Or whether he says the secret to Islam is set down by my noble forefather in the holy *Victory of the Glorious*, before which even the basest infidel would drop to his knees, you say?"

"*Inshallah.*"

"Very good, Kenny," Kamal said, smiling once again.

"Have you read the Uncreated Word of Allah Almighty?" he asked.

"*Inshallah*," I responded.

"Do you believe in Jesus?"

"*Inshallah*."

"Will you become a Muslim?"

"*Inshallah*."

"Are you a Jew?"

"*Inshallah*."

"Ha! Gotcha!" Kamal started laughing. "Trick question."

"Well, what do I say?" I asked, not sure if he was joking again.

"Who's on first?" Kamal said.

"What's the guy's name on first base?"

"No, who's on first."

And this was the heir to the most important clerical family in Islam. More, a son of the ruling elite once jailed at the Care Center for his extremism.

KAMAL NOW LED me inside.

The son kissed his father, who was easily old enough to be his grandfather, on his cheeks, with the greetings of the Bedouins.

"*Assalaamu 'Alaykum wa Rahmatullahi wa Barakatuh*," the old Sheikh said to me in formal greeting.

"*Wa-alaykum assalaam*," I answered, defying Kamal's strict instructions to say only "*Inshallah*."

Kamal had explained that what his father enjoyed the most was the great Bedouin-style framed black-hair "tent" in Nejdi design he had set up inside the palace walls. The traditional "house of hair" was even made with the customary undyed black goat wool. Though to call it a "tent" would be a misnomer. It had the feel of a tent, with tented walls, red and black Arabian carpets covering the floors, and great white draping ceilings, as if a thousand Saudi *thobe*s were hung from the rafters. It was a twenty-first-century, fully air-conditioned, wired (telephones, Internet, TV, etc.) replica of a Bedouin king's desert tent, of the kind his exalted ancestor Sheikh Wahhab might have visited— at least in his dreams.

Here the former Minister Sheikh Abdullah would receive his grown boys (Kamal, the youngest, was already in his mid-twenties) in *majlis,* a traditional gathering where Bedouin supplicants sit around the edges, propped up on golden-thread pillows.

And here Kamal took me to meet his father as well.

While there was no disguising that I was an American, I wondered what the aged sheikh would've thought if he knew his son had brought a Jew inside his "place of special sitting." I had often heard anti-Jewish sentiments in the kingdom, which were confirmed by my nonprofit group's public opinion survey that showed nine out of every ten Saudis had an unfavorable opinion of Jews. Yet I had also come to learn the boundless warmth of traditional Arab hospitality, from strong coffee, sweet tea, and overflowing dates to an extravagant meal and the inevitable after-dinner invitation to spend the night. I just wasn't sure which tradition—magnanimous welcome and acceptance or unbridled hatred and contempt for the American Jewish usurper— would prove more powerful.

Kamal sat on a gold-and-red pillow along the edge of the room. Like Shaheed, his loose-fitting *thobe* and informal headdress without the more traditional *igal* cord showed his Salafi beliefs. I sat right next to him. The entire faux-tented *majlis* was soaked in sandalwood incense from an ancient Wahhabi *mabakhir.* His father sat in the seat of honor, a kind of cushion chair and the only one with a back to it.

Sheikh Minister Abdullah said nothing. After pouring the first cup of the specially brewed *gahwa,* a tall, thin Sudanese servant stood stoically at attention. Of course, Sheikh Abdullah drank first, from the cup passed down from "the Original Sheikh." Kamal followed in ritual ceremony, before translating his father's Arabic speech, which flowed slowly and at considerable length.

In a three-hundred-year-old *dallah* that Abdullah said had also belonged to Sheikh Wahhab himself, *gahwa* was brewed in the ancient way over an open flame by an old Yemeni master. Only the finest masters know how, and only those privileged to serve descendants of the noblest lineage are imparted the right of knowing the secret proportion of coffee beans, cardamom seeds, and pinch of saffron. And Minister Abdullah offered his prized *gahwa* only in cups said to be passed down from no less than the legendary Sheikh too.

The *gahwaji,* who served the *gahwa* in special dress, were all Sudanese servants and descendants of slaves freed by Sheikh Abdullah's cousin King Faisal in 1962. The most important person in the room was always served first, which meant Minister Sheikh Abdullah, unless it was the time when the king himself, the Custodian of the Two Holy Places, partook of the famed Wahhabi *gahwa* as his cousin's honored guest.

Upholding Bedouin tradition, the unique Wahhabi china cups were only half filled, while the *gahwaji* patiently stood without moving a muscle waiting to refill, and only an odd number of cups—one, three, or five—was ever offered. Never sweetened, *gahwa* had to be served with only the finest fresh dates, usually the noble Sukkary from Buraydah. The *gahwa* was followed by honeyed sweet tea from a three-hundred-year-old Wahhabi teapot, delivered in Wahhabi cups by more Sudanese sons of slaves. Even Abdullah's *mabakhir* for his charcoal sandalwood *oud* was handed down from the fabled Sheikh, he told every guest, and now apparently, me.

During his father's perpetual talk, Kamal would occasionally wink at me and smile. He was indeed striking, but not, at least to me, as Abby had described him, in some kind of "God-blessed" fashion. Kamal was Hollywood handsome instead, almost a dead ringer for an Arabian Tom Cruise—only taller with a beard and full Saudi dress, of course.

While his father went on, Kamal began to eat the Sukkary dates, showily sucking off the yellow flesh before mouthing each pit and rolling it under his cheek. Turning away from his father and toward me, with date pit firmly planted underneath his upper lip, Kamal expertly mimicked a monkey. His monkey impression complete, he'd suddenly spit out the sucked-over pit at full force like Ahmad and Grandfather al-Shayea, direct into the waiting brass spittoon—only this one was "naturally" a Wahhabi spittoon, he said, before whispering to me: "Naturally—wasn't he the pitcher?"

"What's on second?" I replied.

"You Americans have Abbott and Costello. Only God's soldiers play on our team."

It could never be said of Minister Abdullah, Kamal now continued his translation, that the Wahhab heir failed to strictly observe the traditions of the Nejd. First, coffee made in the most traditional family fashion, followed by dates, whose cultivation over nearly five thousand years helped give Riyadh ("Gardens") its name. Riyadh was not only the capital of modern Saudi Arabia, he explained, it was the center of Arabia and the heart of the Nejd, birthplace of the Land of the Two Holy Places' two most important families—the Al Saud and the Al al-Sheikh. And the Al al-Sheikh was one of only two families with whom Al Saud royals could marry ("Forget about me marrying one of those porky Al Sauds," Kamal said as an aside in English. "No Lou Costello in *abaya* drag for me"). In fact, ever since Muhammad ibn Wahhab joined with Muhammad ibn Saud in the mid-eighteenth century, this partnership has determined not only both families' fortunes but those of the Arabian Peninsula— and indeed the Muslim world as well. "The oil helped too," Kamal added.

Who else, most importantly, could lay claim to drink from the very cup of the Original Sheikh himself? This was a singular blessing from Allah Almighty in the entire kingdom, an exalted privilege that always impressed every guest—even the times when the Custodian of the Two Holy Places, the king, graced Sheikh Abdullah's ceremonial *majlis* tent. Kamal breathed deeply, as if coming up for air. "Praise God! At last, time for *Isha salat,*" he said.

In a remarkable display, Kamal led the night prayer, joined by not only his aged, slow-moving father but the Bangladeshi driver from Chittagong and the Sudanese *gahwaji,* son of a Saudi slave.

In Isha prayer, they were all equal, bowing to Mecca in the Land of the Holy Prophet himself.

I was relieved that the feast would now follow, as my head was spinning from the strong incense, nonstop coffee, or eating only dates since my lunch almost eight hours before. We all washed together, master, son, servants, and American Jewish guest, in the full bathroom with four toilets and seven sinks that was at the end of the faux-tented building, before being served by even more servants.

As befit a high-ranking member of the Saudi aristocracy, Sheikh Abdullah had a whole army of servants, numbering between fifty and sixty, many of whom I now met. Their function depended on their country of origin, Kamal explained. Cooks were from Lebanon and Syria (the coffee master from Yemen), waiters from Pakistan, drivers from Bangladesh, manservants descendants of the family's slaves from the Sudan, gardeners from Sri Lanka, nannies from Indonesia, cleaning maids from the Philippines, and the servants' manager was a Palestinian.

I waited for the Lebanese *mezze* I'd come to love. Instead, the meal was a cornucopia of traditional Arabian treats I'd never tasted before.

"We'll have Lebanese tomorrow," Kamal said. I couldn't tell whether he was joking again. I felt the line between when he was sarcastic and joking and when piously, even deadly, serious to be precariously thin. And I was constantly on guard not to cross it.

Sitting on the stiff pillows, we ate with our hands in solemn silence, though Kamal would occasionally flash his characteristic shit-eating grin.

After dinner, Kamal led me to his room in one of the outlying homes. "I have two bedrooms," Kamal said. "One where my heart sleeps in the servants' wing and one for my father in the main house."

I had no clue what Kamal meant, though it was hard to believe that this vast bedroom had ever been intended for a servant, equipped with all the latest Western technology (widescreen satellite TV, DVD player, computer, and Internet). Kamal loved American TV shows, especially the classic "funnies," and showed me his vast bootleg collection of DVDs, from *I Love Lucy* and *The Honeymooners* to *Seinfeld* and *The Simpsons*—and "naturally," Abbott and Costello's "Who's on First?"

Most of all, of course, Kamal showed me his two Holy Qur'ans (the well-worn Book that he held and recited from for hours daily and the cherished, antique Book passed down from his pious ancestors).

Putting the Wahhabi Book back in its protected place, he sat on the queen-size bed, which was almost flush with the floor. And as suddenly as Kamal had been deeply reverent, I could see him now winking.

"*Alf Leyla, wa Leyla,*" he said. "Your own personal Umm Kalsoum, but don't look at me to sing." He laughed. "*A Thousand and One Nights* ... the moon and stars will keep us awake all night. Oh, Kenny, spirited away in deepest dark Arabia, you'll be the fabled King Shahrayar and I'll be your muse Shahrazad," he now said, with the wide smile that wouldn't stop, "only the twenty-first-century version."

True to his word, he began his story that very night, the two of us together in his room. "Just like with my Indonesian mom," he said.

THOUGH KAMAL BORE a glorious birthright to lead the faith, his father Abdullah's faith had changed because of 230 riyals, or just $50. That's all the money Kamal's grandfather had when he died. But on his deathbed, the old sheikh had also left Abdullah a vision: "Allah the Most Beneficent and Most Generous will use you to be fruitful in spirit and wealth."

Abdullah had every chance to follow the family legacy and make good on his father's vision, at least in one respect. As a latter-day twentieth-century Al al-Sheikh, the path Abdullah chose was to rise through the kingdom's religious, educational, and judicial establishment, eventually holding the highest positions in key state ministries. As with so many members of the interlocking and intermarried Al Saud and Al al-Sheikh families, the oil booms, with their resulting extravagant ministry salaries and royal budgets—along with secret commissions on government contracts—allowed Abdullah to live a most comfortable lifestyle. In short, he became a billionaire and lived to fulfill at least part of the deathbed vision of his pious father (though, unlike other royals, Abdullah kept his unaccountable billions hidden in dollars and euros in Viennese rather than Swiss banks).

"The Viennese got their coffee from the Arabs," Kamal said, smiling.

Sheikh Abdullah even had the features of his cousin, the great King Faisal, whose mother was a daughter of the Al al-Sheikh family as well. Thin and severe-looking, Abdullah had the strong hooked nose and hooded eyes of an Arabian falcon. And unlike his other brothers, who followed their father's strict clerical path, Abdullah was honored to call himself a descendant of Wahhab. His brothers were so deeply immersed in Wahhabi thought and practice they followed their ancestor's prescriptions exactly and wouldn't even call themselves Wahhab but *muwahhidun* ("Unitarians" or "unifiers of Islamic practice").

Instead, Abdullah bore his famous Wahhabi birthright and its alliance with the Saud royal family proudly, helping him rise in power and fortune. And while in profile he resembled his cousin King Faisal, in spirit Abdullah resembled the legendary King Abdul Aziz al-Saud, who had twenty-two wives and hundreds of concubines. While Abdullah never quite enjoyed the fabled twenty-two wives, he did marry frequently, but always made certain never to have more than the religiously sanctioned four at one time.

Ya'Allah, Abdullah had to be at least seventy when he had his final, "summer" marriage. His new wife was a blue-eyed Syrian woman procured with the help of ministry contacts. Abdullah and his "summer bride" (young enough to be his granddaughter) spent ten days together in Paris and Vienna. It was the Sheikh's last foreign fling. Shopping at Printemps, Galeries Lafayette, Swarovski, and God knows where by day, sleeping at Le Meurice and Hotel Sacher by night, and nine months later greeting his final son, Kamal.

But the mother was simply too young and pretty and Abdullah's other wives too old and greedy to allow her to settle permanently into the royal homestead. After Kamal was born, Minister Abdullah never spoke her name again.

SECRETS HIDE BEHIND walls. And this "summer marriage" for the aging minister sheikh was among the least of them.

In typical Saudi royal fashion, Abdullah's north Riyadh palace was completely hidden behind massive thirty-foot-high desert tan walls (he didn't move to the Wadi Hanifah palace until the beginning of this century). Unlike other royals, who maintained vast summer palaces in Taif or Jeddah (of course, he had a small one in Jeddah so he could quickly travel to Mecca during Ramadan), Abdullah favored his home territory of Riyadh and lavished all his care on his Nejd heartland palace. More than a palace, it was a series of palaces, with each of the last wives holding sway over her own sumptuous turf. True to his wandering Bedouin roots, Abdullah migrated to every one of the separate homes in his family compound to sleep.

Yet by the time little Kamal was born, he was far too removed in age from his siblings to partake in any of the royal honors. Not that his father didn't care. He did everything possible to make sure his last son had the best care, best tutors, best education. Having children perpetuates bloodlines. And Minister Abdullah was from the Al al-Sheikh, a bloodline he did everything possible to glorify. For a Saudi of his noble lineage, having children—more exactly, sons—had nothing to do with Western concepts of paternal bonding and everything to do with the "power of blood."

Of course, none of the sheikh's remaining wifely matriarchs, all well past their fifties and the time of child rearing, wanted anything to do with this suckling babe either. They were more interested in shopping in Riyadh's booming malls—or those of Jeddah, Dubai, Paris, Vienna, or London.

Minister Abdullah had a whole army of servants to take care of the home front. And the servants' quarters were vast enough to match a middle-class Saudi's entire house. So baby Kamal was sent to the servants' wing, a completely separate house on the palace grounds, where he lived his entire childhood, rarely seeing his father and never meeting his mother.

While Kamal was also sent to the very best schools in Riyadh, his father's servants had the responsibility for educating him as well. Nothing was too good for the minister's last son and direct descendant of Wahhab. The tutor servants of little Kamal were a veritable League of Islamic Nations: a noted Egyptian scholar for Classical Arabic and the Holy Qur'an, a Moroccan Olympics contender for horseback riding and falconry, an Iraqi professor from Baghdad for Math, a Lebanese businessman for accounting, an Algerian artist for Arabic calligraphy, and a single Saudi, born and raised in Portland, Maine, through Middlebury College and a master's from Georgetown, who sounded exactly like an American—for English, what else?

And a brigade of servants raised him: a Bangladeshi driver, a Syrian chef (the Lebanese was for the main houses), a Filipino maid for laundry and cleaning, and, towering above them, a formidable and alluring Indonesian woman, Indah, whose sole job was to mother him. Every boy needs a mother.

KAMAL DIDN'T GROW up in the culture of Saudi Arabia alone. He wasn't raised only as a child of Islam's most holy places, sanctified in their most Islamic purity by his very own Wahhabi family. You'd never know it from the outside. Yet the true nature of every family is often the hidden one.

As a boy, Kamal always believed that the famous Indonesian Gunung Merapi, or Mountain of Fire, was in the middle of the Saudi desert. Indah Mother told him all about the fabled volcano, the most magical place on God's blue earth, where heroes would see their fondest wish granted. Kamal's father spent all his free time away camping in the Saudi desert. Little Kamal simply put the two together and wished Mount Merapi would make his dreams come true too.

Until he was six, Kamal thought that Indah was his real mother. You could even say that Bahasa Indonesia was his mother tongue, though Indah was only supposed to speak to him in English. Indah Dharmawan was indeed what anyone would want in a mother. The Maid Agent in Jakarta, Mas Ismail Huda Wiranto, knew she'd fetch a handsome referral fee, and she was, in fact, claimed by the first royal palace in Riyadh where the Maid Agent peddled her.

As Minister Abdullah and the Al al-Sheikh were from the center of the Arabian Peninsula, so Indah Mother came from the heart of the Indonesian archipelago, the island of Java and its very center in the world's largest Muslim country: the royal region of Yogyakarta. Tall for an Indonesian woman at almost five feet, eleven inches, Indah's eyes were completely dark brown, so much so that the iris melted into the pupil, indistinguishable one from the other unless you looked quite closely. And you might, simply because Indah Mother often seemed to be crying.

Traditions can deceive. Despite her hard life, Indah wasn't crying. Her eyes welled up with tears every time she smiled, and in Indonesian culture, you smile at everything. In a custom that makes tourists call them "friendly," an Indonesian smiles when greeting, bargaining, agreeing, or arguing—it doesn't matter.

You could never tell whether Indah Mother was laughing or crying or both.

And in nearly every sentence, she had the strange habit of continually repeating the Bahasa Indonesia word *kenapa*. The word had the chameleon qualities of the jungle or desert, taking on the character of its background. Depending on the context, *kenapa* can mean, in formal Bahasa, "Why?" Yet *kenapa* in Indonesian slang can also mean "Say what?" or, in Indah's words, "What? Come again?" Since the Indonesian jungle had been brought to the Arabian Desert (and her job required her to speak in English), Indah Mother simply translated *kenapa* as *"Why what come again"* to embrace every possible meaning all at once. So that even though Indah Mother was a seer, she always seemed to question life—or to be hard of hearing.

In truth, when Indah Mother read Kamal bedtime stories, she spoke out as loudly as Bilal ibn Rabah, Islam's first muezzin, whose ringing *adhan* (call to prayer) inspired the Chosen One himself.

The stories were their own call to prayer. For nearly every servant in the entire wing could hear Indah Mother each night crank up the volume and recite, in her blaring radio voice, from *The Bobbsey Twins, Where the Wild Things Are, A Thousand and One Nights, Babar the Elephant, Tintin, Emil and the Detectives, The Little Prince*—all for little princely Kamal, whose full name also meant "perfecting perfection in the blessed line of the Al al-Sheikh."

Most of all, Kamal heard Indah's own tales—the story of her life. How could he not hear: "God gave me ears, Indah Mother!"

"On the wings of fire, Almighty Allah has shown," Indah shouted to Kamal as only a true seer could. "Others condemn us, but Allah has marked us as different. '*Why what come again*!' Allah wrote it in a *sawur* across the night sky."

Even as a little boy, Kamal knew he was different. He knew others would not love him, maybe curse him. But he knew that Allah the Most Compassionate had put him on Earth to lead the faith and change the world. He knew it not just because he was a Wahhab descendant but because Indah Mother told him so.

"*WHY WHAT COME AGAIN*???!!!" Kamal now shouted at me, laughing, before just as suddenly turning completely serious:

"*La ilaha illa Allah*" (There is no God but God)," he said.

I wasn't sure whether Kamal was condemning Indah's traditional beliefs or embracing them, as he had her. The center of conflict in the Muslim world was as much among Muslims themselves as with America and the West. Islam has customarily been practiced by the overwhelming majority of the world's Muslims (in Indonesia, Pakistan, India, and elsewhere) by adapting traditional pre-Islamic beliefs to the Arabian import in a syncretic faith. This stands in conflict with the strict, pure Islam epitomized by Kamal's own Wahhab family. Kamal's story—and that of his Indah Mother—embodied this struggle, which was the real war gripping Muslims for "hearts and minds," more than America's "war on terror."

BUT KAMAL LEARNED when still a young boy, he told me, that he wasn't different alone. The story of Indah's life marked her, as well as her father, Luwarso, as "different" too.

Father Luwarso actually thought Indah could go to university. But the only way he could pay was to sell the family land in Cangkringan, their village near Mount Merapi. The year he sold the land, Indah started at Gadjah Mada University. No one was prouder than Father Luwarso.

Except that his family knew it could only be *guna-guna*—the mystical spell of pre-Islamic Indonesian tradition. There was no other reason to sell the family land. Under the shadow of Merapi, blessed by the blood of their ancestors, soon to be a golf course and hotel for *bule* unbelievers, all for the worthless whim of sending a girl to university—a girl!

Indah completed her first year at Gadjah Mada University, excelling in every course, particularly English and literature. She finished with better grades than any of her brothers. But her father had to be proud all alone. No one in the village would talk to him because they were scared they would catch his *guna-guna*.

"Even my mother left him like everyone else," Indah Mother said.

"Don't ever leave me," Kamal told her.

"I will never leave you, Kecil Kamal (little dear Kamal), *why what come again*!" She announced to the world, as if broadcast from Riyadh's tallest minaret.

As time went on, Kamal thought the talismanic words took over more of Indah Mother's stereo loudspeaker sentences.

Father Luwarso soon moved into the royal city of Yogyakarta, not far from Gadjah Mada, to live with Indah, the only one of his children to accept him. But the *guna-guna* followed. At the National Family Planning Coordinating Board, none of his coworkers would talk to him. They didn't want to catch his curse. Then his boss stopped talking to him too and had to fire him because he wasn't following instructions.

Besides Indah, there was only one who still believed in him. His name was Widi, a distant cousin.

Widi went back to the ways of the Prophet. *Guna-guna* was just Indonesian folklore, unworthy of true Muslims, he thought. If anyone had the power to break the legacy of her father's *guna-guna,* it would be this proud son of the fundamentalist Muslim Brothers.

But Widi came too late. When Luwarso poured a glass of water and the bottom fell out, everyone knew it was the sign of drowning. Three days later, Luwarso was found floating in the Progo River, killed by *guna-guna*.

Indah had almost completed her third year at university. Her brothers took what was left of the money, and she had to quit university forever.

Indah was the only girl the *dukun* (a traditional Indonesian holy man) had ever seen who didn't need the *susuk* (a thin gold needle the *dukun* implants under a woman's skin with a blessing from the Qur'an to make her sexually desirable). But no one would marry the daughter of someone carrying the *guna-guna*.

BY THE TIME Kamal turned eleven years old, he had already memorized three-quarters of the Holy Qur'an. His goal was to learn by heart all of the Holy Book when he became twelve, just like his forefather the Original Sheikh. Kamal was a precocious boy, which made him annoying.

"That's enough for now, Kecil Kamal," Indah said the night she told of her father's death.

"Why what come again!" Kamal shouted as loudly as he could. "I've memorized most of the Book! You're not going to tell what happened next?"

"Remember Widi?" Indah began to the boy's insistent pleas.

Widi had always wondered if he were just a stepson. When he was eight years old, he asked his father for schoolbooks, like his older brothers. His father, a hotel chambermaid, said he didn't have the money. Then Widi asked for real shoes, not sandals. "Your brothers need the shoes," his father said. At twelve, Widi ran away from home.

"I would never run away," Kamal said.

"You're loved," Indah said.

"I know *you* love me," Kamal said.

"Your father does too. He may not show it, but I know he is very proud of you, not like Widi's father," Indah said.

Widi grew up on the streets and didn't have enough money to pay even the small entrance fee for the government school. He started living the street life of a *pedagang asongan:* washing car windows, shoplifting shoes, collecting bus tickets, sleeping on the streets or in the abandoned ruins of the Royal Baths. Then he started to go to the library.

Oh, Widi was very diligent about going to the library! First, he'd read every book he could. Like a good student, he collected as many books as possible, before stealing and selling them on the streets to make enough to get by.

One book in particular that Widi stole changed his life. A book with great drawings became his salvation: *Tintin in America*. Tintin was his very own holy book that he always kept it with him. Wherever he lived on the streets, Tintin was his constant companion. It was the only thing he held on to no matter what. While he couldn't read the English, the pictures in the book showed him that if he continued his life of petty street crime, he'd be caught and sent to jail—or worse, be killed on the streets like a dog, with no one even to claim his body.

Tintin led Widi to the Muslim Brothers. Widi could finally leave the streets and stay in the mosque. He could even get Qur'an lessons for free (unlike the government school, where he had to pay). The Muslim Brothers became his new family.

"When my father died and Widi married your Indah Mother, we went back to Cangkringan village. But maybe the *guna-guna* survived. We couldn't have children," Indah continued. "Oh, God in Heaven! After we waited for so many years, Widi told your Indah Mother that if he took a new wife, then he'd finally be blessed with child. But Widi had no way to make enough money. So I came to Saudi Arabia to help support them all: Widi, my mother, and even Widi's new second wife," Indah said, smiling or crying, Kamal wasn't sure which.

It was supposed to be for a couple of years.

"The only problem was that when I came here and met you," Indah said, "I knew my destiny was to raise you." She smiled, a tear falling on Kamal's forehead.

Kamal smiled back. He felt like crying too.

And when Widi started "sweeping" years later, Indah knew that God wanted her to stay here, with Kamal.

"He got a job as a janitor?" Kamal asked.

"I'll only go back when you go to university," Indah said.

———

WIDI WAS A chicken farmer by day and a terrorist by night.

Widi and Indah had been married for four years without children when she left for Saudi Arabia. And he must've been married to this new wife for almost ten years, and a child was not even on the way. Maybe that's why Widi left his second wife alone and went out each night with the Islamic "Brave Enough to Die" Martyrs.

The Martyrs would command the good and fight against the evil. By day, Widi and his men gave rice to the poorest farmers, helped build their homes and many mosques. Widi said he'd defend any true believer like Luwarso against the un-Islamic *guna-guna*. By night, they would "sweep" from the countryside around Yogyakarta and enter the bowels and catacombs of the sinful city, attacking at their roots all the Sodomites: gamblers, drinkers, prostitutes, adulterers, homosexuals.

They went "sweeping" against the evildoers. In a group of between twenty and fifty men, they would come well armed and burn down bars, gambling dens, and houses of prostitutes. They'd hold the evil by force of arms, call the police, and the police would arrest the sinners.

"Most of all, they swept for *banci*."

"Who are the *banci*?"

"*Why what come again,* they are the men who like men. They've always been considered lucky by the good *dukun* to fend off *guna-guna,* but not by Widi and his Islamic Martyrs."

Yet no matter how many times Widi "swept," his second wife, just like his first, remained without child. Geckos had to be living inside her birth canal, Indah Mother explained.

It wasn't until two years later that Kamal finally learned the truth. He was thirteen. Like his illustrious forefather the Original Sheikh, Kamal had memorized the whole of the Holy Qur'an by heart, all 114 surahs. It was a noble accomplishment for a noble boy. Even his father, Abdullah, was proud. Kamal was a true and blessed Wahhab son.

But it was the night when Indah finally finished the story of her life that Kamal felt truly proud for the first time.

Widi was so busy "sweeping," he could no longer work at the chicken farm. He had no way to make enough money or even think of taking another wife.

Indah Mother told Kamal her deepest secret: "God punished him. Widi never had a child. But God has blessed me with you." She smiled at Kamal, a tear from her heart gracing her "real" Wahhab son, the only one she believed in.

Kamal had a secret too: he had an older brother in America, living in San Francisco. He had met him once when he was very little but couldn't even remember what he looked like.

Indah never knew. Every family hid its secrets.

"Maybe one day, we'll all go to America together, *Inshallah,*" Indah said. It was the first time Kamal could remember that Indah Mother had ever spoken in Arabic and said *Inshallah* instead of *why what come again*.

AFTER INDAH REACHED the end of her life story, from age thirteen on, Kamal was always at or near the top of his class at Al Mamlaka. Kingdom High School was one of the best in Riyadh, for the finest royal children and privileged few.

Kamal wanted to excel in school for his father and the entire line of his pious forefathers. He wanted to excel in school because he loved the Holy Qur'an. Kamal wanted to be the best in school so he could go to the best university for Indah Mother.

He knew Indah would go home then. He didn't want to be the one to stop her. He'd miss her, of course, but knew that most of all, he could love Indah Mother the very best by going to the very best university.

As Kamal grew in his teenage years, he curiously seemed to acquire the attributes of Indah Mother. While he never said "*why what come again,*" he was always smiling, something peculiar for a Saudi. Wearing a constant smile, which only half exposed his perfectly white straight teeth, caught the eye of any Saudi and was excused because of his noble lineage as much as his disarming demeanor.

By eighteen, he grew to Indah Mother's exact height too, his black, round eyes and wavy black hair matching hers—only he had a slight beard and the hawklike nose of his cousin King Faisal. And truth be told, unlike his stereo-amplified "real mother," Kamal never raised his voice. He spoke each word softly and distinctly, punctuated by that unexpected smile, which made him stand out in the *thobe* and *shemagh* that were the standard Saudi uniform. In short, he became, for Indah Mother and even his father, "a boy truly blessed." He also became eligible for university.

Given his outstanding marks from the best high school in Riyadh and high scores on his *tawjihiyyah* baccalaureate (let alone who his father was), he was a natural, a shoo-in, for King Saud University (KSU), the best in the kingdom.

Kamal chose King Saud himself. Though his father wanted him to attend the religious university in Riyadh, Al Imam Muhammad ibn Saud Islamic University, where the family held sway and the best religious education could be had, Kamal was passionate. He convinced his father he'd still gain a good religious grounding at KSU and at the same time expose himself to the best courses.

The day he started at King Saud, Indah Mother left for Indonesia. Kamal would never forget her. One day he'd make her even prouder. And he would always stay in touch. Write letters, call on the phone, and now they had the Internet. He'd send her a computer so they could chat back and forth instantaneously across oceans.

One day he would visit her too. They would climb to the top of Mount Merapi at sunrise, right after Fajr prayer. Kamal and Indah would look out at the world from the top of Merapi.

But KSU was harder than anything he had known before. It should've been nothing for him—study was second nature. The "man from Chittagong" took him each morning and home late at night. All he did at home was sleep—that didn't help either.

Among the forty thousand students (all men; the women had a different campus) and hundreds of nearly identical sandstone buildings, all with great Islamic arches and courtyards, Kamal never got over feeling alone. With Kingdom High School left behind, the teachers became "doctors" and the classes "lectures": Qur'anic Sciences and the Construction of Society, Foundations of Qur'anic Jurisprudence, Introduction to the Sciences of Prophet Muhammad's Traditions, and so on. Kamal chose Islamic studies. As a true Wahhab son, Kamal soaked in all the Islamic teachings, but did it for Indah Mother, while his father was endlessly drinking *gahwa* at the new Wadi Hanifah palace.

Well into his eighties, Minister Sheikh Abdullah had shocked the other princes. Unlike his royal cousins, who clung to power until they dropped dead in office, he took the unusual step of actually retiring. Court rumors that King Fahd had forced him out were not true. He retired from the ministry for only one reason: to live his great dream.

As a true son of the Nejd, the minister sheikh enjoyed nothing more than his *estiraha,* a small refuge home in the desert. His dream was to re-create his temporary oasis retreat into a palace *estiraha* fit for a royal. Some court gossip had it that Minister Abdullah spent his worldly treasures to show off his true desert roots; others said that it was to return to the date palms and a religious sense of peace. Certainly that was true for Kamal, who was the aged sheikh's only son to live with him among the date palms of the Wadi Hanifah.

Kamal could find peace at night, walking among the tall, dusty palms and looking up at the stars. In this part of Riyadh, most nights you could actually see the desert stars. Kamal could even see Mount Merapi.

He was also glad that his father had moved before he had started at KSU, since in the notorious Riyadh traffic the old palace could be an hour's drive to the university, while the new one was only twenty minutes away, at most twenty-five with traffic.

AFTER SIX MONTHS, his father received Kamal's first KSU report.

The "man from Chittagong" fetched Kamal early from KSU's great library—the most spectacular building on campus, besides the

Al Nakheel Mosque next door. His father had never summoned him like this.

Kamal came into the *majlis* reception and sat on a gold-and-red pillow. His father said nothing. The son of a Wahhabi slave repeated the *gahwa* ritual as he had thousands of times, the Wahhabi china continually alternating with the flowing green coffee and dead silence. After he dismissed the Sudanese, his father began to mumble something, but the sweet tea was served by a Pakistani. Kamal just wished that the servants would keep coming all night long, until his father dropped to sleep.

When the dates arrived, Kamal had no such luck. His eighty-something, maybe ninety-year-old father, cleared his ancient throat and muttered the few words that were the purpose of their formal *majlis* meeting. Kamal nervously fidgeted on the pillow, chewing a date pit over and over again.

"Spit it out, Kamal son," his father said.

"What, my blessed Sheikh?" He addressed his father with the term of the highest honor.

"Spit out the pit, son."

"Yes, Sheikh Father."

"Tell me. You are a gifted student in our exalted family tradition, of course. I even let you go to KSU instead of Imam U. I never expected to receive a report from the rector with anything short of the top marks," his father mumbled.

Naturally, his father would receive a report from the president of the entire university himself on just one of his forty thousand students! Poor Kamal could not escape his father.

That was all he said. The upshot was that his father decided to take Kamal on a trip to the desert for two weeks. Abdullah, the great Al al-Sheikh descendant of the great Muhammad ibn Wahhab, saw a desert trip as the answer to all the world's problems—or at least Kamal's in university. And Kamal had never been with his father to the desert before.

As on any good desert excursion, they went to hunt desert rabbits and oryx—only those were long extinct from this part of the Nejd. The party was led by his father and Uncle Muhammad, his father's fraternal twin. It was as if the honored sheikhs had taken a five-star hotel and transplanted it into the middle of the Nejd Desert. There must have been some forty servants and vehicles. Kamal couldn't count them all. While his father and uncle stayed in one lavish tent (air-conditioning, television, DVD player, with a fully marbled bathroom!—along with young women they had "married" for the trip), Kamal and his uncle's son stayed in another much smaller, though still fully wired, tent.

Moad was Kamal's first cousin and, like him, the last son. At twenty, he was two years older and had finished his second year at Imam U. While they had seen each other a number of times at family gatherings, they were hardly friends—indeed, barely acquaintances.

THE FIRST NIGHT camping in the red Nejd, Kamal saw Merapi rise from the desert. He was standing outside his tent, looking at the stars he loved, clear in the winter air. What he saw instead was a vision of Merapi growing before him.

Kamal was heir to jihad as none other. He knew the Book by heart, and the Hadith, the sayings and deeds of the Holy Prophet. He knew the writings and words of his great-great-great-great-great grandfather. And the more he studied the words of his famous ancestor, the more he thought the clerics of today didn't understand them.

He felt cold in the desert night. He had refused to eat the baby camel that was lying fully intact and ready to be devoured at his father's vast feast. Kamal spurned the Saudi custom of ripping whole animals apart to eat with your bare hands. Moad wouldn't touch the baby camel either.

"What is this next generation of Saudis coming to?" Kamal's uncle and Moad's father said, laughing, as the old revered sheikhs ate camel and the young future sheiks and rulers, lamb.

Kamal knew what the younger generation would be coming to. He would bring Merapi to the Arabian Desert, as Indah Mother had wanted. And he would bring the true teachings of Sheikh Wahhab for all.

Kamal also knew that his father's servants would next roast the *dhub* lizards over the open fire. He wouldn't touch lizard either. So he left to stand outside his own tent.

Kamal was staring at the Mountain of Fire in his mind when Moad came outside.

Unlike Kamal, Moad hadn't been free to choose which university to attend. Moad's father, His Eminence the Minister Muhammad Al al-Sheikh, had insisted on the most traditional schools, either Umm al-Qura University in Mecca or Al Imam Muhammad ibn Saud Islamic University in Riyadh, where Kamal's father had wanted him to go.

Moad now put his arm around Kamal in a friendly gesture, customary for Saudi men. "See anything good out here, Cousin?" he asked.

Though Moad was two years older, he was two inches shorter. And although Moad was Kamal's first cousin, they could've been brothers. You had to search for the physical differences. His black hair was shorter, almost stiff, and curlier, as was his faint beard, which grew in spots and wasn't full.

Moad's most striking feature was surely his coal black eyes. They fixed on you like stealth radar, not letting go. Good Saudi manners called for you to avert your gaze when talking. Indeed, some thought that a prolonged stare could bring "the evil eye" and blinding bad luck. Yet because he was born to such privilege, Moad felt free to brutally assert himself. Seemingly oblivious to politeness, he would stare straight into you, never giving up.

"I thought I might have seen a *sawur*," Kamal said.

"A what, Cousin?"

"A great flame across the night sky."

"From the roasting fire?"

"From Heaven, from Almighty God. It's a flaming arrow that tells us God's will."

"You mean a comet."

"You can call it what you want. I know what it is."

"Right, Kamal baby, whatever you say, Cousin." Moad said, laughing. Still, Kamal didn't feel mad as Moad hugged him tighter.

"Tomorrow we hunt desert rabbits. Bet you can't wait, Cousin," Moad said, laughing again.

"It's not pious," Kamal said.

"Yeah, I'm sure some servants will just let out some rabbits so Dad and Uncle Abdullah can shoot at will."

"Just like they've always done," Kamal said.

Kamal struck a common note. In truth, Moad and he were of one piece. As first cousins from their twin fathers, they had each been raised by the other half and felt their blood and shared upbringing now racing between them as one, it seemed.

"You got that right, Cousin Kamal. They always shoot what they want and expect us to follow in lockstep."

"But do they love us?" Kamal didn't know where that came from or why it popped out of his mouth. It was an entirely un-Saudi thing to say. You never talked about a father's love like that.

Moad was taken aback, releasing Kamal from his hug. He now fixed his black radar eyes on him instead.

"They love the girls they take in their big fat tent," Moad said.

"What kind of love is that, Cousin?" he replied. Kamal knew what love meant from Wahhab himself, who wrote that any union between two people was blessed only if each respected the other as equals. He knew what love meant from Indah Mother.

"It's cold out here," Moad finally said, taking Kamal by the hand and leading him inside.

Moad tied the flap of the tent with its thick gold rope. The tent also had a door, which Moad bolted. The two first cousins who could've been brothers were alone.

The next day, the two boys didn't even mind hunting desert rabbits or looking into the eyes of another chopped-up baby camel that night at dinner. They didn't even mind their fathers—for the first time in their lives.

They took each of their five prayers together as one and just waited for the magical time after Isha when they could go into their tent in the desert night and wait for another *sawur*.

It was the most wonderful ten days of Kamal's life. It was the most wonderful ten days in Moad's life too. They just didn't know what they would do when they got back to Riyadh, KSU, and Imam U.

"SOUNDS LIKE YOU found someone special," I said sleepily, with Kamal's wide-screen Mitsubishi TV set to KSA2 in the background.

"He's all I ever had, *Inshallah,*" Kamal whispered.

I couldn't tell if he was kidding again. Since uncharacteristically he barely smiled, I thought better of making a joke before he said, smiling, "At least you're not asking 'Why don't you hurry up and get to the terrorism part?'"

"Why? What?"

"Come again!"

We watched a roundtable of "Betty Ford" jihadis being interviewed on Saudi television. The "graduates" of the Care Center had become something of minor celebrities inside the kingdom.

"Quite a dog-and-pony show," I finally said, yawning. We had been talking well into the night.

"As Indah Mother always said, that's enough for one night, *Kecil* Kenny." Kamal switched on his mocking grin again.

I was beginning to be able to discern the fine line between prolific satire and profound piety. And if you're on the right side of this complex cultural barrier, I found, the merciless joking among the seemingly stoic Saudis was an unexpected sign of friendship as well.

"I keep the hours of my cousin the king [which meant staying up most of the night], but you can sleep next door in Indah's old room. I've kept it empty ever since she left. My own special guest room."

"And I'm your own special guest?"

"Your muse Shahrazad will pick up the story tomorrow."

As I left, Kamal prepared to perform the middle-of-the-night Tahajjud prayer, when, he said, "God comes nearest to us in the closest Heaven."

THE BOYS DREAMED of sharing a room. But how could Moad and Kamal explain to their fathers that they wanted to room together when they each had a magnificent space in a royal palace? And Kamal was just twenty minutes from KSU too.

Instead, the boys now studied, ate, and prayed together whenever they could. But they always slept together at each other's homes. Moad would usually come over to Kamal's room, since in the vast maids' wing in the Wadi Hanifah palace no one ever really saw them or even cared. Kamal sometimes went to his uncle's sprawling palace, which also was large enough for the boys to become completely lost. It didn't matter. They had found each other.

Kamal always strove to be a worthy Muslim. He prayed five times a day, Jumu'ah Friday prayers and the voluntary prayers, went on Hajj and Umrah to Mecca, fasted during Ramadan, and gave *zakat* to the poor. Even when he was a little boy, he and Indah Mother together had always sent funds to the starving Indonesians. He could recite the entire Holy Qur'an by heart and knew the Hadith, the sayings and deeds of the Prophet Muhammad, the Sunnah, all with dedicated mind and unflinching devotion. He spoke softly, greeted every soul with peace, and lived with God in his heart, all as the Book commanded.

If God now made him love a man instead of a woman, Kamal wanted to know why. He wanted to know why so many Islamic clerics and scholars thought it was a sin. Kamal wanted to read for himself why God Almighty, whom he prayed to so fervently, would make any kind of real love sinful. And if the Word of God told him it was a sin, Kamal as His humble servant would obey and never love a man again.

Since Kamal was a true descendant, he had as much right as anyone to know from the source himself. And Kamal discovered that what his honored ancestor really had written was far different from what his followers taught in the name of Wahhab.

Kamal found that his love for Moad must be right because Wahhab himself wrote in his *Risalah fi al-Radd ala al-Rafidah* that the true test of love in God's eyes is always whether love is equal. The only practice that his illustrious forefather found unequal in lovemaking was to penetrate another from behind. But Kamal's lovemaking with Moad was equal in practice and in spirit. And it no longer came as a surprise that the Original Sheikh had also written in his *Kitab al-Nikah* that men who loved other men—indeed, any man who could love another—were welcome at the Wedding Feast itself.

After his noble ancestor, Kamal turned to the sayings and life of Prophet Muhammad. "Islam is on the outside, but real faith is in the heart," the Holy Prophet said. If faith was in the heart and not the Islam you wore on the outside, was not love too in the heart? Kamal reasoned.

Now the Glorious Qur'an itself, the very Word of God, told him no less.

HERE I MUST stop again.

At this point, Kamal launched into a lengthy and, at least to my mind, learned exposition on the equality of love, women, men, and human sexuality he found in the Qur'an, far different from not just the radical view but current mainstream Islamic doctrine. The widespread Muslim tradition of treating women as subservient to men was also far removed from the "equal love" his forefather had written about.

But I'll leave it to Kamal to tell the world when he considers the time is right. While I could re-create literally his nuanced and powerful exegesis, it is better voiced by someone with Islamic authority and knowledge.

And, quite simply, it might very well get him killed. Indeed, I have little doubt that his revolutionary—to some, blasphemous—words, though based on deep faith and thorough Islamic scholarship, will result in ostracism, exile, or death. My purpose in revealing Kamal's story now is to open a new window for us in the West. The light for the Muslim world must come from within.

GOING BACK TO the words of the Holy Qur'an, the Prophet Muhammad, and the Original Sheikh to understand every word for himself, Kamal discovered a new world. He just wasn't sure whether to tell Indah Mother.

He knew from her too that Allah the Most Compassionate had failed to bless Widi with children because he "swept" for *banci*.

The empty computer left him no choice. At the other side of the world, its warm screen was waiting patiently.

Across oceans, God spoke. Man could just write.

"Hey, Indah Mother," Kamal wrote in English on his laptop.

"Kecil," Indah wrote. It didn't matter how many times he told her he was no longer little. He'd always be her *kecil*.

"*Why what come again?*" Kamal replied.

"Ha ha."

"Widi still 'sweeping' the floor like a good maid?"

"Always the joker. But you, Kecil?

He couldn't escape before her. Not like when his father the Great Sheikh asked something and he could hide behind all the intricate customs of Bedouin traditions. Kamal had no place to hide. Besides, Indah with her secret spirit knew what was right. He had no one else to ask for the truth.

"I'm in love." It just popped out.

"I'm surprised your father picked a wife for you before you completed university," Indah wrote.

"Is that love? What's custom isn't love," he now wrote in the Instant Messenger. "I have Equal Love. You remember Moad?"

The screen went blank. He waited for her to type something. Maybe he should've just told her over the phone. Like a schoolboy, he couldn't wait. What if she thought it a sin?

Kamal knew that many latter-day, so-called Wahhabis preached that love between men was a sin. Certainly his uncle, Moad's father, did; his own father likely felt the same way. But Kamal thought he and Moad were following the true teachings of Wahhab, with equal love before God (and no penetration from behind). He also knew Indah Mother would give him the right answer now too.

"Didn't you tell me that you don't believe in Widi *sweeping?*" Kamal wrote, filling the blue space that was waiting too long for an answer.

"My dream last night saw you, Kecil," Indah wrote. "You had a long beard and wore the white robes of the Prophet himself, peace be upon him. Abu Bakr, the Prophet's most loyal follower, was now an imam from Yogya's Round Mosque. He was holding your hand, and the two of you were addressing the entire *umma*. Everyone was there: Widi, his Islamic Martyrs, and the *banci* all together, listening in peace to your words of love. Now, Kecil, you know."

"*Mash'Allah,*" Kamal wrote back.

"You have the truth. Moad is blessed as your lover. Just remember your mission," Indah wrote.

"I cannot forget," Kamal promised.

"The best in university, so you can be the best leading the faith."

KAMAL WAS NOW the best in his class—no mean feat among the more than ten thousand in his year. Moad excelled at Imam U. too. Their fathers would never need to speak to them again. Over the next three and a half years, they could just be the equal lovers their famous ancestor had written about, praising God in all His infinite glory.

With Indah's blessing too, Kamal and Moad became inseparable. On weekends, they loved to go to the Tahlia. No Riyadhi called the street by its true name. Even Kamal sometimes had trouble remembering what it was really called, though named after one of his relatives (Prince Muhammad bin Abdul Aziz). Like so much else in the kingdom, there was one reality, official and approved for all, and an entirely different reality, which reflected how lives were lived in the world's richest kingdom. Sometimes you only wanted to know the second reality.

Every Thursday and Friday weekend evening, when the curfew extended closings, they strolled down the Tahlia, where other young men would speed by, showing off their best cars and motorcycles. It was a time and place where traditional Saudi *thobe*s and *shemagh*s weren't required and the *mutaween* wouldn't show. (Moad called the religious police by their slang name, but Kamal refused and still called them by their rightful title of Hai'a.) Still, Kamal and Moad *thobe*d and kept a certain bemused decorum in their strolls, a tourist's kind of clinical detachment in their vicarious pleasure.

For "faith was in the heart," as Kamal repeated.

The boys would usually eat outside when the Riyadh dust and sand were not too thick. Afterward, they'd go for American coffee, lattes and cappuccinos, and walk until midnight.

They were no longer "Kamal" and "Moad." The closest term of endearment for any two men—even closer than for many husbands and wives—was to call each other "Abu" (father of), then the name of their first son—whether or not they had a son. So Kamal became "Abu Muhammad" (who else could he be?) and Moad, "Abu Musa" (after one of the first prophets, Moses): affirming their heritage, living their faith, and loving the future to be born. In their own world, they meant everything to each other. To others, the first cousins were the sons of privilege, the future rulers, whether loved or not, of simply Al Mamlaka—The Kingdom.

For "Abu Muhammad" and "Abu Musa," while their love did not give birth to first sons, they were reborn together instead.

Kamal even took a bold step.

He wrote an e-mail to his older brother Faisal in San Francisco. He barely knew his fourth eldest brother. Faisal was well into his fifties, had gone to Stanford University, worked in Silicon Valley, and never come home. But Kamal knew he'd never married a woman and lived in San Francisco, so he wrote an e-mail hello, hoping for what kind of answer, he had no clue.

Kamal heard nothing back. He did not exist for Faisal. His e-mail was dead to his "brother." Indah was his real family—and now his true and equal brother in blood, Moad.

So, for almost four years at KSU, in God's great blessing, with Indah and Moad's love, Kamal was the best.

KAMAL AND I were at the InterContinental gym. It could've been a Gold's or LA Fitness, with the customary props of iron free weights, LifeCore elliptical cross-trainers, PaceMaster stationary bikes, even the overhead color TV monitors broadcasting CNN and *Oprah*. All of the Saudi men were sheared of their traditional robes and headdresses, sporting the ubiquitous gym shorts and shirts that have become something of a global uniform. And like a McDonald's or KFC, the gym seemed to blur national boundaries, until I realized there wasn't even one woman in sight—not counting Oprah, of course.

I helped Kamal while he bench-pressed, spotting him 110 pounds.

"What if your father found out about you and Moad?" I asked. "Wouldn't you lose everything?"

Kamal pushed the weights even harder. "Am I a fool—a real idiot or what," he said, more a statement than a question.

"For watching so much Bugs Bunny?"

"For never being able to love who I choose, openly, without fear of being found out and 'losing everything,' as you say."

"You can still love in private."

"Not the same. It makes something that should be beautiful shameful instead."

In interviewing jihadis, I knew I had to take risks. And with Kamal, I felt I was becoming close enough to roll the dice. "It does seem like a lonely life."

"That's why half the guys become jihadis."

"They're gay?"

"Or frustrated in love."

"And the other half?"

"Fools like me. I guess I have both halves in one. Can't love who I want to love—and a fool for believing that I can."

"Your father's worth how many billions?"

"In euros or dollars?"

"And you stand to inherit how much?"

"More than I'll ever need. I'm now his favorite son."

"You're no fool," I said.

"Thanks, my American friend. What a big help you've been."

TAKING OFF FROM King Khalid International Airport, Kamal would soon taste the meaning of jihad firsthand.

Kamal was the first in his class in Terminology of Prophet Muhammad's Traditions, the Scientific Rules of Qur'anic Recitation, and the Jurisprudence of Islamic Jihad. More: He had faithfully studied for himself jihad from the Holy Qur'an and Hadith, as well as the writings of his great ancestor, who wrote in *Kitab al-Tawheed* that Islam could be spread only by the heart and not the sword.

Kamal was twenty-two and had never left his Wahhabi homeland before. When he had traveled to Mecca for Hajj (the greater pilgrimage) and Umrah (the lesser pilgrimage), it had always been with his father, whom he barely saw in the swirl of officials. But his dream was to go on Hajj with Indah Mother. For Hajj was the blessed time and place where servant and master, royal and nonroyal, man and woman, mother and son, indeed all mankind were equal.

As the airplane's wheels now left the ground, Kamal thought the only way he should ever leave his country was for jihad. He was a born jihadi—a *muwahhid* true believer by deed, a Wahhab by birthright.

Looking out the window of his first-class cabin on Saudi Arabian Airlines, he didn't see the brown desert below but the miraculous green of the Mountain of Fire growing before him—the mountain that God had now shaken to open the earth.

When he'd told Moad he must go to Indonesia, Moad had understood. When he'd told his father, even his father had understood and told him to go too. But now he was alone.

Kamal was just finishing his term at KSU when he heard the news of the earthquake on Al Jazeera. He immediately called. There was no answer. He opened his laptop. He searched the screen in vain. He wouldn't give up until he found Indah, no matter how much the screen's empty light seared his eyes, no matter how much it hurt to miss her.

It was like a miracle when her name appeared in blue relief: Indah. Indah Mother at last.

The earthquake was the worst to hit central Indonesia in some fifty years. More than five thousand people were dead and millions homeless, but the epicenter was well south of Merapi, near the coast. Indah's village was safe. It made Kamal miss her all the more.

But Indah wanted nothing more than for him to finish his exams. It was hard for Kamal to concentrate, even with Moad by his side. His heart was in Indonesia. And he felt the same headache attacking him between the eyes every time he went online.

When he next heard from her, he had just finished taking his last exam in the Islamic Jurisprudence of Family Affairs. He somehow knew that no matter what happened, Indah would never contact him until his exams were finished for the term.

Indah Mother then told him what had happened to Widi.

After the earthquake first struck, Widi had joined other volunteers from the Islamic Martyrs to rescue as many victims as they could. God had spared Widi and his family from the earthquake's wrath. Widi wanted to help others; God had saved him for a purpose.

Bantul, just south of Yogyakarta, was the hardest hit. Widi and his fellow rescuers' callused brown hands were their only shovels. As Widi had built his own home by hand, so he dug through the jagged, cracked pieces of other people's crushed homes by hand. The flies led the way to the dead. Three or four face masks couldn't stop the rotting stench of human flesh from burning his nose. He breathed death.

On day three, when the rescuers had lost hope, they found little more than the skeleton of a spotted black-and-white dog wildly barking next to a small hill of rubble. The debris looked as if it had once been a small motorcycle repair shop. Widi and the other Islamic Martyrs began to uncover the fallen shop piece by piece. After digging for hours, they came to a place where the wooden beams had formed a cross against each other and seemed to support a small space below. Only since they had God with them could they hear a soft moan.

Widi needed the help of ten other men to carefully pull the beams apart so they would not collapse on the faint sound. And dusty, short of breath, lay a small boy, no more than seven or eight years old.

Widi and another Islamic Martyr rushed the boy to Wattes Hospital in an American Red Cross jeep. The traffic jam to the hospital was worse than in Yoyga's Central Square. The parking lot was overflowing with makeshift Red Cross tents, wandering survivors, and victims lying on cots or the exposed earth, their sounds and smells overpowering any sense. If not for the American Red Cross official who plowed his way through, Widi could never have delivered the barely breathing boy to the harassed emergency room doctor inside (despite all the resentment, foreigners, especially white ones, were afforded a certain continuing colonial deference in Indonesia).

The boy lived but was the last survivor the Islamic Martyrs found. Widi continued the recovery work for ten long days. Moving from rescuing those who survived to removing the dead bodies of those who did not, the task after day five was to take down the shaky houses and mosques before they fell from the aftershocks.

On day eleven of the rescue, Widi was on the roof of a ruined house, ready with his fellow Islamic Martyrs to take it down. A powerful aftershock hit, sending Widi to the ground. He didn't seem too badly hurt at first, as another Martyr took him by motorcycle to the nearest hospital.

Wattes Hospital was where Widi's troubles truly began. With Indah by his side, the doctors told Widi they would set his broken leg first thing the next morning.

The nurses wheeled him into the operating room for 6:30 A.M. surgery. The doctors began to take off the remnants of clothes from his battered leg when at exactly 6:39, another aftershock struck. This one came directly from God Himself, it was so powerful. The entire hospital moved up and down. The doctors and nurses fled in panic, leaving Widi trapped on his abandoned cot, trembling as he watched the hospital walls shake.

He lay there for half an hour, unable to move, until a doctor and nurse finally came back. The doctor didn't have time to clean the wound. Another shock might hit any minute. He quickly put on a temporary cast, as the hospital staff frantically moved Widi and all the other patients out of the fragile hospital.

They took him first to Dr. Sardjito Hospital, then Panti Rapih Catholic Hospital—more precisely, its parking lot. There, along with thousands of other patients waiting for medical help, Widi lay on the stretcher for five long days. As the nurses passed through with the bare food and water, no one knew what lay underneath. Since his leg was already covered by a cast, the triage left him way back in the pack. Until, on day five, his soul seemed to leave his body.

The doctors rushed Widi, now unconscious, to the operating room and found a massive infection. Under the temporary cast, his left leg had become full of gangrene. They had no choice but to amputate and hope the infection hadn't spread to his internal organs. But the hospital didn't have enough antibiotics. Only God's hand could save his life.

Widi was in a coma for twenty days before Kamal touched down in Jakarta.

KAMAL ARRIVED AT Soekarno-Hatta International Airport in defeat. This wasn't how it was supposed to be. He was supposed to arrive in triumph, greeting his beloved Indah Mother as the new leader of Islam she wanted him to be—or at a least as a new university graduate, degree in hand. What did he have for her now? Just one lousy suitcase? He was returning for a burial, not a birth. And for the burial of a man who'd followed his great-great-great-great-great grandfather by "sweeping" away those who loved like his great-great-great-great-great grandson.

Kamal had to wait forever in the immigration line, though the officer smiled when stamping his Saudi passport. Chaos took over as people randomly grabbed for suitcases, whether they belonged to them or not. The steel baggage conveyor was rusted and chugged forward in fits and starts. He had to fight his way through to grab his lone black suitcase before finding his connecting flight to Yogyakarta in a different part of the steamy airport. He felt as if he pulled his shoulder out from its socket in rescuing his suitcase and felt ashamed that it was all he had managed to bring with him.

The Garuda Indonesia plane to Yogyakarta was cramped, hot, and noisy with Indonesians. Silver duct tape held the compartment above him in place, while chewing gum had been applied to the window to seal a crack. The airplane felt like a hearse.

Approaching Yogyakarta's airport, even though fog or volcanic smoke covered the summit of Merapi, he could see through to the lush green below. Repeating the baggage fight all over again, people swarmed everywhere like flies.

He fought his way out to the taxis and immediately saw her round brown eyes stand out from the crowd. He ran toward her, oblivious to all around him. They hugged and said nothing at first. Kamal felt the tears in his eyes.

"This is not how I wanted to come back," he said.

"I am blessed to see you, Kecil."

"I didn't want to come until I graduated."

"You look wonderful."

"I'd wanted to come leading the change."

"*Why what come again,* no matter how you come, I love you, Kecil." Indah smiled, and Kamal could see the tears laughing in her glorious eyes.

They got into a minivan driven by Widi's eldest brother, who praised Wahhabis and said Widi's only regret was that he had never made the Hajj to Mecca.

The streets of Yogya were like the baggage claim: everyone going his own way. Cars went around on sidewalks; people ran in the middle of the street; bicycles cut in front of buses; motorcycles circled horse-drawn carts: all the anger of being poor was let loose on the road. Worse were the traffic circles, where the signals meant nothing and teeming people poured in from every direction. And every time the minivan stopped, beggars surrounded them. It must be worse from the earthquake. Why was God testing these people?

Indah told him they would pay their respects to Widi before going to Cangkringan village, where they both really wanted to be.

Panti Rapih Catholic Hospital smelled of death. The halls were filled with men missing limbs, women covered by white bloody bandages, and children screaming in pain: all the hell of the streets dumped inside its falling walls. The rooms and halls, even the stairs, were stained with blood, while Catholic nuns patrolled its crammed corridors like gray vultures.

Kamal couldn't even tell whether Widi was in a room or the hall. He had a bag of salty water hooked into his left arm and was dead in all but name. Widi's sister or one of his other wives stood against the wall nearby, keeping vigil.

Widi's brother, then Indah, and finally Kamal took turns holding Widi's icy hand. It was stiff as an American doll any good Wahhabi child was forbidden to play with, a toy reminiscent of idol worship.

As Kamal held Widi's cold hand, he felt the sweat on his own forehead. Did he want Widi to wake from his deathbed, so that in the name of Islam he could beat men who loved other men? Why was this the legacy that Widi thought Kamal's ancestor had brought? Only if Widi woke would he know. Kamal wondered if Indah prayed for Widi to wake or die.

"It's time for prayer, but there's no place anywhere," Kamal said and felt like adding "No wonder so many are dying."

"We do it here," Widi's brother said. In the hall with the victims, half-dead men, the maimed, uncovered women, motherless children, even the roaming Catholic nuns—no room even for prayer rugs, Kamal thought.

He could barely breathe. Perhaps he was just overtired from the long trip, the hospital smell. He had longed to see Indah again in triumph, coming to Indonesia leading the faith and not still just a boy. Indonesia was unlike his dreams too. The tropical paradise of great spirits serving God was a deadly jungle of battered cars, dirty motorcycles, broken airplanes, lost suitcases—its people as torn up as the ripped earth beneath them.

At last they got into the minivan to Cangkringan village—except Widi's brother drove as if he were leading a burial procession on steroids. The rusty van took on a new life, jolting back and forth like a rocket. The brother's right foot was firmly planted on the accelerator pedal, while his left foot applied equal if not greater force to the brake pedal. It was nothing less than another miracle from God that Widi's brother didn't increase the death toll from the earthquake that very day.

Driving past the white stucco campus of Gadjah Mada University, Kamal wondered how Indah Mother felt. If she had completed university, she wouldn't be here now and she wouldn't have been his "real mother" either. He owed her everything and didn't want to die before he could give something back.

Past the university, the countryside of Indonesia grew before him. Kamal opened the window to take in its steamy air, to breathe the ash from the Mountain of Fire itself as they climbed the twisted roads closer to its summit.

Hidden in the foothills of the village, the family homes were clustered together, the dusty jungle surrounding them. They were more like cement shacks than homes, and the toilet wasn't even in the house. Kamal was glad he was staying in the nearby five-star Merapi Golf resort (and got Indah a room too).

Waiting in the outer living room of the humid cement shack with the other men, Kamal sat cross-legged on the floor, his bare toes pointing inward in the Muslim way. Indah went with the other women to prepare the Selamatan welcome feast or the Tahlilan ceremony for the wake. Nobody was sure which.

They talked in broken English but mostly Bahasa. The men of Widi's family told Kamal how much they admired the Arabs, especially the Saudis from the Land of the Two Holy Places, and how much he was their honored guest. Kamal just wanted to eat Indah's cooking and go to the hotel.

Instead, he asked one of the men for the Holy Qur'an. While he knew God's Uncreated Word by heart, he wanted to hold the Book in his hands in the heart of Indonesia under the great mountain he still hadn't seen. Widi's eldest brother, the maniacal driver, got a battered silver box from inside a dark mahogany chest. Opening the Holy Book's resting place, Kamal saw something else in its place. Yes, there was a worn copy of the Book of God inside, but also an equally tattered copy of *Tintin in America* next to it.

Kamal took the dented silver box with both books and laid them before him. The direction of Mecca was the same as Merapi, the men said, and Kamal led them in prayer.

The meal then served by Indah and her cousins had all of Kamal's favorites. Except it should have been for the wake instead, as they got word that Widi had died before they even finished eating.

The next day, they buried Widi's body, wrapped in *kafan* cloth, in the family cemetery. As his skinny body was lowered into the earth, the mourners were graced by the presence of no less a celebrity than the leader of the Islamic Martyrs himself. Following the burial, the leader laid out all of his jihadi credentials to Kamal and the other mourners.

Before Indonesia had become independent some sixty years ago, the leader explained, his grandfather had fought for Sharia and Islamic rule. His father had then fought against the Communists in 1965, when Muslim true believers and the army killed 500,000 infidels, Christians, and Communists. It wasn't enough, he told Kamal. The family tradition would never stop; all of his brothers were now jihadis, like their grandfather, like their father, like the noble Widi whom Allah Almighty now sent to Heaven above. "It doesn't matter how many generations it takes," the leader said. "Our blood never stops flowing, our jihad never ends, until we bring Islam to all of God's Earth and meet again as martyrs in Heaven."

Dressed completely in white, the "Great Martyr to Islam" had just a scraggly, wispy beard growing from his sharp chin—not a full jihadi growth. And his small head seemed mismatched, Kamal thought, on top of an overly muscular and squat frame, as he wildly threw his arms in the air with each word: "From across oceans, the Crusader Christians and Jews invade our land to destroy true Islam." The fiery Martyr's face turned from light brown to red when he ended in a hail of glory to jihad: "We will not die until we kill every last Christian," he almost shouted. "Rescuing our Muslim brothers, the holy *shaheed* Widi was martyred at the unclean hands of infidel Christian doctors and Catholic nun nurses. As the blood of base infidels is drawn, the blood of holy martyrs shall flow. The Word of God Himself in the Holy Book has commanded us: 'When the sacred months are over, fight and slay all the infidels wherever you find them, and seize them, attack them, and lie in wait for them with every strategy of war.' *Allah-u-Akbar!*" he shouted.

"*Allah-u-Akbar!*" the others repeated in turn. Kamal could see that even Indah Mother joined the cry.

The next great feast prepared by Indah Mother could have been the food of Heaven, for Kamal never loved any food more than the sweet delicacies and curries of Indonesia. And after he relished Indah's bounty, Kamal at last walked outside with her and saw the miracle of Merapi rising behind them from the smoke and clouds. It was all he ever dreamed of in its towering majesty.

Indah Mother told him how much it meant to her that he was here, and Kamal felt his tears. Held by Indah, the Mountain of Fire above them, he began to miss Cousin Moad, his Abu Musa, too.

When Widi was safely resting inside the earth, Kamal and Indah could finally stay together at the five-star Cangkringan resort on the land her father had once sold. They had the entire Royal Villa to themselves, with an unobstructed view of the Mountain of Fire and the championship Merapi Golf Course.

The following day, after Fajr prayer, they finally climbed near the summit of Merapi, their sandaled feet darkened by its sacred ash. Back at the hotel on the land that had sent Indah to university, they washed the Merapi ash off their feet together before sunset and Maghrib prayer.

Kamal and Indah even prayed together every one of the five prayers—something they had not done since he was a boy. Kamal dreamed of the day they could go to Mecca on Hajj together. In the clothes of pilgrims, they would be equal in the sight of God. Yet, whatever they wore on the outside, he knew that their faith now burned true in each heart.

After five miraculous days, it was time for him to go home. Indah still had to take care of her elderly mother and other children in the extended family. Kamal didn't want to say good-bye. Not all over again. Worse, he had come empty-handed, not yet a leader of Islam or even a university graduate.

But Indah would not let him leave empty-handed. She hugged him at the airport. "Kecil, always remember."

"How can I forget?"

"Always remember—"

"Your love—"

"My blessing—"

"Your gift—"

"Kecil, I have a gift."

She reached into her large blue-and-white batik bag and pulled out Widi's beaten silver box. Why would she now give him the Holy Qur'an, he thought. If there were one thing this great-great-great-great-great grandson of Wahhab had, it was plenty of Holy Qur'ans!

Indah handed him Widi's copy of *Tintin in America*.

"Honor Widi," Indah said.

Kamal wondered which of Widi's legacies Indah wanted him to follow: as a martyr for Islam by the sword or a rescuer of lost souls by the pen.

Widi had always dreamed of writing a sequel that could save more lost boys from a life on the streets, as the Tintin book had once saved him. But he had never written the new *Tintin*. Instead, he had fought for Islam with his blood.

Kamal would wait for the path that God would require of him.

KAMAL AND I were having dinner at the InterContinental's "Asian-Western fusion" restaurant Mondo, on the other side of the hotel's gym and mosque. He loved the chicken satay. I had to admit it was quite good. Indah could even have made the meal, he said.

I told him about my son at Middlebury College, who spoke fluent Japanese.

"Like 'Middlebury Ali,' my favorite tutor, who spoke fluent English," Kamal said.

I then told him about my daughter, who had just turned sixteen.

"Ah, sweet sixteen," he said. "What's that episode of *The Patty Duke Show* when the good Patty Duke and her bad twin both turn sixteen?"

I'd thought that I had Talmudic knowledge of obscure TV trivia until I met this Saudi aristocrat and devout jihadi. "Your commentary on current events?" I joked.

"Saudi Arabia and America. Twins by black blood, right? The one can never tell the true motives of the other. Good or bad."

"And you get this all from Patty Duke?"

"You'd be surprised what I can get from American TV."

WHEN KAMAL RETURNED from Indonesia to KSU for the next semester, he continued with religion but also started to study literature. Only God could tell him which of Widi's legacies to follow.

His father didn't mind either. "If that's what you want, Son" was all he said.

And for the next year and a half, Kamal loved Moad all the more.

After Kamal's very last exam (Islamic Jurisprudence of Transactions: B), first semester 2008, they could lie together in his room in the servants' wing at the Wadi Hanifah palace and simply celebrate another successful year.

They had been among the most outstanding students (particularly Kamal) ever since they'd fallen in love five years before.

"So what is your great dream, Cousin Abu Musa?" Kamal said.

"My cousin, Abu Muhammad. You always have your head in the clouds," Moad said. "Never here on Earth."

"I'm here now."

"In a desert wind—you tell me your greatest dream first, lover boy?"

"That we find the true path of the Prophet, peace be upon him."

"Shit, I knew you'd say something like that!"

"Or go on Hajj together again. Not just Umrah. But stop joking around for once, Cousin. What greater dream can there be than that we find the true path of the Prophet together, peace be upon him? Not Islam on the outside, but the true faith?" Kamal asked.

"You want me to stop joking for once? To go with you to America, Cousin—I really mean Massachusetts or Vermont—where we can live in peace. Or Canada," Moad said.

The TV was set to KSA1. It was nothing less than a soccer match between Riyadh archrivals Al Hilal and Al Nasr, broadcast live from King Fahd International Stadium. Moad was a fanatic "blue" Hilal fan, rooting most of all for its star, number 20, Yasser al-Qahtani. Qahtani was the "Sniper Robin Hood" in his ability to score goals no matter how the odds were stacked against him. Unmarried though in his late twenties, Qahtani was his hero—besides Kamal, of course. Moad always joked that Kamal better watch out, or he'd hook up with the famed number 20 instead.

Kamal loved to see Moad passionate, even though Qahtani hadn't scored. "Not yet, Cousin," Moad said, his large eyes glued to the wide-screen TV, which hung on the wall opposite Kamal's bed—really, their bed.

They were tired from their last exams, drifting off into the King-dom of Dreams on the wide queen-size bed during half-time. Kamal's head was still in the clouds and Moad's feet were still on the ground, so Moad was the first to hear the noise outside their door.

He thought it might be thunder. Maybe the *shamal* wind. There was a thud, as if something dropped on the floor, but dreamy-head Kamal just dozed off.

Of all the times to sleep . . . to dream!

Moad felt too good in his embrace to break the bonds. Even though Hilal and Nasr were still tied at 1, he felt too alive to worry. For truth be told, how many good Saudi and Arab boys did exactly what they were doing now? Oh, so many did—the only difference is, they marry the women assigned to them. Then they can be with men as much as they wanted. Moad just didn't like that secret bargain. He loved Kamal and Kamal loved him, so why should they pretend not to? The grand mufti, their uncle, told Moad it was *halal* to look down on Jews but *haram* to look up at the ass of another man during prayer—who had this all fucked up? Moad or Mufti Know-it-all?

didn't have to bother to go either, for just one wife had died. You'd think it was something that mattered more. He even forgot to move Kamal's room and never said another word to him on the subject—or even spoke to him about finding a wife.

But Moad's punishment was swift and severe. Sheikh Muhammad told him that he'd soon be exiled to America and that if he ever had just the slightest contact with Kamal again, one look, one e-mail, one IM, one phone call—*anything at all*—he would cut him off completely, by the knees, at his nuts. Moad would never receive one riyal again. Two weeks later, he shipped Moad off to the United States—California—and eventually university there (UCLA). Through friends, he was able to tell Kamal the bare minimum of what had happened, but he dared not do more. His father was dead serious, and with the Ministry of Interior behind him, Moad knew that his father would somehow find out and leave him with nothing.

"I know you understand. Don't worry. Maybe one day . . ." the message came from Moad.

KAMAL DIDN'T UNDERSTAND. He loved Moad with all his heart, just as he loved Indah Mother. He had never felt so sad and abandoned. It was as if Indah Mother had left for Indonesia all over again.

Indah was his only consolation. Maybe he should just join her in Indonesia. Indah was the rock of peace. What mattered to Kamal now? He had no one. Indah was his balm. Where could he go? What could he do? Indah was his soul.

"You have your God-given mission, Kecil," she wrote online. "God Almighty will show the way. God put you on this earth to change, the *sawur* told us that. You must lead the faith."

But Kamal could only miss Cousin Moad, his "Abu Musa," his only true and equal love.

"You will love again, but follow your mission," Indah wrote.

Kamal felt lost.

"God will show you," she wrote.

Yes, thank God, it was midyear break. Kamal could live on the

Internet instead of at KSU, chatting with Indah Mother, praying five times a day, and surfing the Web like a true American university student. For he was still just twenty-four and only left the screen for meals with the other servants, and once every Friday for Jumu'ah prayer at mosque. All other prayers he did in his room, the computer blazing away in the background. It stayed on 24/7.

Was he waiting for another message from Moad? He got none. Maybe that lost brother in California too, he almost forgot his name— right, that worthless Faisal. No word from him either.

Indah Mother was often online. They much preferred chatting online to talking on the phone. It felt so much more private and thoughtful. Written words had a way of lasting. They did not disappear in the air like talk.

And Kamal could reread her words over and over again, her words in English and a few special ones in Bahasa . . . words only the two of them truly understood.

And in his loneliness, in his search, Kamal found a new world. More precisely: the World Wide Web.

There was nowhere he didn't search. Every site was fair game.

In San Francisco, he found every gay bar and Human Rights Campaign site that slipped through the Saudi censors. There was no "brother" Faisal.

In Los Angeles, every gay and student chat room at UCLA or in nearby Brentwood or the beach at Santa Monica. There was no Moad.

In Indonesia, he found the gay sites too, the chat rooms with *banci:* boys with men and women with women and boys to men and to women and men, each with his own golden *susuk.*

"What a wild jungle Muslim paradise," Kamal wrote to Indah.

"Mind your mission," Indah wrote back. "Honor Widi."

So Kamal did.

He now found the sites of jihad. He would fight for the poor and suffering Muslims of Indonesia. He would fight for Muslims everywhere.

He would fight for God.

———

KAMAL HAD SPOKEN with his father only a few times since the final night with Moad. He had asked his father if he could live in a dorm at KSU the coming semester. His father didn't mind. "If that's what you want," he said.

With his father's help, Kamal got a single room, though it had to be specially converted from a double. He even got a single room in the most sought-after dorm at KSU: Number 12, directly across from the main entrance of the university's great Al Nakheel Mosque.

So when he left for KSU to begin his second semester 2008, Kamal had only his well-worn laptop, several *thobe*s and *shemagh*s, underwear, toiletries, and a small suitcase to take to his new room in Number 12—a single facing the Al Nakheel Mosque, just as he wanted. The "man from Chittagong" said he'd miss the everyday back-and-forth.

"Maybe one day," Kamal replied.

Setting up in his sandstone dorm room, Kamal turned on his laptop. Nothing else mattered. He trolled the jihadi sites, one more beautiful than the next.

He found a site with photos of all the 9/11 martyrs. He fell in love all over again. He surfed another site with photos of the London bombers. Not quite as moving, but still, there was a force.

Ah, but then he trolled the Indonesian jihadi sites of Widi's Islamic Martyrs and Jamaah Islamiyah, Al Qaeda's local allies. And God now showed him the path.

"I will honor Widi," he wrote to Indah.

"Only God will lead you," Indah wrote back.

"He has. I must fight in His way."

Everything now looked different. He still went to class, ate his meals, performed his prayers, and sat through the lectures, but he lived online.

Inside the jihadi Web, Kamal could enter Paradise with every martyr. He saw the before and after.

Before their martyrdom missions, the photos and videos of their dying declarations revealed Arab, Pakistani, and Indonesian boys like him.

After their ascent to Heaven, though, their faces turned from dark-skinned to white, the clouds of Heaven casting a pale shadow, each one more beautiful than the next.

Kamal imagined his own white future.

Who had worn the white of the Wahhab? Kamal knew: the Ikhwan, the Brothers, who loved each other till death and lived together as first cousins equal to one another in the *hujar* communes—the Army of the White, which had once fought for pure Wahhabi rule throughout Arabia.

There was no sin in white.

Kamal now saw for the first time: his father was perhaps old enough to have lived, if still only a boy, with the Ikhwan. For though his father's twin, Uncle Muhammad, had condemned Moad, his own father never judged or condemned Kamal. His father must have worn the white; he must've tasted the power of the Ikhwan, the men who love and honor the faith of the heart as first cousins or brothers to one another.

Kamal then had a dream. In the early morning before Fajr prayer, he saw his great and holy ancestor the Original Sheikh Wahhab dressed completely in white, skiing down the steepest snow-covered slope of Merapi itself until he landed at the five-star resort hotel below.

AS DREAMS HAD once changed Shaheed and Malik, Mullah Omar's seer, even Ahmad and Abby and Maryam, so this dream changed Kamal.

His bloodline gave him a unique role; his heritage ordained a powerful fate. He even bore the very name of Sheikh Abd al-Rahman ibn Hasan Al al-Sheikh—whose great book *The Victory of the Glorious* bin Laden himself told all Muslims held the key to understanding their faith. Kamal was the direct heir to bin Laden's most revered thinker. Every word of Osama's favorite author flowed through his blood and beat faithfully with his heart. He was heir to jihad as none other. It was clear what the dream meant: he now had to carry the jihad into our times.

Kamal soon knew he was on the right path too when he saw on Al Jazeera the dying declaration of a suicide bomber for Al Qaeda. Kamal looked straight into the jihadi's eyes, heard every word pour from the jihadi's lips, and watched every wave of the jihadi's hands as he told of his sacred mission, his jihad for God the Most High. Watching the jihadi's dying declaration on Al Jazeera, Kamal felt an uncontrollable force take over. Mysteriously rising in him, it struck like the *sawur* out of nowhere. It struck like Mount Merapi on fire. Jihad took him over in one violent tsunami.

It was now three months since Moad had left. It was three in the morning. But for the first time since Moad had been taken away, he felt alive.

Because watching this jihadi give his dying declaration, Kamal saw Moad (only with a full beard): his unblinking, dark eyes, his curling lashes and wavy brown eyebrows, loose and free. And Kamal felt as if Moad were in bed next to him: he now knew the way.

Before long Kamal took a brave step forward.

In between visits to gay chat rooms—Gulf Arab Love Online Live—he now began chatting in radical jihadi forums—Al Mahbubat—with other young men and boys.

They chatted about the injustices of Iraq and Palestine. Kamal told them of the pure brotherhood of the Ikhwan. They talked of the evil of America. He told them how the Original Sheikh rose from the desert to cleanse the land of false idols and restore the heart of submission to God. They chatted about Jews raping Muslim women and the virgins who'd greet them in Heaven. Kamal wrote of Indonesia and the sacrifice of Widi and the Islamic Martyrs.

Chatting in the virtual jihad, trading photos of men from around the world, sharing secrets, Kamal surfed and found a new world. It was as if he found Heaven's promised rewards, the immortal boys of youth, God's greatest servants, right here on Earth.

Toward the end of second semester, he went on a particularly intense Internet binge. It was two in the morning. He had a wicked headache. He had stayed up for two days now and, except for his five daily prayers, was lost in time, his thoughts lost in chat. Maybe he kept too many windows open. He couldn't keep track of who he was chatting with or which room he really was in. He even thought he might be getting sick, and he never got sick.

Until he met "Al Akbot," as he called himself, or "The Love Jihadi." Al Akbot asked to meet, in the flesh, so to speak. He wasn't too far from KSU, in Al Wisham, he wrote on Kamal's laptop screen. He'd come to him. Not a problem. He could even come right now. Straight to his lonely dorm room at KSU in Dorm Number 12. They could meet together that very night. He could be there before Fajr prayer.

Al Akbot was going to Iraq for jihad and wanted Kamal to come with him. They could be Ikhwan in jihad. Love Brothers in Martyrdom.

Al Akbot sent his photo. Kamal racked his soul to know where he had seen him before; he looked so familiar, so striking: Al Akbot—the Love Jihadi.

And for the first time since Moad had left, Kamal would have a companion to perform the nighttime Tahajjud prayer, when God is closest. He would finally not be alone.

Kamal gave the Love Jihadi his dorm address. The Americans had attacked a Muslim nation. Innocents were vilely tortured at Abu Ghraib. Fighting in defense of believers was the classic definition of jihad. Together with the Love Jihadi, Kamal could become a true brother in arms, a White Ikhwan, perhaps like his father—even a *shaheed,* if God so willed, to love again in Paradise. Kamal was ready to join Al Qaeda in Iraq. He would honor the Ikhwan path of his father; he would honor the sacrifice of his other "father," Widi.

Waiting for the Love Jihadi and Iraq, Kamal's head was floating; his eyes red; his stomach dizzy. He felt as though he were, in truth, skiing down Merapi, free fall. He opened a separate window in a Los Angeles chat room and, leaving the chat window with Al Akbot still open, he trolled for Moad at the same time. There was no Moad. It didn't matter. Kamal could dream of Iraq and the Heaven that waited. He would follow the Way of God in jihad.

But as Moad had left and was now in Los Angeles, the Love Jihadi seemed to leave him all alone too: it was almost time for Fajr prayer and he hadn't arrived at his dorm. Kamal didn't know whether to try to contact the Jihadi on the Internet again or just wait for him to come, if God so willed.

The next morning following prayers, Kamal went to his Islamic Jurisprudence of Penalties class, followed by Biography of the Prophet Muhammad and Umayyad Literature later in the day.

Kamal now planned how he would join the jihad. He was ready to fight in Iraq but knew he could have an even greater impact than a single soldier. As a Wahhab heir, he could write the ultimate religious justification, which would carry his family's holy seal, on the inherent individual duty of jihad. Kamal also knew that his cousin from Imam U. could move large sums through Doha and a shadow *hawala* network to Al Qaeda and Taliban headquarters in Pakistan. He also believed his cousin even had a way to wire the funds to Al Qaeda. Like thousands of other Saudis, who were the most significant source of financing for Al Qaeda, Kamal could simply donate the money directly. Though Kamal hadn't yet inherited his share of his father's more than $2 billion, he did have access to a personal trust account at Bank Julius Baer (Vienna branch) of some $143 million.

Al Qaeda and the Taliban, while not broke, were struggling for funding. Bin Laden himself had run through his personal fortune of no more than $30 million almost five years before 9/11. The 9/11 attacks themselves had cost at most only $500,000. Imagine what Al Qaeda and the Taliban could do with a sudden infusion of even a small portion of $143 million. In one moment, Al Qaeda would likely have more money than it had in the entire life of the group since 9/11—easily enough to purchase a nuclear weapon on the black market.

That night, after final Isha prayer at Al Nakheel Mosque across from his dorm, Kamal went to the Internet. As soon as he turned on his Sony laptop and before he could contact his cousin the Imam U. professor or search for the Love Jihadi again, an IM from Indah popped up. And before Kamal could tell her his plans, she wrote that her mother had died. Kamal immediately remembered how the death of Moad's mother had changed everything too, and now felt his own childhood die as quickly as the pop-up had interrupted his thoughts of jihad.

Lying on his bed with the laptop as his only light, an Indah-tear welled in his eyes. He knew that, whatever happened, he was on his own. He couldn't forever be her little Kecil. Now many Indah-tears fell.

He heard the red wind outside whipping through the KSU build-ings. He tried to smile through the tears like Indah. But the door broke open and the world busted in.

The time for dreams was over. The time for nightmares had begun.

HIS THIN WOODEN door burst off its hinges. Shadows of men flew everywhere, surrounding Kamal, curled up and shaking on his dorm bed barely off the floor. Lights like the BMW's set to high beam burned his eyeballs until he couldn't see; evil jinn shouted so loudly he couldn't hear. A sharp claw pulled his arm from its shoulder joint to the cold dorm floor.

The first thing that hit was a heavy black boot squeezing his head flat to bare ground. They didn't even push him to his prayer rug, which he kept right by the bed. They couldn't be Muslims: the Devil's very jinn!

The yelling attacked his ears. Curses like *guna-guna:* asshole dog, son of a whore. A new boot in the center of his back dug in even harder. A fiendish hand now grabbed one arm, then just as suddenly the other.

Metal cut through his skin as his left wrist was uncleanly latched to the right, before he was spun over from his back. Kamal now knew for sure: these monsters couldn't possibly be Muslims, grabbing his left hand first.

All he had on was a thin Speedo for bed. His legs, arms, and feet were naked. He felt himself shivering before a large stinking clam of spit landed directly between his eyes, running down his King Faisal nose directly onto his thin lips.

"You fucking piece of faggot terrorist swine!" the man yelled as if he were Dajjal the Deceiver standing in judgment. But Kamal could now see that this representative of Satan had a machine gun aimed directly at his head.

The dorm room lights abruptly went on for the first time. And Kamal could finally make out all the soldiers in desert camouflage standing around him—MOI, National Guard, or only God-knows-who.

He began to silently ask Allah the Most Compassionate to save him. For Allah knows best. He didn't want to open his mouth and say his prayer out loud, or he'd swallow the soldier's spit. He couldn't wipe it away. His hands were handcuffed behind his back. His shoulder hurt as if it had been broken. He couldn't talk. The spit would go in his mouth.

Kamal prayed with his sinking heart as the soldiers tore open his room, flinging the bed, tearing the curtains, ripping through his clothes, smashing his IKEA cabinets and drawers. One grabbed his Sony laptop. One grabbed his *thobe*. What were they looking for?

As quickly as the mayhem started, his room stripped with the force of a desert *shamal,* it all just stopped. The soldiers parted in the middle like the Red Sea before Moses. Abu Musa, Kamal thought, and felt his sudden loss.

Yet through the center of his tossed and twisted Number 12 converted double dorm room, dressed in a traditional white Saudi *thobe* with matching white *ghutra* headdress, he came. The only thing that marked him as different was the black pistol attached to his waist. Kamal felt a strange and unexplained hope before this man screamed as vilely as the others, "You fucking pieces of idiot scum!"

"Didn't mean to, Major" . . ." Didn't know, sir" . . . "Just followed procedure, Major H." . . . "So sorry, Major H.," different soldiers' voices mumbled back in turn.

"Secure him first before you start!" the new man shouted violently. "Damn!" he screamed. He almost began to take the name of Allah in vain as he held Kamal's official Saudi ID card in his hand.

"I'm Major Hameed," he now said. Kamal hated the relentless shouting that drowned out all sense. Thank God the new man spoke in a normal voice, without taking the name of the Bringer of Benefit and Harm in vain.

"I am sorry, you must be Sheikh Minister Abdullah's son, am I most correct?" the major asked in formal and official Arabic, still holding Kamal's ID.

Major Hameed had Moad's penetrating dark eyes, Indah Mother's red lips—though he wore a well-groomed but prominent mustache above them.

Kamal couldn't stop shaking. "Major H." took out a small white handkerchief and wiped all traces of the foul spit from Kamal's face.

Suddenly he kissed him on each cheek. He then gently lifted him by his shoulders—so gently in fact, that it didn't even hurt his sore shoulder. Just as quickly, Major H. jerked his head and shouted, "Get 'em off, you idiots!"

Kamal felt the handcuffs fall from his bruised wrists. The major now helped him up, while another soldier handed Kamal one of his white *thobe*s.

"I am most sorry; please now get yourself most fully dressed. You are indeed the most noblest born of His Eminence Sheikh Minister Abdullah . . . ?" Major H. tried again to speak in the highest obsequious language of formal Arabic.

"My father?" Kamal asked. He couldn't believe that his father would ever send the MOI—no, if anyone, it had to be his Uncle Muhammad who'd order up the MOI to teach Kamal a lesson. He wondered whether Moad might be back in the kingdom. Or perhaps the MOI was coming to tell him that his father had died.

"Is my father okay?" That's all Kamal could now think of as he unexpectedly felt the tears come back from earlier in the evening. It seemed like a lifetime ago.

"Most Honored Son of His Eminence Sheikh Abdullah," Major H. said. "Everything's okay. Please do not worry your noble head, but we must talk together at ministry headquarters. I must get official clearance. Please, most noblest son." The major kept trying to speak in formal Arabic but did not succeed. "We are most sincerely sorry, but we had no knowledge it was your room. The official records didn't list you as the occupant. It only showed a double room—not even a single. It wasn't our fault," he pleaded. "It's standard MOI protocol to secure the location first."

Major H. now put his right arm around him, as Kamal finished putting on his *thobe*. Another soldier brought him his sandals and slipped them on his bare cold feet.

Major H. held Kamal close. His arm felt warm. He smiled, and Kamal smiled back. The major was more handsome than any jihadi or gay man Kamal had ever seen online. He was as striking as Moad.

The major now ordered his men to find a *ghutra,* the all-white headdress, and a traditional *igal* with double black cords to secure it. But following in the footsteps of the Prophet, Kamal had abandoned his more formal wear and the soldiers searched in vain.

Major H. had to help him put on his red-checked *shemagh* head-dress instead. And since there was no *igal* to hold it in place, he had to delicately fit it to Kamal's head before carefully guiding him into the narrow dorm elevator. The small elevator barely had room for just the two of them.

The major was as tender now as Moad had ever been, as soft as his men had been hard and brutal, gently leading Kamal into an official Ministry of Interior car parked in front of the Al Nakheel Mosque. It was a black Ford Lincoln. One of the other soldiers—Kamal couldn't tell if he was one of the fiendish ones—drove.

Major H. sat close in the comfortable back leather seat. And for the first time since his dorm room had been busted in, Kamal didn't feel cold.

"Will I see my father there?" he asked.

"We must notify him. We have no choice. You understand that we had to secure the room first. Standard procedure. We meant you no harm of course, " he said.

Kamal didn't know what to say.

"You understand, honored son, don't you?" The major was now the one who seemed nervous.

Kamal still didn't know what he was supposed to say.

"You must understand. There was no record that you were the dorm occupant. I don't know how that happened. It was even listed as a double. It's an understandable error. I wouldn't want you to tell your most honorable father anything else."

Kamal felt light-headed. It was past midnight. He'd hardly had any dinner. "We just have to ask you a few questions," Major H. wouldn't stop nervously talking. "We'll give you *gahwa* and tea. We even have dates—the very best from each region: Sukkary, Khlas, and Ajwah, of course. Are you hungry? We'll get you something to eat. Please do not worry, we'll call your most noble father so he can come and get you as soon as we clear procedure."

Accompanied by a phalanx of black GMC Yukons, the Lincoln pulled up to the concrete barriers and more soldiers. Kamal could see through the darkened window the massive Ministry of Interior headquarters building before him, a giant desert pyramid turned on its head.

The soldiers waved the Lincoln through the maze of cement barriers directly to the front door. As the major helped him from the car, soldiers stiffly saluted.

And as they went through the glass doors into the vast open-air marbled lobby, it looked more like the spectacular ground floor of one of Riyadh's best malls, the Al Faisaliah or Al Mamlaka, than the headquarters of the most powerful government agency in the kingdom. Kamal didn't want his father to come and get him. He felt sure the "man from Chittagong" could just drive him home—he couldn't return to his broken dorm.

They took one of the mall-like glass elevators to the highest floor. The elevator quickly flew to the top, and Kamal felt even more light-headed. He needed food. He didn't want to face his father.

The elevator door opened silently, and Major H. put his strong arm around his shoulder, leading him down a bright white corridor. Kamal's shoulder no longer hurt, though his eyes had trouble adjusting to the burning fluorescent light—brighter than the midday sun, even though they were inside the MOI headquarters in the middle of the night.

Major H. held him close—too close. Kamal couldn't help it. He was trying not to. With all the strength he had left—he was exhausted, drained, wasted—he tried his best. But with Major H. holding him so tenderly, he now felt Moad's sweet embrace. Oh, Moad! Where was he now? My Abu Musa! If they had just been able to be together, none of this would have happened.

They went into a large wood-paneled conference room with a great mahogany table, a hanging bright green flag of the Kingdom of Saudi Arabia, and oversized full color portraits of Kamal's cousins: the Custodian of The Two Holy Places, the king, and His Royal Highness, the Minister of Interior.

A lieutenant handed Kamal a cup of *gahwa,* which he downed in one shot before the officer poured his cup half full again, waiting for him to finish before pouring again. It was as if he were an honored guest of the ministry, now served sweet tea and dates, which he devoured like a starving Bedouin.

"I will order a lamb *kabsa* for you, or would you prefer *korsan?*"

"Doesn't matter, don't trouble yourself, Major," Kamal said.

"Please, Abu Zaki," the major said.

"It's Abu Muhammad," Kamal said, extending his hand.

"Honored to officially meet you," Major H. said, shaking his right hand and then kissing him on both cheeks again.

The major now tried to make small talk: first about soccer, then cars and desert hunting, none of which worked.

"Maybe we should pray together instead," Kamal finally said. The Tahajjud, his favorite prayer, when God is closest. At least Kamal would not be alone.

Major H. got another officer to bring them prayer rugs. As they laid the prayer rugs together, the major did another incredibly kind act and let Kamal lead them in prayer.

"*Shukran,*" Kamal said after prayer. "Allah the Gentle knows best."

The food came, and Kamal ate with the speed of a true *bedu*. Even though his fingers were still cold, he finally felt he was beginning to relax.

"I've called your father. He's on his way here to fetch you," Major H. said.

"You mean he's coming himself?" Kamal said, wishing his father were just sending the "man from Chittagong" instead.

"I need to ask you one question, if you don't mind, honored son, I mean, Abu Muhammad, if you don't mind, before your father, I mean His Eminence, arrives," the major said, more nervous than Kamal. "I need to—must—protocol, just one question; you understand, of course, the clearance is official, just procedure. What were you doing on that kind of site? I mean, how did you get there? Did someone tell you about it?"

Kamal didn't know whether the major was asking about a gay or jihadi site. He didn't know whether the MOI had come to question him for visiting a gay site, a jihadi site, or both. He wondered if there were any gay jihadi sites and smiled at the thought.

"I fail to see the humor," the major now said in a more formal tone.

"I am sorry, major. I was just surfing the Internet, not really thinking, mindlessly going from one site to another."

"I see, and . . ."

"And? Youthful curiosity. I was lonely. It passed the time. I never would've done anything. Allah knows best."

Kamal was no fool. After the food and the initial shock had worn off, it was time to protect himself. He knew that a ministry major, no matter how handsome and gentle, was questioning him. And even though a religious aristocrat, he knew what to say.

"Did anyone tell you to go to the site?"

"I was just surfing around."

"Did you ever meet anyone?"

"All talk."

"And what if Al Akbot, the Love Jihadi from Al Wisham, had come to take you to fight in Iraq?"

"He's come now," Kamal said, realizing for the first time that it was Major H.—though much younger—in the photo. No wonder he looked so familiar. Kamal must've met him when he guarded his father. Kamal smiled.

But the major had to follow protocol and official decorum. "You know it's a crime?" he quickly added.

Kamal could only smile again but, like Indah Mother, didn't know if he was really smiling or crying.

"It'll be all right. Please do not worry your most noble self." The major turned to look Kamal in the eye. "Please just don't tell your father about the rough stuff. I mean, if anyone would understand MOI protocol, it'd be your father. But we wouldn't want to get an officer into any unnecessary trouble, now would we?" The major finally smiled.

"It's okay," Kamal said, smiling in turn.

Major H. winked. And Kamal thought that the major really liked him too.

EVERYTHING WAS DIFFERENT when his father came.

Left alone in the cavernous conference room, Kamal felt an overwhelming urge to pee and called for an officer to take him to the toilet. Returning to the empty room, he felt he had to pee again. Was Major H. now talking to his father? Telling him that his boy had been arrested for going to a gay site? To a jihadi site? To both? Kamal didn't know what his father would say. He just felt glad that no one knew of his plans to donate part of his fortune to Al Qaeda.

But when the major and his father finally came through the conference room's grand door, as the officers had burst through his dorm door earlier that same eternal night, his father suddenly said, "You know, Kamal, it's the middle of the night. Time for Tahajjud prayer."

Oh yes, Kamal knew, when God is in the closest Heaven. He also knew the overriding power of royal influence (*wasta*) and the official privilege and immunity afforded to the ruling aristocracy.

"I am sorry, Father," he said. Kamal deliberately chose not to address him as Sheikh but Father. He wanted to show his love. He wanted to receive his father's mercy.

But the sheikh addressed the major instead: "Tell him the sentence for his offense, Major."

"Yes, sir, Your Eminence. It's three years, one hundred lashes."

"Did you hear that, Son?"

Kamal heard nothing. He couldn't believe his father would do this to him.

"Well," his father said.

"I never meant to hurt anyone," Kamal said. "I never meant to hurt you, Father."

As the major proved kind, given his role and position, Kamal was now proved right about his father too.

"Kamal, I know. I'm not your Uncle Muhammad. You are my last son."

Kamal now looked into his eyes, and another Indah-tear fell, one left over from the beginning of the evening so long ago.

"But Kamal, I cannot just let you go home, like nothing happened, like you're special only because you're my son," he said.

Could Kamal be wrong about his father?

"The major and I have discussed it. We agree. There will be no record of your arrest, no judge, no time in prison for what you did. Do you understand me, Kamal?"

"Yes, Father," Kamal said softly. He didn't know what to think.

"I will tell the rector that you need just a little time away from school, and . . ."

Kamal didn't know what would happen. He was in his father's hands.

"I can't say," the former minister said. "I can't say the words. Major, tell him."

"Yes, Your Eminence. Kamal, the MOI has a Care Center just outside Riyadh. It's not a jail, don't worry—" He stopped himself in midsentence.

Kamal swallowed. The tears dropped from his eyes, and exactly like Indah Mother again, he was smiling through his tears, not knowing why.

"We have psychological counseling there," the major continued, "religious reeducation, vocational training—I guess you won't need that—art therapy, writing, sports. We even call it 'The Resort.' It's like a halfway house to get you back on your feet."

"Then you can go back to KSU," his father quickly added, "resume your studies. Think of it as a short trip to the desert, 'get you back on your feet,' as the major said."

"Your Eminence is most correct. Truly, Kamal, we have a lot of success at the Care Center. There'll be no record of your arrest. No record even of your stay. And you don't have to be there for very long. Once released, none of our guests has gone back to his former ways. We are certain you won't either, *Inshallah*."

"*Inshallah*," Kamal replied.

"He's a good boy, Major. Make sure he's well taken care of," his father said, as he called for the Bangladeshi driver to lead him away.

Kamal wondered if he would ever see his father again.

MAJOR H. DROVE Kamal to the Care Center that very night. It was the longest night of his short life.

As a sign of friendship, the major held his hand in the backseat of the ministry Lincoln. Another officer was at the wheel, while more official black Yukon SUVs accompanied them on all sides.

Speeding over Riyadh's superhighways even faster than Widi's brother had plowed through the back roads of Indonesia, Kamal felt safe with Major H. holding his hand, until he finally remembered.

"What's going to happen to my stuff?" he asked.

"Don't worry, we packed everything up," the major said.

"My laptop?"

"That's what got you into trouble in the first place."

"You don't understand. I need it." Kamal was frantic. How would he reach Indah? "It's not fair. It's not what you think," he pleaded.

"What do I think?" the major asked.

"It's for my mother, I mean my nanny, the woman who raised me. We chat online all the time. When she doesn't hear from me, she'll worry."

"Well, we can send her something."

"She's in Indonesia, Major." Kamal thought he was about to cry. It was the long night, so much had happened. He was just twenty-four years old.

"Don't worry." Major H. squeezed his hand. "I'll tell the general to let you on the Internet. We'll make an exception. But someone will be with you the whole time. You're forbidden to surf any sites, do you understand?"

"Thank you. Thank God."

"Just go on to chat and e-mail her in the Philippines."

"Indonesia."

"Same difference."

"Indonesia's Muslim."

"Right."

"The world's largest Muslim country."

But what could he tell Indah? He knew for the first time in his life that he'd lose the truth that had always bound them. It was just another way things were changing for him; just another way he knew that when he did get out, he'd have to change even more.

The officer driving sped over the highways as if he were late to an Indonesian burial. It didn't matter that it was past three in the morning, Riyadh's freeways always had traffic and many official checkpoints—only they didn't have to stop.

Kamal stared out the window. As they left the city proper, he could see the ATVs dodging barbecue grills and ice cream vans in the rocky desert. They went through the resort of Al Thumama, famous for its *estirahas*—though none even remotely approached the grandeur and opulence of his own in the Wadi Hanifah. They finally passed "Al Fantazi Land," the "Magic Kingdom" inside the Magic Kingdom, where Kamal never had the chance to go.

It came after Fantasy Land. Kamal heard dogs barking. The Yukons and then the Lincoln went through an unmarked gate, and a stray white cat jumped out of the way.

"Welcome home," Major H. said, smiling as he let go of Kamal's soft, sweaty hand.

The MOI Lincoln pulled up to the entrance of a tentlike *majlis* reception area—similar to his father's, only not so fancy, of course.

Kamal could finally see a sign: MINISTRY OF INTERIOR, DEPARTMENT OF PUBLIC RELATIONS, CARE CENTER, MAJOR GENERAL YOUSEF MANSOUR, COMMANDER.

As soon as the Lincoln came to a full stop, someone short, not even five foot six, quickly opened the door. The first thing that greeted Kamal was a large belly, which lifted the short man's white *thobe* like a blimp hanging over Fantasy Land. With a crooked-toothed smile, his face was clean-shaven (although it looked as if he'd missed a day), except for a faint, gray pencil-thin mustache above his narrow lips. His fat hand slapped Kamal hard across the back. Maybe it only hurt because of the boot that had been planted there seven hours before.

"My noble son, my noble son, not to worry, not to worry, welcome to the 'oasis of knowledge,' great to have ya here," the man barked like a small dog. "I'm General Mansour, but you can call me Abu Yousef," he said, shaking his hand in greeting.

This was General Mansour? Oh well, Kamal felt certain that the camp commander never personally greeted any of the other newly arrived "guests" at four in the morning!

Kamal put his right hand over his heart in a sign of respect.

"Not to worry, not to worry, you're just in time for Fajr prayer," the general said.

"Major," Kamal said, "could you please tell General Mansour."

Major H. took General Mansour aside. When the general emerged, he clung to Kamal like a long-lost buddy, kissing him on both cheeks and shaking his hands incessantly up and down.

"Not to worry, not to worry, Kamal, sweet boy, my noble son. You need a computer to write your nanny. You can use mine," the general said, placing the tip of his right forefinger to the tip of his nose—a traditional Bedouin gesture meaning "consider it done."

"For you," the general continued. "You can use my very own computer indeed. The very one in my personal office. Whenever you want. But not during class or prayer time."

"Class? I'm already in class at KSU," Kamal said.

"Not to worry, not to worry, these are our classes; you'll like them just fine. We even have some professors from KSU too, the dean of the Psychology Department. We're all nice here."

Major H. now gave Kamal the traditional kiss good-bye.

"You will not forget me here," Kamal said.

"We'll have you home before you know it," the major said. "You'll be well. Everything will work out, *Inshallah*." Holding hands, they walked together to the Lincoln. Behind the car, Major H. leaned over to kiss Kamal again on the cheeks. Whatever happened, Kamal had faith in him. *"Inshallah,"* he said as the major quickly retreated inside the Lincoln.

"Not to worry, not to worry," General Not-to-worry now said, the Lincoln pulling away.

Kamal was still smiling Indah-like through his tears.

The general started babbling on about all the professors from KSU at the Care Center, the art therapy, Kamal would be in a special "rest home," Unit 2; he'd like the other boys there, not to worry.

Kamal already missed Major H. He missed Indah. He missed his special room in Dorm Number 12 and the Wadi Hanifah dream *estiraha* with its bright stars. He missed his father.

"You stand by me," the general said. They were together at the place of honor in the *majlis* tent. "I'll take good care of you, not to worry, my noble son."

"Allah knows best," Kamal said.

Dr. Ali, the psychological counselor and KSU professor, was the first in line. He warmly took Kamal's hands and greeted him profusely with kisses on both cheeks.

Next came Dr. Awad al-Yami, another KSU professor and art therapist, and Dr. Sheikh Ahmad Hamad Jelan, the religion professor, followed by Dr. Hamid al-Shaygi, the sociological counselor, Dr. Nasser al-Arifi, the criminal psychiatrist, and Dr. Turki al-Otayan, the chief psychologist and yet another professor—it was indeed as if Kamal were back at KSU.

Then one by one, they began to trickle in, the halfway house inmates from Unit 2—no, no, "our resort guests, my noble son, *guests,*" the general corrected Kamal.

As the other "guests" arrived for dawn prayer in the *majlis* greeting tent, the men all had the long beards and white robes of the Holy Prophet. With General Not-to-worry standing next to him, the men formed a long line, welcoming Kamal with the customary cheek-kissing.

Each of Kamal's jihadi Internet photos had come to life. Oh, did his father have any idea what he was sending him to? Then again, from his ancient Ihkwan past, maybe he did.

As Kamal knelt with the other men in dawn prayer, he knew he was blessed. Kamal thanked God for His wisdom. He thanked God for His compassion. He thanked God for His infinite mercy and judgment. He thanked Allah the Well-Acquainted. Kamal thanked God for his father.

After prayer, the boys all huddled around him before leading the way to his new "rest home." They walked across grassy courtyards and a soccer field.

The "rest home" for Unit 2 was a long cement dorm, with bunk beds and ten boys all sleeping in rows. Kamal was given a bunk near the door. Someone had put his suitcase on the bed already, along with a "welcome package" of gifts: *thobe*s, notebooks, soap, candy bars (Twix, his favorite) and a wristwatch set to the lunar calendar and Islamic holidays.

Kamal was smiling away. Everything seemed just fine—until he saw the toilet. It was simply a hole in the ground covered by porcelain, with a chain pulley to flush but no seat. He knew this was the traditional Saudi way—he had just never used one. At twenty-four years old, Kamal, a Saudi, had never squatted before. Even the Merapi resort in Indonesia had real toilets.

"Oh well, not to worry, not to worry," he said to Falah, another "guest."

Falah started laughing silently like Mumbly, the cartoon dog with the wheezing laugh.

RIGHT FROM THE start, Kamal knew he liked Falah the most.

Falah was twenty-four, the same age as Kamal, except a month older. In the past, Saudis had never kept track of their birthdays or ages. Not this new generation. They knew.

The boys were about the same height too, around five feet, eleven inches or so, and not into soccer either, though Falah said he liked to swim in the Care Center pool.

Falah had the brown eyes of a desert oryx. Unlike Kamal though, his teeth could rarely be seen, with a shy smile reflecting good Saudi manners. Whenever Falah glanced your way, he'd give a quick wink too—not like Moad's endless stare. Kamal wondered where Moad was now but just wanted to forget.

And unlike most of the other boys, Falah had a thin beard, not very full, and was thin in frame as well. He showed only a little fat around his belly. And Kamal could hear his breathing every night, as his bunk bed was next to him.

Falah's offense was that his father had suddenly dropped dead of a stroke and, just as precipitously, Falah had then taken off to fight in Iraq. He had spent six months fighting for Al Qaeda when the Americans bombed his safe house. One of the few survivors of the attack, he had been held at Abu Ghraib before he was shipped back to Saudi Arabia. From Ha'il north of Buraydah, Falah was studying air-conditioning repair at vocational college.

Three years, two months, and three days in jail for "associating with deviants." He had served every day of that sentence at Al Ha'ir prison, and now had been at "the Betty Ford Jihadi Clinic" for six months, counting the unknown months and days before he would "graduate."

Jamil was in the bunk across and became Kamal's second-best friend. He was slight like Falah, but only twenty-three. From Asir, the province in the far south of Saudi Arabia, his lilting voice sounded almost Indonesian. Maybe that's just an Asiri accent, Kamal thought. He had never met anyone from Asir. Jamil had been at the Care Center for only two days and stayed close like a brother—or first cousin.

Kamal never had a group of friends like this before. He had no friends in primary, middle, or secondary school. At university, there was only Moad. Kamal had always stood apart. Now, for the first time in his life, he was " one of the boys."

Abdullah al-Gilani from Taif, whom everyone called just Abby, became Kamal's third close friend. Abby was tall and thin, with an equally thin mustache (no beard) and quiet smile. Abby had also gone to Iraq to fight but had always known that jihad in the Way of God was love. And Kamal was the only inmate at the Care Center that Abby had told about his "secret angel Maryam." He had even shared with him all of their poems and Maryam's last letter good-bye.

Kamal also got to know the "graduates" of the Care Center who came to visit. In his twenties as well, Ahmad al-Shayea ("Bernie") from Buraydah was his favorite. Even though his face was disfigured by the misplaced force of his suicide bomb, Kamal could see inside his eyes, as limpid and watery as Indah's. (Kamal smiled at his American nickname too but didn't tell him why he was called Bernie.)

THE JIHADIS FROM Guantánamo were from a different planet.

The most famous recent "graduate" of the Care Center after Ahmad al-Shayea was Juma al-Dosari. He really wasn't all that bad-looking, Kamal thought. At five feet, five inches, he was skinny from stomach-stapling surgery. It was hard to believe he'd once weighed 274 pounds. His nose hooked a bit, though that just made it take after Kamal's cousin King Faisal. Kamal saw his eyes only once for a second or two. They weren't bad either, with a slight hazel tint to the brown. He didn't know why Juma always kept them covered with dark sunglasses, as if totally veiled like a woman.

When he was sixteen, Juma had left Dammam on the eastern shore of Saudi Arabia for Afghanistan. More than any other act as a Muslim, Juma said, becoming a jihadi would "make him a hero." He had chased that dream from Saudi Arabia to Afghanistan, Bosnia, and the United States before returning to Afghanistan after 9/11.

While in the United States, Juma boasted, he had inspired the only American-born group ever to attend Al Farooq, Osama bin Laden's Afghan training camp. The American men were in their early twenties and had graduated from Lackawanna High School. Juma had met with them regularly at a small apartment above the Arabian Foods deli in Lackawanna, New York, where he was a guest imam at the Guidance Mosque.

"They were all-American boys," Juma said.

"Like Marcia's brothers on *The Brady Bunch*?" Kamal asked.

Juma had challenged the American boys: they could be Muslim heroes, jihadis who could fight for their brethren, as Juma had in Afghanistan. "What kind of Muslims were they now? They knew the names of sports stars better than the companions of the Prophet. They could recite every Hollywood movie, but not every verse of the Holy Qur'an. They had easy, beautiful women, while Muslim women were raped in Afghanistan. "

The boys became famous. Singled out by the president of the United States, they were even called the "first American Al Qaeda sleeper cell." Yet Juma did not become the jihadi hero he had always longed to be.

Picked up in Afghanistan after 9/11, Juma finally found the key to his dream at Guantánamo, where he was confined for seven long years.

He discovered that being an American victim made him a Muslim hero. He told Kamal and the other boys how he now met official delegations from Western Europe, Japan, and the United States, and even sat down for a private meeting with British Prime Minister Gordon Brown. While claiming his complete innocence, Juma recounted his torture at Guantánamo on Saudi television—in Arabic on KSA1 and in English on KSA2. He appeared on Al Jazeera and Al Arabiya across the Arab world. In the United States, Juma was featured on the front page of *The Washington Post*. He was the subject of a half-hour interview on the BBC. And the Associated Press quoted Juma among "world leaders." The Americans had turned him into a jihadi hero at last.

But Kamal could never trust any man who couldn't look him in the eye.

Juma's best friend at the Care Center was a fellow Gitmo jihadi, Ghanim Abdul Rahman al-Harbi. Leaving his father's car dealership in Dammam, Ghanim had also gone to Afghanistan in 2001, before the Americans arrested him. Large and fat with a long beard and wide yellow-toothed smile, Ghanim had spent seven years at "the different planet" too, where for seventy-two straight hours, baby naked, his hands had been bound to his feet, without food, bathroom, or shower. He'd had to live like a tortured fetus.

Ghanim and Juma had another Gitmo jihadi friend at the Care Center too: Said Ali al-Shihri. Said had much the same story as Ghanim and Juma. He'd gone to Afghanistan to purchase carpets for his family's store in Riyadh. He had never fought for Al Qaeda and promised to happily return to the family furniture store in Riyadh if released.

Except it was a "lie for jihad." Said was an Al Qaeda fighter fleeing Afghanistan when the Pakistanis turned him over to the Americans for a $5,000 bounty. And despite his cries that "bin Laden had divorced himself from Islam," Said was Al Qaeda throughout his years at Guantánamo and an Al Qaeda warrior when he was sent from Gitmo back to Saudi Arabia. He "stayed below the gaze of infidels," saying whatever his captors wanted to hear while remaining steadfast throughout his confinement and "reformation" in Saudi Arabia. He was still a soldier set to fight when released again from the Care Center, leading the bombing that killed sixteen people at the U.S. Embassy in Yemen before becoming the mastermind behind the 2009 Christmas day attack on Northwest flight 253 over Detroit, and a top leader of Al Qaeda in the Arabian Peninsula. Said was now committed to transforming Saudi Arabia into a gas station for Al Qaeda, pumping its vast reserves into a dedicated "killing America project." This was the hatred that in the name of the purest Islam turned his blood black as oil.

Yet Kamal understood something about Said (and Osama, for that matter) that no Westerner could really understand. Kamal knew the power of God's words, in the Holy Book and the Hadith of the Prophet, of course, but also in the writings of his Wahhabi ancestors, which Kamal as heir had the right to interpret for our times. His words would matter to the jihadis.

Kamal now also learned the "magic" of the kingdom's prisons. You were given a choice: rot away like a caged scorpion in jail or be released with the Ministry of Interior's full blessing, the ministry buying a new house for you and your family, securing a desirable job or helping with further education, even paying the rather steep price for a handsome dowry. In Egypt, the leading jihadis, Sayyid Qutb and Ayman al-Zawahiri, had been tortured in Egyptian jails and had come out more radical than when they went in. But in Saudi Arabia, the price of freedom came with a handsome bounty. Every single jihadi who emerged from the Betty Ford jail with a message of love was bought and paid for with a home, job, spending money, even a new dowry and wife. Kamal had to admire Said al-Shihri in at least one respect: he wouldn't be bribed. He had to admire Osama bin Laden for the same reason.

Yes, his forefather Muhammad Wahhab was willing to sacrifice all worldly comforts for the glory of God. In our times, Kamal had to acknowledge, it was only Osama who gave up everything for faith.

Kamal started to talk to these Gitmo refugees from another planet. He now began to see that Al Qaeda's jihad fell short. Despite bin Laden's sacrifices, his jihad wasn't about finding the difficult struggle to better himself and others before God. Instead, Al Qaeda offered too much of a quick-and-easy path, a simple shortcut with ready-made answers that can lure someone from the long and hard true jihad of God.

"The idol-worshipping Indians gave us Gandhi. Where's the Muslim Gandhi? The Christians, who even worship a human prophet as divine, delivered Nelson Mandela. Where's the devout Muslim now following in the footsteps of the Prophet Jesus and most of all, Prophet Muhammad, who'd renounce everything for love?" Kamal said, "A leader who'd follow not only what the Prophet did fourteen hundred years ago, but what the Prophet would do, from his heart, if he were with us today."

Kamal knew he had to find a different way to reach Al Qaeda's followers. He was not sure yet how, but felt blessed, for now, to be in Unit 2 with his new friends.

EVERY PRAYER, five times a day, Kamal, Falah, Jamil, and Abby prayed together. Every meal they ate together (the cook was Syrian, and the food tasted almost Lebanese). And practically every class, from The Holy Qur'an in the Correct Path to Scientific Understandings of Jihad to Islamic Art Therapy and True History of Muwahhidun Thought (naturally his favorite, though he told no one, not even Falah, that he was an Al al-Sheikh), the four men were together.

There were some classes they didn't share, of course (Kamal never went to vocational training). It didn't matter. There were plenty of other nice jihadi boys. All the MOI guards were great too. The jihadis and guards even swam as a group, played soccer on the same teams, prayed as one, and ate as one. The only thing missing was sleeping together. It was all part of the "Jihadi Reformation Project" to reha-bilitate the holy warriors into productive, loyal citizens of the King-dom of Saudi Arabia.

Then Kamal had a dream. "Like Martin Luther King," he said to me, smiling.

He had been at the Care Center for a little more than two weeks. He sent an e-mail to Indah that everything with him was *"why what come again"* (though he didn't say where he was now living). He even told General Not-to-worry to let his father know that things were going well.

"Oh, I will, my noble son, not to worry, not to worry." General Mansour was grateful for another chance to call His Eminence the Sheikh with a personal report.

It was a morning dream, an hour before dawn prayer. Kamal was even a little awake while he dreamed, and could hear Falah breathing.

In the dream, he was praying with Falah when Major H. came to him. "I'm not Moad, you can trust me," the H Man said. Then the face of his father appeared instead, first red, then dripping with blood.

"I'm not just your 'father' any more. I come with love. For His Holy Word says in Surah al-Ma'idah, 'If He had wanted, He would have made all of you the same.'"

Then Kamal saw the earthquake victims, half-dead men, maimed, uncovered women, and motherless children. They were not alone. Swimming with the clouds, Kamal also saw the Indonesian *banci* and Widi's Islamic Martyrs, the American Red Cross workers and even the Panti Rapih Catholic nuns. With God in their heart, they all wear white, drinking of the milky river. Free as green birds, all are now ageless, all can see Allah together, yet Kamal is still himself; floating above yet still on Earth, praying to Allah but witnessing His almighty power through the bare flesh of his feet planted to the ground.

Still dreaming, Kamal grew on the tips of his toes, tall enough to hover above Falah—and dark-skinned Falah turned completely white too, another martyr ascending to Heaven.

Kamal woke up. All his bunkmates were still asleep. He got up from his dream and stood next to Falah's bed.

Falah was breathing in and out in sleep, but his wide mahogany-colored eyes were, curiously, still completely open. Kamal could see inside. He reached out with his right fingers, as if to touch the whites of Falah's eyes. But Falah woke. Turning his head, he reached out to hold Kamal's hovering fingers before getting out of bed and leading him to the shower.

Kamal was the first person Falah, the Al Qaeda in Iraq fighter, had ever loved. And Kamal had never thought it possible after Moad to love another man again. But once more, miraculous Mother Indah had the power of a seer. She had said that Kamal would find another man. And *why what come again,* he did. Allah knows best.

For three weeks the lovers were in bliss, and since they never announced themselves as lovers (and Falah never even thought of them that way), all was well in the Betty Ford jihadi jail behind Fantazi Land and the Lebanese Fruits Restaurant, in the Al Thumama resort just northeast of Riyadh.

Kamal and Falah were on the greater jihad of love.

———

IT WAS the kiss. Sure, it was fine for men to kiss on both cheeks and embrace. That's the traditional *bedu* greeting. It's just that Kamal and Falah's kiss . . .

"Well, there are rules for this kind of thing," Kamal told me.

The Unit 2 boys were splashing in the pool during free swim time, chasing one another, some playing tag, some tossing a volleyball in a game not to let it touch the water. The jihadis were carrying on. There were even a couple of MOI guards swimming with them, and Falah and Kamal were in the shallow end, laughing about something, when Falah grabbed Kamal by the shoulders and Kamal just as suddenly gave him a quick kiss on the lips.

The other boys started cheering and splashing them. The guards didn't seem to mind either.

Two days later, General Not-to-worry met with Kamal and Falah in the prison's ceremonial *majlis* tent. It was strange that the general asked them to appear together. He was constantly solicitous of Kamal but had never once met with Falah the entire seven months he had been at the Care Center.

A Bangladeshi servant first served them the ritual shot of *gahwa,* followed by a small glass of highly sweetened tea, accompanied by fresh Sukkary dates. Kamal thought they were particularly good and told Not-to-worry to his face, "General, these are the best dates I've tasted in ages." He let loose a particularly wide smile. "Particularly sugary sweet." (A pun in Arabic, as *sukkary* means "sugary.")

But Not-to-worry seemed worried. He didn't laugh at Kamal's joke, as he always had before. He didn't even answer him. It was the first time he failed to address him "my noble son." It was the first time he didn't say "not to worry."

Kamal was worried.

Sure enough, after the traditional coffee, tea, and dates, the general got straight to the business of the day. General Mansour offered each of the boys a $25,000 dowry to marry a wife.

"Does that mean I'm going to be released?" Falah asked.

"You mean 'graduated.' If your family has a girl for you," the general said.

Falah had always wanted his second cousin because she had blue eyes and was not like the others. And Falah knew he was a little different too. Having loved Kamal, he was ready to love again—and this time, he thought, in the accepted way with a wife. Jihad didn't seem to matter as much as love or his freedom. His second cousin's mother was actually Palestinian or something, and now, with $25,000, he finally had enough for a dowry. His family could never afford such a dowry.

As he dismissed Falah, the general said he could "graduate" in a week and go back home to Ha'il, six hundred kilometers from Riyadh.

Kamal looked down. All he could think of was Moad.

The general had a big potbelly that shook when he laughed and said "not to worry." And he wore a full-toothed grin when talking to any of the "guests"—or "beneficiaries," as he now preferred to call them.

"Well, well," the general said, the sounds coming from deep in his chest—or belly. "Not to worry, not to worry . . ." he started. Kamal was worried sick.

"Time for Kamal," the general said, at last flashing his toothy smile. "Time for my noble son, the other half of the Care Center Siamese twins here, to speak his piece."

Kamal couldn't find the words. Was his dream a lie? No, he had faith in his heart, in Almighty God the All-Compassionate, All-Merciful, and All-Knowing.

"I don't have anyone," he said to the general. "*La ilaha illa Allah*— There is no God but God," he said, feeling the tears collect in his eyes, the smile then come reflexively to his face.

"That's all right, my noble son, not to worry, you'll have someone someday, *Inshallah,* it is God's will." The general downed another shot of Arabian coffee in one gulp, and an African servant, another descendant of a slave freed in 1962 by Kamal's cousin, promptly refilled the general's cup.

"*Inshallah,*" Kamal said.

"We'll *graduate* you next week anyway, Kamal, most noble son of His Eminence, if you promise your General Yousef on just one little matter." The general now turned to look at him directly.

Kamal didn't know what to say. "Yes, General," he said. The African servant waited to refill his cup.

"I don't mind who you're with," the general began. "Your noble family will find you a little sweetieheart, even if you're passing up a handsome dowry now. It's not that you need our dowry, of course. Just promise your dear old general friend here that you will not forget me, and from now, you shall only . . ."

Kamal caught his breath and looked at the ground again. He didn't want to lie in front of God. He would not lie, no matter what, before God. But he wanted to get out of this jail—sorry, halfway house. He had to get out now since Falah would be gone.

"Just go back to King Saud U. and study hard. Study hard, my noble son. Your esteemed father can always find you a little sweet-heart—or two," the general said, laughing and putting his right index finger to the tip of his nose. "Not to worry. You just make sure to tell your father, His Eminence, that I took good care of you here. Don't forget. You're all better now. You just tell him."

Kamal was dying to say "Not to worry," but with his and Falah's freedom on the line, he had no choice but to be dead serious.

"Yes, sir, General Mansour. I will tell my father how much you've helped me, how much I've changed."

Kamal would not lie and didn't now. He knew he had truly changed. He would find the path to show Said and the Al Qaeda soldiers the true jihad to lead the faith, as he had showed to Falah with love. As Indah had always told him he would—and God had begun to show him the way.

Bin Laden, Al Qaeda, and other radicals were steadfast in their belief that their jihad, as passed down from Kamal's family, meant to attack America and wage a holy war. Imbued with the God-given heritage of his pious forefathers, Kamal now knew he had the right, above these so-called radicals, to pronounce the meaning of jihad from the Wahhab line.

Kamal hardly talked to Falah again. They were both released the next weekend, on Thursday, before Friday Jumu'ah prayer. Falah's family had come to take him home.

The boys didn't even get to say good-bye. And, of course, they never took another shower together again. Or stole a single kiss. Their freedom was at stake, and at least for Falah, it might be his only chance. God knows how long he'd be confined if he dared spend any time with Kamal again. Jamil now stayed closer to him than before, but Kamal had the only thought anyone ever confined clings to the most: to get out.

At last, the "man from Chittagong" came to collect his master's son. Falah had been at the Center for seven months, eleven days, Kamal for forty-one days.

KAMAL KEPT HIS promise to General Mansour, sang Not-to-worry's praises to his father, and told him how the Care Center had changed him. He was a Betty Ford graduate, cured of his jihadi addiction— but entirely on his own terms.

From the other jihadis, Kamal saw firsthand the easy path of Al Qaeda and its allies: how seductive it was to turn God's demanding gift of mercy inside each human to simple anger; how glamorous and self-important to switch the painful continuing struggle to better yourself before God (the Greater Jihad) into black-and-white contempt for others. He'd learned too from his time at the Care Center that only those who love one another were on jihad for God.

Kamal redoubled his studies at King Saud U. He continued with Qur'anic classes and Islamic studies but also concentrated on poetry and literature. His father didn't mind, particularly since the rector told him that Kamal had become the best again. And as the Book says, it is by the pen that God teaches man what he doesn't know.

Kamal even started to pray with his father faithfully in their *majlis* and at mosque. He also wrote to Indah Mother, as he always had, and promised her that things had changed.

Kamal wasn't lying to his father or Indah. He felt his change. His jihad—his struggle for God—could either take the words of his ancestors and fight against the Americans in the path of Osama bin Laden and Said al-Shihri or, understanding the spirit of what his forefathers had really written, wage an entirely different American jihad. He realized that the legacy of his great-great-great-great-great grandfather had been distorted by bin Laden and those with worldly goals. At last he could convey the truth of his noble ancestor: it wasn't the Islam you wore on the outside that mattered; faith was in the heart.

Over the months ahead, Kamal continued to excel in every possible course at KSU. He understood as never before Prophet Muhammad's command "to seek knowledge everywhere, even if you have to go to China."

Kamal now knew that in the twenty-first century, Indonesia was as close as China or as far as America.

"Not to worry," he took to repeating to his many new KSU buddies, laughing and smiling profusely.

And as his father aged into his nineties, he became strangely gentler and closer to Kamal, the one son who every week prayed Jumu'ah prayer and ate Friday dinner with him. At the end of his father's long life and the beginning of Kamal's new one, Kamal saw in his father's acceptance of him the spiritual strength the Wahhabi legacy could represent.

Above all, Kamal had to be who he was, a Muslim across borders: the faith of Wahhab with a direct line to God in Heaven, in all His majesty, and the spirit of Indonesia, living with God as His closest companion on Earth, with all His compassion. Kamal at last could embrace both.

He told Indah that this year was finally the time he could take her to Mecca for Hajj. In his heart and before Allah Almighty, they will pray as one.

And not just with Indah. Kamal now wanted to pray with the earthquake victims, every infirm man, destitute woman, and orphaned child.

For the first time, he had found the path to reach Al Qaeda fighters and those who saw violence as their first response. Kamal had begun the true jihad, the one he told Indah, where "only the pen shall lead God's Way":

Kamal started to write the sequel to *Tintin in America* that Widi had always dreamed of writing—the book to save the lost boys at last. This was the true legacy of Widi that he would honor. Only this time, Kamal would write of Tintin leading to a different Muslim brotherhood—with all men and women.

Kamal was also writing down Indah's miraculous life tales into *A Thousand and One Nights* for our times: stories with every lover equal in the sight of God.

Most of all, as the heir to Wahhab, Kamal began the book he was born to write: the new *Victory of the Glorious*. In it, he would render *Tawheed* for the twenty-first century in the line of his forefathers and reveal Islam's unwavering stand against the killing of Al Qaeda and its allies. Their hate was not jihad.

"REMEMBER THE DREAM?" Kamal asked me.

With so many dreams that Kamal and the other jihadis had told me, I didn't know which one he meant.

"My dream at the Care Center," he added. "The earthquake victims, the poor, the sick and the motherless children float with the clouds in the closest Heaven. There're also the Indonesian *banci* and Widi's Islamic Martyrs, American Red Cross workers and Panti Rapih Catholic nuns." He stopped.

"Even the Jewish men." He winked. "All are now free as green birds. Any person who has ever loved another is equal and sheltered by God's shade."

Kamal looked me in the eye and smiled widely. "One day I'll see you, Kenny, in my dream too," he said.

AFTERWORD

O N A spring day in 2009, Kamal and I were together in Riyadh on the "Street of Sweetness." I wasn't sure whether Kamal called it that in memory of Moad, his former lover, or simply because of its nickname, "Tahlia." As if to close the circle, we were sitting outside in the cool Saudi evening at Abdel Wahab Lebanese Cuisine— Kamal and Moad's favorite restaurant.

Amid the endless *mezze* again, I told Kamal about Shaheed. In particular, I recounted in detail my dream at the Serena Hotel in Islamabad, with its Al Maghreb Restaurant and the Jerusalem back home. I told him how my dream had changed Shaheed's perception of me and allowed him to see me as a "brother," not simply the American Jewish "other."

A shared experience seemed to be the catalyst that broke hardened stereotypes. That the American Jewish enemy could have Shaheed's cherished dream shocked him into human recognition. For Ahmad ("Bernie"), it was that Americans at Abu Ghraib treated him better than his fellow Muslim brothers of Al Qaeda; for Abby, it was the surprising generosity of the Iraqi boy. And for Kamal, befriending the other jihadis and Al Qaeda leaders at the Care Center, he saw what motivated them, and it wasn't the path of true jihad. Jihad in the Way of God, Kamal now believed, was a more demanding struggle than the quick and simple illusions of Al Qaeda.

"Inshallah," Kamal said softly after I told him about Shaheed, but he did not smile or even wink in his usual manner.

Unexpectedly, he asked me about the Jerusalem Restaurant in Falls Church, Virginia, and what it was really like to live nearby in Washington, D.C.

I told him that I had grown up in New York but now liked Washington as well.

Kamal wondered if New York, or perhaps Portland, might have "the spirit" of San Francisco or Yogyakarta. Maybe Washington could even have some of the heart of Riyadh too, and Riyadh could have some of the heart of Washington.

"Two halves now part of one whole," Kamal said, "just like the Circle K—Kamal and Kenny," he said, winking. "Wasn't that the name of the ranch on *Bonanza*? You know, I heard that *Bonanza* was Osama's favorite TV show."

Kamal's mastery of American TV trivia must have approached his encyclopedic Qur'anic expertise. Even in the time I knew him, his illicit DVD collection of the classics had grown, with new episodes of *Family Guy* and *South Park*.

"Osama loved *Bonanza*?" Kamal continued, "With that idiot Lorne Greene, who always knows everything, blah blah blah, busy telling everyone else what to do. The Ugly American stereotype himself. You Americans should've known that stupid show couldn't possibly be Osama bin Laden's favorite. Must be a CIA disinformation campaign or Mossad conspiracy," he joked.

From South Asia to East Asia and the Middle East, my journey throughout the Muslim world was about making unexpected links and unconventional friendships. It was that human bond, after all, in all its inherent messiness, that had provided the bridge over differences between Kamal and me. It wasn't about who I was or what I thought, any more than it was about who he was and what he believed.

Kamal helped me understand what I had learned from five years of research and hundreds of interviews. American policies, of course, play a large role in fomenting radicalism. Without U.S. troops in Iraq, would Ahmad ever have gone off to fight? Perhaps to some degree, you could even say the same about Malik, the Taliban seer, fighting in Afghanistan. Hating/blaming (and secretly loving/envying) the all-powerful enemy, as Zeddy said, creates a powerful motive to fight back.

Yet the notion that America is at the center of everything, which Kamal had mocked, was dear to the heart of not only too many Americans but, even more, all too many conspiracy-minded Muslims.

While misguided U.S. policies can help create jihadis, the far greater force propelling Islamist radicals comes from their own societies. It wasn't America that had sent Abby and perhaps Maryam to Iraq, but a love denied and the certain belief that by sacrificing their own lives to God they would be reunited—literally—as husband and wife in Heaven. And though America was the rationale behind Ahmad's journey to Iraq, his desire to fight came from a complex of religious, psychological, nationalistic, and simply the idealistic urges of a young man for adventure. Without the U.S. invasion of Iraq, he or at least some of his friends would have found another religious reason to fight. And for Zeddy, it was equally about rebellion and fame, where America had but a small part.

Above all, looking at Malik, Mullah Omar's seer, Shaheed and his university Taliban peers, and Kamal himself, it was a deep religious fervor that drove them—and to fight against other Muslims even more than the United States. Their jihad is about giving your life for a holy cause. And as Kamal told me, radical Islam, which presents itself as the purest Islam, is a seemingly easy and glamorous path, or, as Zeddy said, "an exciting shortcut" when there are few jobs and much drudgery. While the United States certainly matters, these stories show us that, if nothing else, we shouldn't view their world simply from our own American perspective.

The jihadis I encountered had been pushed away from the security of traditional beliefs, with little in the way of tangible hope or opportunity to replace it. They had imbibed an alienation and searched for something more real—it must be the forgotten religion of a lost past Islamic glory. The alienation endemic to young Muslims can also be found, to a lesser degree, among non-Muslim youth in the West. But among Muslims struggling between the old world and the new, a divided self infects on some level everyone. Kamal hit the nail on the head (or "in the coffin," as he said): out of this conflict between static tribal tradition and unyielding faith on the one side versus fast-forward modernization and Internet-age communications on the other, there comes a profound loneliness. In this world, who can you love?

Yes, the story of Islamist radicals and terrorists, I found, is as much about love as hate. A missed love, a love you cannot have, a love you can find only in God and not your fellow man, a love a man can never have with a woman or a woman cannot have with a man (or in Kamal's case another man). It is about a love that turns violent and cruel, a love that is never allowed to grow, to be just what it is, a simple feeling of caring toward another human being.

Kamal also embodied what I learned in another important respect: He didn't impose his beliefs on me, and I in turn couldn't impose mine either. Americans still carry Rudyard Kipling's "white man's burden." We are weighed down by the old baggage of American exceptionalism, the "City on the Hill" lighting the way for all mankind. In our globalized Internet world, people can see for themselves. Shining our light at others only makes them feel as if they're under our microscope, an object of the American experiment, not a fellow human deserving of respect.

Muslims must find their own answers to extremism. We in the West can listen; we can help when asked. Of course, we must defend ourselves against attack. Some of our enemies, as we have seen in this book, unshakably believe, to their death, in our annihilation. They are religiously convinced that by killing Americans and all "infidels" they will earn a place for themselves and their families in Heaven. We delude ourselves by not seeing clearly the implacable character of their religiously determined genocidal intentions. Witness Malik, Mullah Omar's seer, whose faith told him to kill every Jew, every Christian, every infidel.

The line between success and defeat for Al Qaeda, the Taliban, and other Muslim radicals, as this book also demonstrates, is a precariously thin one. In Pakistan, as Zeddy exposed, generals and other high-ranking officers in the Pakistani army with access to its nuclear weapons are radical sympathizers—willing to covertly support Islamist terrorists from the Taliban and even Al Qaeda and Osama bin Laden. Shaheed, the son of one of the guardians of the country's nukes, was indeed once part of the terrorist cell responsible for the Marriott Hotel bombing. The line is also dangerously close in Saudi Arabia, the religiously fundamentalist home of more than a quarter of the world's oil reserves. Saudis are still the principal funders of Al Qaeda and the Taliban. Terrorist attacks are not expensive. Suppose Kamal had not been arrested and instead had transferred even part of his fortune of $143 million to Al Qaeda—more than enough for the terrorists to obtain access to black-market nukes. Equally troubling, what if another wealthy Saudi decides to turn over his fortune to Al Qaeda, or one of its many allies, now? Complacency on our part against people who are dedicated to nothing less than the genocide of Americans would be the gravest mistake we can make—one from which there is no turning back.

At the same time, it's a deadly mistake to draw a picture of our enemies too broadly. They are, in fact, a small group that can be isolated and defeated. We must be vigilant not to fall into Al Qaeda's trap of defeating ourselves by overreaching. One finding in my nonprofit group's poll of Saudi Arabia kept coming back to me. The highest priorities Saudis had for their country were a free press, elections, freedom of speech—in other words, democracy. Yet the policy of the United States that Saudis hated the most, even beyond what they viewed as unconditional support for Israel, was America trying to promote its own vision of democracy in the Middle East. Lasting change for Muslims must come from their vision.

Kamal, Shaheed, and Ahmad are the hope. And as we've seen, that hope is as real as the hateful ideology of the terrorists. The journey from Malik, who believes all Jews should be killed, to Kamal, who told me that Jews and Christians can be welcomed in Heaven too, is an epic one. Indeed, these individuals and others in the book illustrate a missed opportunity in the ideological battle against Islamist extremism. Their personal stories can be a powerful deterrent to young people tempted by Al Qaeda's violence. But the stories must be owned by Muslims themselves.

Americans have much to be proud of. In every poll I've conducted, most of what we stand for and have achieved is the envy of the rest of the world—even of Muslim radicals! It is time we let the American Dream speak for itself. It is time we let the United States be the leader by example.

Which I felt was true for Kamal with me. I suspected Kamal would have liked nothing more than if I converted to Islam too, especially after I related my Serena dream. But he never asked, taking to heart the Qur'anic injunction that "there should be no compulsion in faith."

It is an injunction worth heeding in any kind of faith, secular or religious. It is a worthy ideal for any people or nation—particularly the most powerful one in the world.

ON FEBRUARY 11, 2011, the day the Egyptian dictator Hosni Mubarak was forced to resign, Kamal wrote to me:

"Now you see the hope for the future of Islam, not Al Qaeda. Against the odds, the people in Tahrir Square stood for love and respect of their fellow man. In their Liberation, Muslims with Christians, the young and old, poor and rich, men and women were together. With each person equal, they all bow only before the Sole Sovereign, God Almighty."

A Note on Sources and Methods

I CONDUCTED MOST of the initial and follow-up interviews of the six jihadis one-on-one. Half (Shaheed, Kamal, and Zeddy) spoke fluent English. I took extensive contemporaneous notes and engaged in much follow-up for three years. All of the radicals featured were eager to present their point of view and knew that I would write about them. Indeed, for almost all, I read my final chapters back to them. For two of the Saudis interviewed (Ahmad and Abby), I conducted most of the interviews with Dr. Ali, their Saudi psychologist, present, along with Majid, an Arabic interpreter, both of whom spoke fluent English. The Saudi psychologist played an important role in prompting questions and encouraging answers. For the final Taliban fighter portrayed (Malik), the initial interpretation from Pashto was provided by a Pashtun-speaking reporter, with subsequent translations provided by Shaheed and another reporter, over the course of more than two years. Shaheed assisted me with follow-up for both Malik (chapter 3) and Zeddy (chapter 4). I conducted all of the interviews from 2008 through 2011, in Pakistan, Saudi Arabia, Indonesia, Qatar, Austria, the United States, and elsewhere.

I have corroborated the core facts of each person's biography with independent sources. By chapter:

1. Ahmad's role as a suicide bomber in Iraq is confirmed by contemporaneous news accounts, official government documents, and his Saudi psychologist. I use Ahmad's real name with his permission.

2. Abby's illicit love affair and his time as a jihadi fighter in Iraq are corroborated by a lengthy contemporaneous letter from his girlfriend, as well as Saudi government sources, news accounts, and his Saudi psychologist. I had essential help corroborating the biographies of Ahmad and Abby from private conversations and official government records provided by two senior officials of the Saudi Ministry of Interior, as well as the Saudi psychiatrist and psychologists who treated Ahmad and Abby.

3. Malik's membership in the Taliban and closeness to the enigmatic Taliban leader Mullah Omar were confirmed by a senior American intelligence official and by interviews with Malik's colleagues.

4. Zeddy's career as a self-described "captain of terror," paid by the Pakistani army, was corroborated by his colleagues, as well as contemporaneous news accounts and American intelligence sources. Shaheed assisted me with follow-up for both Malik and Zeddy.

5. Shaheed's role in a cell responsible for the suicide bombing of the Marriott Hotel was confirmed by a high-level U.S. intelligence official.

6. Kamal's identity as a member of the royal family—in particular, its clerical branch—has been corroborated by two high-level sources at the Saudi Ministry of Interior, as well as my personal visits, along with interviews of his relatives and colleagues. His radical activities were confirmed by Abby and other inmates, in addition to Kamal's own contemporaneous documents. His account was also corroborated by my interviews throughout Indonesia.

7. The people portrayed corroborated each other. Kamal knew both Ahmad and Abby (and even saw Maryam's letter), and Ahmad and Abby could also corroborate parts of Kamal's account. Similarly, Malik, Zeddy and Shaheed all provided contemporaneous and independent corroboration of key facts in each of their stories.

8. I have also corroborated all of the stories by close to seventy additional interviews, including with many Guantánamo detainees, as well as extensive independent information, which is documented in the online source notes for the book at its website www.terroristsinlove.com

9. Abby, Malik, Zeddy, Shaheed, and Kamal's identities have been changed at their request. For Abby, it was his request for privacy. For the others, it was to protect their lives, which still, to some unknown degree, may be at risk because of their candid disclosures.

I still doubt that everything the radicals told me was the truth. Everyone sees his own past as he wants it to be viewed now. It is no different with Islamist radicals. I am certain that they embellished some incidents and colored others. I also believe those embellishments are important to understanding not only their view of themselves but their perspective on the world. Emotions and memory are, of course, always seen through the present—a process inherent in any memoir or biography. These memories, in particular, are not all objective facts. They comprise the protagonists' feelings, family myths, dreams, and religious visions. These subjective phenomena have largely been avoided by analysts of terrorism. My hope is that they can open a deeper window into the world of extremists than we have had before.

Of course, the freedom I take in documenting the lives of the radicals in a narrative form is not unique. Presenting their lives as stories, the dialogue necessarily re-creates what was said to me. I have also, as mentioned, disguised some identities, time sequences, and incidental details at the request of those featured and, given the nature of Al Qaeda and the Taliban, to protect their lives. Still, I was able to check the final versions of the chapters with almost all those I have portrayed. I also relied on numerous other sources, which I detail in the online source notes at www.terroristsinlove.com.

Needless to say, any errors are my own.

ACKNOWLEDGMENTS

T O BEGIN, I must acknowledge Shaheed in Islamabad and Kamal in Riyadh, whose inspiration led me to write. Without their extraordinary stories and fearless help—indeed friendship—this entire book would have not been possible. Of course, I also must thank the other men featured, who also gave so much of their time and effort: Ahmad al-Shayea, Abby, Zeddy, and Malik, as well as all those around them whose help was unstinting, including Hamid al-Shaygi, Nasser al-Arifi, Turki al-Otayan, Sheik Ahmad Jelan, Sheik Salman al-Awdah, Prince Mohammed bin Nayef, Mansour al-Turki, Abdul Rahman al-Hadlag, Yousef al-Mansour, Ambassador Hussein Haqqani, Muhammad Aslam Khan, and numerous other Saudi, Pakistani, Indonesian, and American intelligence and law enforcement officials who provided corroboration on background.

For the Saudi individuals profiled, I also corroborated—or discounted—important facts in the jihadis' stories with the psychiatrist and psychologists who treated some of them, and for all of the Saudis, two senior officials from the Saudi Ministry of Interior, who have asked to remain unidentified. For the Pakistani/Afghan accounts, I received on background necessary corroboration from three leading Pakistani journalists and a high-ranking senior American intelligence official who oversees Pakistan and Afghanistan in his portfolio. While they must remain nameless, I cannot thank them enough for verifying some of the most critical points in the Pakistani/Afghan stories. I was also helped by so many from the Middle East, South and East Asia, including, among others, Faisal al-Mahmoud, Juma al-Dosari, Ghanim al-Harbi, Abdul Azziz al-Attalhi, Ibrahim Gazi al-Hazmi, Abdul Rahman Nasir Shahrani, Ayad al-Amri, Rudud al-Yezeedi, Hammad al-Otaibi, Yousef al-Matrafi, Bandar Abdullah Saidi, Amin Ali Twaijri, Abdul Majid Ashabanat, Mahal Rashid Saidi, Mansoor Olayan al-Jihani, Falih al-Otabi, Ahmad Howaiyar al-Enize, Muhammad Isam Beghdadi, Majid Omar Wali, Mohammed al-Fauzon, Ahmad al-Mahbob, Ali al-Hassan, Hussein Salih Moathin, Said al-Gaimdi, Jamal Khashoggi, Muhammad Hanif, Daniyal Noorani, Shabbir Shah, Rashad Bukhari, Shahab Shakil, Hamid Mir, Syed Saleem Shahzad, Noor Huda Ismail, Nasir Abas, Muhammad Qodari, Ray Rangkuti, Imam Nur Aziz, and too many more to name, and others who asked to remain unnamed.

David Shipler, Peter Marks, Karin Green, David Sadkin, Bonnie Anthony, Nick Hardison, Michael Raphael, Andy Klingenstein, and Azadeh Pourzand were all tremendous readers. I also wish to thank Ilsa Brink, Suzanne Spaulding, Diara Holmes, Denise Halter, and, in particular, Fadil Bayyari.

I need to single out four people who read the entire book at least twice and whose generous editorial help and unquestioned expertise did more to shape this book than anyone else: Peter Bergen, whose knowledge and insight of Al Qaeda and Islamist radicals is unparalleled among all experts; Ammar Abdulhamid, a former Islamist radical and skilled author himself who provided me with singular first-hand corroboration and confidence; Steven Hirsch, a questioning, clear-eyed editor, and above all, Joe Kertes, a powerful novelist whose dedication and belief in my writing now spans two decades.

I would also like to thank the following individuals who remained my foundation to research, write, and complete the book:

My indefatigable agents Jim Levine and Victoria Skurnick, who believed in this book from the start;

My outstanding, insightful, and patient editor Alessandra Bastagli and her able assistant Sydney Tanigawa, as well as Dominick Anfuso,

Amber Qureshi, Carisa Hays, Jill Siegel, Suzanne Donahue, Laura Cooke, Claire Kelley, and Carol deOnís, all at Free Press;

William I. Koch, the book's dedicatee, Gisela Garneau, Andy and Julie Klingenstein, who all provided invaluable support in so many ways.

In addition to those singled out, the board, advisory board, and staff of Terror Free Tomorrow, who enabled everything with grace and generosity;

Josephine Dansby, Anna Sagmeister, and Minnie Klingebiel, whose spirit has led me;

Christine Ballen, whose belief in me covered nearly two decades of marriage;

Andi Budi Hutomo, whose confidence sustains me now;

And to my wonderful children: my indomitable son, Nicholas, and my always inspiring daughter, Cecilia.

INDEX

About Terror Free Tomorrow

LOCATED IN WASHINGTON, D.C., Terror Free Tomorrow is a non-partisan, not-for-profit organization, which investigates the causes of extremism. Since 2004, Terror Free Tomorrow's research has been featured in *The New York Times, The Washington Post,* CNN, CBS, NBC, and cited by Presidents Barack Obama, Bill Clinton, and George H.W. Bush, among others. Terror Free Tomorrow's Advisory Board is led by former Democratic Congressman and Co-Chair of the 9/11 Commission Lee Hamilton and John McCain, senior Republican Senator from Arizona.

All royalties from this book will go to Terror Free Tomorrow, instead of the author.

www.terrorfreetomorrow.org

ABOUT THE AUTHOR

Ken Ballen is President and founder of Terror Free Tomorrow. Ballen has spent nearly two decades on the frontlines of law enforcement, international relations, intelligence oversight, and congressional investigations. As a federal prosecutor, Ballen successfully convicted international terrorists. He also prosecuted major figures in organized crime, global narcotics trafficking, and one of the first cases in the United States involving illegal financing for Middle Eastern terrorists. Ballen served as Counsel to the House Iran-Contra Committee, where he was a lead investigator responsible for questioning key witnesses during the nationally televised hearings. Among other assignments on Capitol Hill, Ballen also was Chief Counsel to a bi-partisan Senate special investigative committee and Chief Counsel to the House Steering and Policy Committee, where he directed initiatives on crime prevention, intelligence oversight, and select national security matters for the U.S. House of Representatives. Ballen has regularly contributed to CNN, and its companion website CNN.com. His articles have also been published in *The Washington Post, Financial Times, Los Angeles Times, The Wall Street Journal* and *The Christian Science Monitor,* among others.

Ken Ballen was born in New York City. He graduated from Tufts University in 1977 and has a Masters in International Affairs from The Fletcher School and a J.D. from Columbia Law School. He lives with his son and daughter near Washington D.C. Learn more at www.terroristsinlove.com.